BEHAVIORAL HEALTH
CRISIS AND DE-ESCALATION INTERVENTION TRAINING

ADVANCED STUDENT GUIDE

David Fowler

Founder and Author of
AVADE® Training Programs

EDUCATION, PREVENTION, AND MITIGATION FOR VIOLENCE IN THE WORKPLACE

Behavioral Health Advanced Student Guide

Copyright ©2024
David Fowler, Personal Safety Training, Inc.
All Rights Reserved.

ISBN: 9798329982947

No part of this publication may be reproduced or transmitted in any form by any means, electronic, mechanical, photocopying, recording, or otherwise for any purpose without written permission from the author.

Printed in the United States of America

Personal Safety Training, Inc.
P.O. Box 2957, Coeur d' Alene, ID 83816 USA
(208) 664-5551
www.PersonalSafetyTraining.com

Also by David Fowler

AVADE® Defense Baton™ Training

AVADE® Handcuffing Tactics™ Training

AVADE® Defensive Tactics System™

AVADE® Pepper Spray Defense™ Training

AVADE® Healthcare Defensive Tactics System™

AVADE® Retail Loss Prevention™ Training

AVADE® Safety Incident Reporting System™

SOCS® Safety Oriented Customer Service Training

AVADE® Workplace Violence Prevention Training

AVADE® De-Escalation Training

AVADE® Active Shooter Training

Violence In The Workplace

Be Safe Not Sorry

To Serve and Protect

The Plan: Building a Safe Workplace

Acknowledgements

I would like to thank the many teachers, instructors, mentors, and friends that have helped make this program a reality. Without your help, inspiration, and invaluable knowledge, this wouldn't have been possible.

To all of you, I am eternally grateful.

I would also like to thank the thousands of individuals that I have worked with whose direct and indirect contribution to this program has made it possible for me to do what I feel on purpose to do.

Special thanks to the following individuals for their support and technical advice: Steve Baker, Genelle Fowler, Patrick Gibney, Brian Goodwin, Jamie Lang, Cosmo Rowell, and Devin Yates.

I would also like to thank my family for their support; I love you all so much!

David

David Fowler
Founder, AVADE® Training Programs
President, Personal Safety Training, Inc.

The information within this training book/program is presented in part/summary form as a supplement to, not a substitute for, the expertise of qualified psychiatrists, psychologists, physicians, and healthcare professionals. The details on AVADE® Behavioral Health are sourced from reasonably believed accurate and reliable sources. By acknowledging, understanding, and agreeing, you recognize that this material/training, its content, and educational resources do not constitute the practice of any medical, nursing, or other professional healthcare advice, diagnosis, or treatment. The content accessed on or through AVADE® Behavioral Health is not exhaustive and does not cover all disabilities, diseases, illnesses, physical conditions, etc., or their management, diagnosis, or treatment.

It is essential to consult your healthcare provider for specific guidelines and instructions, particularly those related to the diagnosis and treatment of any medical or behavioral health condition. In providing the content, information, and resources and offering any related products or services, we do not represent or warrant that such information, content, and resources are applicable or appropriate for anyone's needs and/or conditions. We also do not claim that any particular technique, strategy, intervention, service, or product is safe, appropriate, or effective for you and your agency.

The author and the publisher, Personal Safety Training, Inc., do not dictate policies or procedures for the use of any violence prevention, self-defense, or any physical intervention authorized for use by a department/agency or private individual. The suggestions/options disseminated in this book are simply that, suggestions or options. Each individual, department, or agency is responsible for developing their own policies and procedures regarding the use of violence prevention, self-defense, and physical intervention for their personnel and for themselves. Although every effort has been made for this book to be complete and accurate, it is impossible to predict, discuss or plan for every circumstance or situation which might arise in the course of defending yourself during any contact with a violent or aggressive person(s) or during a crime.

Every reader must always take into consideration his/her experience, physical abilities, professional responsibilities, agency and department procedures, and local, state, and federal legal requirements. With this in mind, each reader must evaluate the recommendations and techniques contained in this book and decide for himself/herself, which should be used, and under what circumstances. Each reader assumes the risk of loss, injury, and damages associated with this book and the use of the information obtained in it. The author and publisher, Personal Safety Training, Inc., cannot guarantee or warrant the legal, medical, tactical, or technical suggestions/options in this book.

ANY IMPLIED WARRANTIES ARE EXPRESSLY DISAVOWED.

Table Of Contents

Introduction 1
AVADE® Behavioral Health Crisis and De-Escalation Interventions 1
Commonality and Importance of the Term "Behavioral Health" 2
Do Individuals with Mental Illness Commit Violence? 3
The State of Behavioral Health in America 3
Systematic Training Methodology 4
The AVADE® Safety Principles for Workplace Violence Prevention 5
AVADE® Mission, Vision, and Philosophy 8
Workplace Violence Defined 8
Evidence-Based Training 9
Barriers to Reporting Incidents of Workplace Violence 10
Three Training Levels 10
Six Core Strategies© for Reducing Seclusion and Restraint Use Alignment 10
AVADE® Behavioral Health Crisis and De-Escalation Intervention, Level I Modules and Objectives 13
AVADE® Self-Defense Tactics and Techniques, Level II Modules and Objectives 16
AVADE® Defensive Control Tactics and Techniques, Level III Modules and Objectives 17
Creating an Effective Workplace Violence Prevention Plan 18
Proactive Response Planning 18
Personal Safety Habits 18
Developing Personal Safety Habits 19
   Exercise: Commitment 21
Benefits of AVADE® Workplace Violence Prevention Training 22
   Exercise: Spatial Empathy 23

Behavioral Health Level I:
Crisis and De-Escalation Intervention Training 27

Module 1: Trauma-Informed Care 29
Trauma-Informed Care Defined 30
What is Trauma? What Do We Mean by Trauma? 30
Adverse Childhood Experiences (ACE) 31
What Are Some of the Short and Long-Term Effects of Trauma? 31
Key Elements for Providing Trauma-Informed Care 32
Six Principles for Trauma-Informed Care 32
Key Ingredients of Trauma-Informed Organizational Practices 33
Best Practices of Trauma-Informed Care 34

Module 2: Interpersonal Communication 37
Interpersonal Communication (IPC) 38
Interpersonal Communication Fundamentals 38
Maslow's Hierarchy of Needs 40
Understanding Interpersonal Communication Skills 42
Facial Expressions 42
Eye Communication 43
Reading Eye Communications 43
Body Language, Postures, and Gestures 44
Hand Positions (Universal Signals) 44
Developing and Improving Your Interpersonal Communication Skills 45
   Exercise: The Miracle 45
The Law of Reciprocation 46

Module 3: The Assault Cycle 47
The Assault Cycle Defined 48

Behavioral Health Advanced Student Guide ... continued, Table of Contents

The Five Stages of the Assault Cycle ... 49

   Exercise: Reactionary Gap ... 50

Module 4: **De-Escalation Tactics and Techniques** ... 55

Have You Encountered an Escalated Individual? ... 56

De-Escalation and Escalation Defined ... 56

What is Conflict? ... 57

De-Escalation Ingredients ... 58

The Aim of De-Escalation: Calm, Empathic Communication ... 58

Response vs. Reaction ... 58

The 5 Habits of De-Escalation and Making a Positive Impression ... 59

   Exercise: The 5 Habits of De-Escalation ... 60

De-Escalation for the Triggering Phase (upset/stressed individuals) ... 61

Triggering Phase De-Escalation Techniques ... 61

De-Escalation for the Escalation Phase (angry/aggressive individuals) ... 62

Escalation Phase De-Escalation Techniques ... 63

Avoidance for the Crisis Phase (physically combative/violent individuals) ... 65

Strategies to Avoid Physical Harm from the Assault Cycle of Crisis ... 65

Security/Code Team Responses to Workplace Violence Incidents ... 66

The Recovery Phase: Submission ... 66

Post-Crisis Phase ... 67

Module 5: **Anxiety Disorder** ... 69

Anxiety Disorder Defined ... 70

Anxiety Disorder Facts and Statistics ... 70

Signs and Symptoms of Anxiety ... 71

Anxiety Causes ... 71

Anxiety Risk Factors ... 71

Types of Anxiety Disorders ... 72

Anxiety Disorder Crisis ... 72

Crisis and De-Escalation Interventions for Anxiety Disorder 73
Anxiety Disorder Treatments 75
Panic Attack Assessment and Monitoring 75
Helping Someone During a Panic Attack 76
References for Module 5 78

Module 6: **Depression Disorder** 79

Depression Disorder Defined 80
Depression Disorder Facts and Statistics 80
Signs and Symptoms of Depression 81
Depression Causes 81
Types of Depression Disorders 81
Depression Disorder Crisis 82
Crisis and De-Escalation Interventions for Depression Disorder 83
Depression Disorder Treatments 85
References for Module 6 86

Module 7: **Bipolar Disorder** 87

Bipolar Disorder Defined 88
What is Mania? 88
What is Hypomania? 88
Bipolar Disorder Facts and Statistics 89
Signs and Symptoms of Bipolar Disorder (Mania/Hypomania) 89
Mixed Episodes in Bipolar Disorder 90
Anosognosia 90
Bipolar Causes/Risk Factors 90
Types of Bipolar Disorder 91
Bipolar Complications 91
Bipolar Disorder Crisis 91
Crisis and De-Escalation Interventions for Bipolar Disorder 92

Bipolar Treatments 94
References for Module 7 96

Module 8: **Schizophrenia Disorder** 97
Schizophrenia Disorder Defined 98
Schizophrenia/Psychotic Disorders Facts and Statistics 98
Signs and Symptoms of Schizophrenia Disorder 99
Schizophrenia Disorder Causes 101
Types of Schizophrenia and Other Psychotic Disorders 101
Schizophrenia/Psychotic Disorders Crisis 102
Crisis and De-Escalation Interventions for Schizophrenia/Psychotic Disorders 102
Schizophrenia/Psychotic Disorders Treatments 104
References for Module 8 106

Module 9: **Obsessive-Compulsive Disorder (OCD)** 109
Obsessive-Compulsive Disorder (OCD) Defined 110
Obsessive-Compulsive Disorder Facts and Statistics 110
Signs and Symptoms of Obsessive-Compulsive Disorder 111
Obsessive-Compulsive Disorder Causes 112
Types of Obsessive-Compulsive Disorder 112
Obsessive-Compulsive Disorder Crisis 114
Crisis and De-Escalation Interventions for Obsessive-Compulsive Disorder 115
Obsessive-Compulsive Disorder Treatments 117
References for Module 9 118

Module 10: **Post-Traumatic Stress Disorder (PTSD)** 121
Post-Traumatic Stress Disorder (PTSD) Defined 122
PTSD Facts and Statistics 122
Signs and Symptoms of PTSD 123
PTSD Causes 123

Risk Factors for PTSD	124
Types of PTSD	125
PTSD Crisis	125
Crisis and De-Escalation Interventions for PTSD	125
PTSD Treatments	127
References for Module 10	129

Module 11: Substance Use Disorder (SUD) 131

Substance Use Disorder (SUD) Defined	132
Substance Use Disorder Facts and Statistics	133
Signs and Symptoms of Substance Use Disorder	133
Substance Use Disorder Causes	134
Substance Use Disorder Risk Factors	134
Types of Substance Use Disorder	135
Substance Use Disorder Crisis	136
Crisis and De-Escalation Interventions for Substance Use Disorder	136
Substance Use Disorder Treatments	138
References for Module 11	140

Module 12: Co-Occurring Disorder 141

Co-Occurring Disorder Defined	142
Co-Occurring Disorder Facts and Statistics	142
Signs and Symptoms of Co-Occurring Disorder	143
Co-Occurring Disorder Causes	143
Co-Occurring Disorder Risk Factors	144
Types of Co-Occurring Disorder	144
Co-Occurring Disorder Crisis	145
Crisis and De-Escalation Interventions for Co-Occurring Disorder	145
Co-Occurring Disorder Treatments	147
References for Module 12	149

Behavioral Health Advanced Student Guide . . . continued, Table of Contents

Module 13: **Neurocognitive Disorders** 151

Neurocognitive Disorders Defined 152
Neurocognitive Disorders Facts and Statistics 153
Signs and Symptoms of Neurocognitive Disorders 153
Causes of Neurocognitive Disorders/Dementia 154
Risk Factors for Neurocognitive Disorders 154
Types of Neurocognitive Disorders 155
Understanding the Progression of Neurocognitive Disorders 155
Neurocognitive Disorders Crisis 156
Crisis and De-Escalation Interventions for Neurocognitive Disorders 156
Neurocognitive Disorders Treatments 159
Sundowning 160
References for Module 13 162

Module 14: **Borderline Personality Disorder** 165

Borderline Personality Disorder (BPD) Defined 166
Borderline Personality Disorder Facts and Statistics 166
Signs and Symptoms of Borderline Personality Disorder 167
Borderline Personality Disorder Causes and Risk Factors 168
Types of Borderline Personality Disorder 168
Borderline Personality Disorder Crisis 169
Crisis and De-Escalation Interventions for Borderline Personality Disorder 169
Borderline Personality Disorder Treatments 171
References for Module 14 173

Module 15: **Autism Spectrum Disorder (ASD)** 175

Autism Spectrum Disorder (ASD) Defined 176
Autism Spectrum Disorder Facts and Statistics 177
Signs and Symptoms of Autism Spectrum Disorder 177
Autism Spectrum Disorder Causes 178

Behavioral Health Advanced Student Guide . . . continued, Table of Contents

Types of Autism Spectrum Disorder 178
Autism Spectrum Disorder Crisis 179
Crisis and De-Escalation Interventions for Autism Spectrum Disorder 180
Autism Spectrum Disorder Treatments 181
References for Module 15 183

Module 16: **Suicide Prevention** 185

Suicide Prevention Defined 186
Suicide Facts and Statistics 187
Warning Signs and Symptoms of Suicide for Adults 187
Warning Signs and Symptoms of Suicide for Youth 188
Suicidal Ideation and Planning 188
Suicide Risk Factors 189
Suicide Methods 189
Crisis Warning Signs for Suicide 190
Crisis and De-Escalation Interventions for Suicide 190
References for Module 16 194

Module 17: **Post-Incident Response, Debriefing, and Documentation** 197

Post-Incident Response 198
Post-Incident Debriefing 199
Conducting an Incident Debrief 200
Debrief Process Form 201
Post-Incident Documentation 202
Elements of Reporting Self-Defense Force 202

Level I Training Review 205

Behavioral Health Level II: Self-Defense Tactics and Techniques 207

The Goal of Self-Defense 208
AVADE® Training Safety Rules 209
AVADE® Level II Self-Defense Tactics and Techniques Modules 210

Module 1: **Self-Defense Fundamentals** 211

Self-Defense Fundamentals Overview 212
On Target Training 213
Exercises 214
   Stance | Balance | Stability (The Bladed Stance) 214
   Defensive Movements—Forward Shuffle 215
   Defensive Movements—Rear Shuffle 216
   Defensive Movements—Side-to-Side Shuffle 217
   Defensive Movements—Forward and Rear Pivoting 218
   Robot Exercise 219
   Core Energy Principle 220
Defensive Verbalization 221
The Art of Distraction 221
Escape Strategies 222
   Exercise: Reactionary Gap 222
Hand Positions 225

Module 2: **Defensive Blocking Techniques** 227

Defensive Blocking Techniques Overview 228
Exercises 229
   Shoulder Block Defense 229
   Elbow Block Defense 230
   Turtle Block Defense 231

Behavioral Health Advanced Student Guide ...continued, Table of Contents

High Block Defense 232
Middle Block Defense 233
Outside Block Defense 234
Low Block Defense 235

Module 3: **Self-Defense Techniques** 237

Self-Defense Techniques Overview 238
Self-Defense Caution 238
Vulnerable Areas of the Body 239
Exercises 240
   Wrist Grab Defense 240
   Two-Hand Wrist Grab Defense 242
   Bite Defense 243
   Rear Hair/Collar Pull Defense 246
   Front Hair/Lapel Pull Defense 247
   Front Strangle Defense 248
   Front Strangle Defense (Special Situation) 249
   Rear Airway Choke Defense 250
   Rear Carotid Choke Defense 251
   Rear Bear Hold Defense 252

Module 4: **Post-Incident Response, Debriefing, and Documentation** 255

Post-Incident Response 256
Post-Incident Debriefing 257
Conducting an Incident Debrief 258
Debrief Process Form 259
Post-Incident Documentation 260
Elements of Reporting Self-Defense Force 260

Level II Training Review 263

Behavioral Health Level III:
Defensive Control Tactics and Techniques 265

Introduction to Defensive Control Tactics and Techniques 266
AVADE® Training Safety Rules 267
Level III Defensive Control Tactics Modules 268
Use of Force 268
Use of Force Awareness 268
Center for Medicaid Services (CMS) 268
Violent or Self-Destructive Behavior Continuum 269

Module 1: Fundamentals of Defensive Control 271

Fundamentals of Defensive Control Overview 272
On Target Training 273
Exercises 274
   Stance | Balance | Stability (The Bladed Stance) 274
   Defensive Movements—Forward Shuffle 275
   Defensive Movements—Rear Shuffle 276
   Defensive Movements—Side-to-Side Shuffle 277
   Defensive Movements—Forward and Rear Pivoting 278
   Robot Exercise 279
   Core Energy Principle 280
Defensive Verbalization 281
The Art of Distraction 281
Escape Strategies 282
   Exercise: Reactionary Gap 282
Hand Positions 285

Behavioral Health Advanced Student Guide ...continued, Table of Contents

Module 2: **Contact and Cover Positioning** 287

Contact and Cover Overview 288

Exercises 289

    Initial Contact Front—1-Person 289

    Initial Contact Front—2-Person 291

    Initial Contact Rear—1-Person 293

    Initial Contact Rear—2-Person 294

    Contact and Cover—2-Person 295

    Contact and Cover—3-Person 297

Module 3: **Escort Strategies and Techniques** 299

Escort Strategies and Techniques Overview 300

Exercises 301

    Escort Strategies and Techniques—1-Person 301

    Escort Strategies and Techniques—2-Person 302

    Hands-On Escort Technique—1-Person 303

    Hands-On Escort Technique—2-Person 304

Module 4: **Control and Decentralization** 305

Control and Decentralization Overview 306

Exercises 307

    One-Arm Takedown 307

    Prone Control Position 309

    Standing the Prone Subject 310

    Escorting the Combative Subject 312

    Rear Arm Control Technique—1-Person 313

    Rear Arm Control Technique—2-Person 314

    Wall Control Technique 315

    Restraint Chair Holds and Application 316

Restraint Chair Holds and Application Studies 318

Exercises 320
   Child Control Technique—Standing (Optional) 320
   Child Control Technique—Seated (Optional) 321

Module 5: Post-Incident Response, Debriefing, and Documentation 323

Post-Incident Response 324
Post-Incident Debriefing 325
Conducting an Incident Debrief 326
Debrief Process Form 327
Post-Incident Documentation 328
Elements of Reporting Self-Defense Force 328

Module 6: Healthcare Restraint Holds/Applications 331

Use of Restraints 332
Exercises 333
   Supine Holding Position 333
   Supine Restraint Position 334
Supine Holding Hand Positions 335
Restraint Placement 335
Restraint Fit 336
Locking Restraints 336
Six Core Strategies© for Reducing Seclusion and Restraint Use Alignment 337
Risk Factors for Restraints 338
Strategies for Reducing Risk 339
Chemical Restraints (Emergency Medications) 339
Positional Asphyxia 340
Excited Delirium 340

Level III Training Review 341

About the Author 343

Bibliography, Reference Guide, and Recommended Reading 344

Training Courses for You and Your Agency 355

Introduction

Even before the onset of the COVID-19 pandemic in 2020, the prevalence of mental illness among adults was on the rise. The National Alliance on Mental Illness reports that one in five adults in the United States experiences mental illness during their lifetime. The impact extends to our youth, with 10% grappling with severe depression. According to the CDC, suicide stands as the 11th leading cause of death in the country. The current mental health crisis not only affects individuals but also has broader societal repercussions. It contributes to issues such as homelessness, poverty, employment challenges, compromised safety, and economic downturns. This widespread mental health challenge adversely affects the productivity of local businesses, escalates healthcare costs, hinders the educational success of children and youth, and causes disruptions within families and communities.

The largely unaddressed mental health issue may pave the way for an escalation in violence and aggression within workplaces, hospitals, schools, and psychiatric facilities. Mental illness, to varying degrees, can contribute to aggressive and heightened behaviors, consequently increasing the risk of workplace violence. Regardless of whether one works in an inpatient psychiatric facility or not, the likelihood of encountering individuals at risk due to suffering from a mental health crisis is currently significantly high.

With compassion, empathy, and a focus on safety, there are steps you, as an individual, can take to diffuse and de-escalate individuals in a mental health crisis—whether they are upset, angry, experiencing a substance use disorder, or exhibiting violent or self-destructive behavior toward themselves or others.

AVADE® Behavioral Health Crisis and De-Escalation Interventions

> **The AVADE® Behavioral Health Training is a systematic methodology designed to educate, prevent, and mitigate the risks associated with escalation, aggression, and violence toward individuals in the workplace. This training focuses on behavioral crisis and intervention strategies to effectively manage and de-escalate these incidents, ensuring the safety and well-being of all individuals involved.**

The AVADE® Behavioral Health training program is a crucial element in fulfilling the obligations outlined by state and federal guidelines, including OSHA's General Duty Clause, to ensure that employees are afforded a workplace devoid of recognized hazards.

The AVADE® Behavioral Health Training course is designed to empower you to:

- Identify, prevent, and respond to mental health crises that could involve escalation, aggression, and violence with composure, compassion, and empathy.
- Gain universal precautions for mental health crises that involve violence/aggression by applying the principles of the AVADE® Behavioral Health training program.
- Understand the aggressive and violent characteristics of individuals suffering from a mental health crisis in the workplace environment.
- Improve your safety by employing verbal and non-verbal techniques to de-escalate, diffuse, and prevent violent and aggressive behavior.
- Acquire best practices for crisis interventions and de-escalation with individuals experiencing a mental health crisis.
- Gain knowledge about the predicting factors of aggression and violence in the workplace, their correlation with the components of the assault cycle, and learn appropriate response strategies.
- Acquire strategies to prevent physical harm by applying the principles of time and distance.

The AVADE® Behavioral Health Training Program has undergone extensive research and development to emerge as the most comprehensive and effective training program for crisis intervention and de-escalation in corporate and healthcare environments, particularly when dealing with individuals undergoing a mental health crisis. This program is adaptable, allowing customization to address the specific needs and dynamics of your workplace.

Commonality and Importance of the Term "Behavioral Health"

Behavioral Health vs. Mental Health
The biggest differentiation between the two terms is that behavioral health is a blanket term that encompasses mental health.

Behavioral Health
Behavioral health relates to the connection between behavior and the health of the mind, body, and spirit. It is the way habits affect mental and physical health and wellness.

Behavioral Health Disorders
Behavioral health disorders involve a pattern of disruptive or destructive behavior that lasts several months or more.

Mental Health
Refers to a person's emotional, social, and psychological wellness. It affects how we think and feel, how we act, how we relate to others, and how we handle stress. Mental health is important from childhood through adulthood.

Mental Illness
Mental illnesses are health conditions involving changes in emotion, thinking, or behavior (or a combination of these). Mental illnesses can be associated with distress and/or problems functioning in social, work, or family activities.[1]

Mental Health Disorder
Also known as mental illnesses are a broad range of conditions that can affect a person's thinking, mood, feelings, and behaviors. They can be short-lived or long-lasting and can range from mild to severe.

Psychiatric Illness
Also known as a mental disorder or mental health condition, is a medical condition that can affect a person's

---

1 https://www.psychiatry.org/patients-families/what-is-mental-illness

thinking, emotions, or behavior. It can cause significant distress or impairment in a person's ability to function in their personal life, at work, school, or in their community. Mental illnesses can be occasional or long-lasting.

Psychiatric Disorder

Also known as a mental illness or mental health condition, is a behavioral or mental pattern that can significantly affect a person's thoughts, feelings, mood, or behavior. These disorders can be occasional or long-lasting and can make it difficult to function at home, work, school, or in your community. They can also impair a person's ability to maintain healthy social relationships.

All these terms relate to aspects of an individual's mental, emotional, and behavioral well-being. The common thread is the impact on a person's ability to function and maintain health in various aspects of life, including emotional, social, and psychological domains.

The term "behavioral health" best describes all these conditions because it encompasses the broad spectrum of issues related to behavior and its effects on mental and physical health. It highlights the interconnectedness of behavior and overall well-being, acknowledging that habits and actions play a crucial role in one's mental and physical health. This comprehensive term allows for a more holistic approach to health care, addressing not just mental disorders but also the behaviors that contribute to overall wellness.

Do Individuals with Mental Illness Commit Violence?

NO! It's important to recognize that the majority of individuals with mental illness do not engage in violent behavior. While some individuals with certain mental health conditions may exhibit aggression or violent tendencies, it's not accurate or fair to generalize this to everyone with a mental illness. Research consistently

THE STATE OF BEHAVIORAL HEALTH IN AMERICA
(NATIONAL INSTITUTE OF MENTAL HEALTH)[1]

Did you know....?

- Over 20% of adults are experiencing a mental illness, equivalent to over 50 million Americans.
- Almost 15% of Americans had a substance use disorder in the past year. Over 90% did not receive any treatment.
- Almost 5% of adults reported serious thoughts of suicide, equivalent to over 12 million adults.
- Over 16% of our youth reported suffering from at least one major depressive episode in the past year.
- Over half of all adults with a mental illness receive no treatment, which is equivalent to over 28 million people.
- Over 60% of youth with major depression receive no mental health treatment.
- Almost one-third of adults with a mental illness reported that they were not able to receive the treatment they needed.
- In the U.S., there are 350 individuals for every mental health provider (350/1).

[1] https://mhanational.org/sites/default/files/2023-State-of-Mental-Health-in-America-Report.pdf

shows that most people with mental health disorders are not prone to violence, and various factors, such as substance abuse, play a more significant role in the relationship between mental illness and violence. It's crucial to approach these discussions with sensitivity and avoid stigmatizing individuals based on their mental health status.

Systematic Training Methodology

The goal of the AVADE® Behavioral Health De-Escalation and Crisis Intervention Training is to offer a trauma-informed care approach characterized by compassion, empathy, and safety. The focus is on implementing safety measures when interacting with individuals experiencing a mental health crisis. The overarching objective is to equip individuals with the skills and knowledge necessary to navigate such situations with respect, dignity, sensitivity, and effectiveness.

The AVADE® Behavioral Health Crisis and De-Escalation Intervention Training program is a systematic methodology that integrates a trauma-informed approach, emphasizes interpersonal communication, comprehends the assault cycle, and utilizes best practices for crisis and de-escalation interventions to ensure the safety of all.

- **Methodology** is a systematic way of doing something, typically involving a specific process or procedure. It is an organized and planned approach to achieving a particular goal or outcome.
- **Trauma-Informed Care** is an approach to providing support and services that recognizes and responds to the effects of trauma.
- **Interpersonal communication** is a transactional process through which people share their ideas and feelings by simultaneously sending and receiving messages. This includes, but is not limited to:
  - **Compassion** motivates people to go out of their way to help the physical, mental, or emotional pains of another and themselves. Compassion is often regarded as having sensitivity, which is an emotional aspect to suffering.
  - **Empathy** is the capacity to understand or feel what another person is experiencing from within their frame of reference; that is, the capacity to place oneself in another's position.
  - **Respect** is the recognition and consideration of the inherent worth and rights of individuals.
  - **Dignity** is the state or quality of being worthy of honor, respect, and ethical treatment.
- **The Assault Cycle** is a theoretical model that describes the stages through which an individual may progress when escalating toward aggressive or violent behavior.
- **A crisis** is a significant and often sudden event or situation that disrupts normal functioning and map pose a threat to individuals, organizations, or communities.
- **Crisis intervention** is a set of immediate, short-term actions and strategies aimed at assisting individuals or groups experiencing a crisis. The goal is to stabilize the situation, reduce the immediate

distress, and provide support to help those affected cope with the crisis and begin the recovery process.

- **De-Escalation** is a strategy for reducing the intensity of a conflict or potentially violent situation. It involves techniques and communication methods for calming an agitated person and preventing further escalation.
- **Safety Measures** encompass a range of actions, precautions, and methods implemented to enhance safety and mitigate risks associated with human health. These measures commonly involve maintaining awareness of one's surroundings and environment, employing effective verbal and nonverbal communication, utilizing de-escalation techniques, and, when necessary, implementing physical maneuvers. The overarching goal is to reduce the potential for harm and create a secure environment conducive to well-being.

The AVADE® Safety Principles for Workplace Violence Prevention:

AWARENESS
A

VIGILANCE
V

AVOIDANCE
A

DEFENSE
D

ESCAPE
E

The AVADE® approach to safety incorporates learning new habits, skills, and actions that employers and employees can use to enhance their personal safety and their ability to de-escalate/defend themselves or others from dangerous situations, crime, and violence.

A Awareness

Awareness is the foundation for everything in life and is crucial for safety in the workplace. We've all said that we would have done something differently if we had just been aware.

> Awareness is a mental state or ability to perceive, feel, or be conscious of people, emotions, conditions, events, objects, and patterns.

Levels of Awareness:

- **Personal Safety Awareness:** Knowing that your safety is ultimately your responsibility.
- **Self-Awareness:** Your ability to think, reason, choose, exercise free will, evaluate options, and make decisions.
- **Emotional Awareness:** Your ability to recognize and feel the emotions and feelings of others, as well as your own.
- **Situational Awareness:** Being aware of what is happening around you and making decisions about this information for your personal safety.

- **Environmental Awareness:** Your ability to understand and recognize the many factors relating to your environment and how they can benefit or limit you.
- **360° View of Awareness:** Being aware of your surroundings and who and what is in your surroundings as much as possible at all times.
- **Unconscious Awareness:** Taking your awareness to a habitual level.
- **Higher Awareness:** Using your intuitive ability to navigate challenging situations.

Developing and increasing your awareness through training, planning, and a positive attitude can significantly enhance your safety and ability to handle workplace violence and other at-risk situations.

Vigilance

Vigilance involves actively paying attention to internal and external cues to enhance personal safety. It emphasizes being alert, cautious, and trusting gut feelings, utilizing all senses to respond effectively to potential dangers.

> Vigilance is the practice of paying attention to our internal and external messages with regard to ourselves, other people, things, and events. Vigilance is taking your awareness and putting it into action.

Vigilant Actions:

- **Alertness:** Being constantly aware of your surroundings and potential risks.
- **Caution:** Exercising carefulness in actions and decisions to prevent harm.
- **Attention:** Focusing on both internal signals (like gut feelings) and external cues (like body language).
- **Trust intuition:** Relying on intuitive feelings to guide actions and decisions.
- **Avoid hyper-vigilance:** An excessive state of awareness leading to anxiety and exhaustion, which is counterproductive.

Vigilance is about transforming awareness into actionable steps to maintain safety and well-being. It requires continuous attention to both your environment and internal signals, helping you to preemptively address potential risks.

Avoidance

The ability to calm a tense situation before it escalates into crisis and workplace violence is crucial for preventing physical harm to anyone. It serves as the last opportunity to avoid physical engagement, which inherently carries the risk of injury.

> **Avoidance involves recognizing and steering clear of potentially violent situations and individuals by being aware and prepared while using interpersonal communication skills and de-escalation techniques to avoid conflict/crisis.**

Strategies for Avoidance:

- **Structural avoidance:** The use of barriers and security measures in your environment.
- **Behavioral avoidance:** Recognizing and responding to escalating behaviors with positive interpersonal communication skills and de-escalation strategies.
- **Psychological avoidance:** Maintaining mental awareness and preparedness to recognize dangers and make decisions, choices, and responses that always keep you safe.
- **Physiological avoidance:** Being physically capable of defensive actions as a last resort.

- **Environmental avoidance:** Awareness of and adapting to different environments.
- **Intuitive avoidance:** Trusting gut feelings and instincts, and acting upon them.

By incorporating these strategies into your daily routine, you can proactively manage risks and enhance your personal safety, ensuring a safer and more secure environment for yourself and others. Practicing avoidance through awareness, preparation, and effective communication can significantly reduce the likelihood of encountering violence.

D Defense

Any time force is used to defend yourself or others, it must be a last resort and reasonable, and you must be able to articulate what you did, why you did it, and how you did it.

> Self-defense is the right to use reasonable force to protect oneself or others from bodily harm if there is a credible and immediate threat.

Defense Rules:

- **Reasonable force:** Force used must be proportional to the threat and is justified only as a last resort.
- **Avoidance first:** The best self-defense strategy is to avoid the situation or escape if possible.
- **Legal and policy compliance:** Self-defense actions must comply with agency policies, procedures, and relevant state and federal laws.
- **Seek assistance:** Know how to contact security and law enforcement in emergencies.
- **Reporting:** Notify security and supervisors immediately about incidents.

The use of force and self-defense is about using reasonable force as a last resort, prioritizing avoidance, and ensuring all actions are legally and ethically justified. Post-incident protocols and documentation are crucial for managing and preventing future incidents.

E Escape Planning

Having an escape plan in all environments is an act of committing to be aware until it becomes a habit. As the old proverb goes: "He who fails to plan, plans to fail" (Winston Churchill).

> Escape planning involves recognizing and preparing for potential escape routes in all environments to ensure safety during an aggressive or violent incident. It combines physical escape routes with quick verbal responses to avoid or defuse negative situations.

Escape Strategies:

- **Awareness of exits:** Know all exits in your environment and develop the habit of identifying escape routes.
- **"Own the Door" concept:** Position yourself so that others cannot block your escape route. If the environment doesn't allow this, have backup support.
- **Dominant hand awareness:** Position yourself on the dominant side of potentially aggressive individuals to make it harder for them to strike.
- **Optimal positioning:** Maintain a safe distance and position yourself at a 45-degree angle to upset individuals, which is less threatening and allows for easier escape.
- **Spatial empathy:** Be aware of personal space zones and respect others' comfort levels to avoid escalating situations.
- **Commitment and practice:** Pre-plan escape routes, ensure all staff know the plan, and regularly practice escape scenarios.

- **"What If?" Game:** Mentally run through potential scenarios and responses to stay prepared.

By implementing these escape strategies, you can enhance your preparedness and safety in potentially dangerous situations, ensuring you are ready to act effectively if the need arises.

AVADE® Mission, Vision, and Philosophy

AVADE® Training Mission
Our mission is to provide training and education aimed at preventing and reducing the risk of violence towards individuals in the workplace.

AVADE® Training Vision
Our vision is to assist organizations in cultivating a culture of safety where workplace violence is not a necessary component of the job.

AVADE® Training Philosophy
Preventing conflict, violence, and aggression through clear communication and de-escalation techniques to address potential conflicts early and prevent escalation.

> The overall essence of what AVADE® workplace violence prevention training and its team members are about is the desire that all would live a safe and positive life with peace, security, harmony, and freedom of choice.

AVADE® has been taught in private corporations, healthcare agencies, schools, community programs, and civic institutions for many years. The founder of the AVADE® Training programs, David Fowler, has over thirty years of experience and has made personal safety training his life's work. He has an extensive background in training, martial science, and all functions of security management and operations. He is also the author of *Be Safe Not Sorry: The Art and Science of Keeping You and Your Family Safe from Crime and Violence*, available on Amazon.com or at www.avadetraining.com.

The **AVADE® Behavioral Health Crisis and De-Escalation Intervention Training Program** is designed to equip individuals with the skills and knowledge needed to prevent and mitigate workplace violence effectively. This program focuses on teaching de-escalation techniques, understanding the assault cycle, and implementing best practices to create a safe and secure work environment. By addressing both behavioral health crises and potential violent incidents, the training helps participants learn how to prevent, defuse, and manage escalated, aggressive, and violent situations in the workplace.

Workplace Violence Defined

> Workplace violence is any act of aggression, verbal assault, physical assault, or threatening behavior that occurs in the workplace environment and causes physical or emotional harm to guests, staff, patients, or visitors.

OSHA® The National Institute for Occupational Safety and Health Administration (NIOSH) and the Occupational Safety and Health Administration (OSHA) define workplace violence as any physical assault, threatening behavior, or verbal abuse occurring in the workplace. Violence includes overt and covert behaviors ranging in aggressiveness from verbal harassment to murder. (NIOSH, OSHA).

Currently, there is no federal standard that requires workplace violence protections. However, **The Occupational**

Safety and Health Act of 1970 (OSH Act) mandates that, in addition to compliance with hazard-specific standards, all employers have a general duty to provide their employees with a workplace free from recognized hazards likely to cause death or serious physical harm.

OSHA will rely on Section 5a-1 of the OSH Act, the "General Duty Clause," for enforcement authority. Failure to implement these guidelines is not in itself a violation of the General Duty Clause; however, employers can be cited for violating the General Duty Clause if there is a recognized hazard of workplace violence in their establishments, and they do nothing to prevent or abate it. These standards address employee safety and security risks.

In September of 2011, OSHA announced a new directive targeting workplace violence prevention. In this directive, OSHA is actively investigating and citing employers for failure to keep their workplace safe from threats and incidents of workplace violence. Some states have sought legislative solutions, including the mandatory establishment of a comprehensive prevention program for employers and employees.

Workplace Violence Disclaimer

This instruction manual and the information contained within is *not* an exhaustive program on workplace violence prevention. The AVADE® Workplace Violence Prevention Training program is the most comprehensive workplace violence prevention training in the country. For more information, go to avadetraining.com.

Evidence-Based Training

AVADE® Behavioral Health Training is based on research from OSHA, CDC, NIOSH, NAMI, SAMHSA, NIMH, MHA-NATIONAL, APA, CMS, BLS, State WPV Laws, Department of Labor and Industries, the DSM-5, and more.

A comprehensive look at the AVADE® Training's research can be found in the bibliography.

The AVADE® Workplace Violence Prevention system is designed to give you the training and education you'll need in the prevention and mitigation of violence in the workplace. Agencies must also consider and implement the appropriate administrative, behavioral, and environmental categories for developing protocols and procedures for their workplace violence prevention plan.

Barriers to Reporting Incidents of Workplace Violence[2]

- A culture that considers workplace violence part of the job: "It's just part of the job."
- Fear of being accused of inadequate performance or of being blamed for the incident, and fear of retaliation by the offender and or the employer/supervisor.
- Lack of awareness of the reporting system.
- A belief that reporting will not change the current systems or decrease the potential for future incidents of violence (complacency).
- A belief that the incident was not serious enough to report. Unintentional violence, e.g., incidents involving Alzheimer's patients, behavioral health, on/off meds, etc.
- Lack of manager and employer support and training related to reporting and managing workplace violence.
- Lack of agreement on definitions of violence, e.g., does it include verbal harassment?

Removing these barriers requires **a multifront strategy and the buy-in** from staff and their employer.

---

[2] https://www.nursingworld.org/~495349/globalassets/docs/ana/ethics/endabuse-issue-brief-final.pdf

Three Training Levels

The AVADE® Workplace Violence Prevention Training Program is incorporated into three training levels:

- Level I: Behavioral Health Crisis and De-Escalation Intervention
- Level II: Self-Defense Tactics and Techniques
- Level III: Defensive Control Tactics and Techniques

The AVADE® Workplace Violence Prevention Training program will teach you how to recognize emerging situations, how to deal with someone before they become violent (de-escalation), how to survive and escape a violent attack, and much, much more. Read carefully. Integrate the lessons you learn here. Unfortunately, one day you may be responsible for saving your own life—and the lives of your co-workers.

Six Core Strategies© for Reducing Seclusion and Restraint Use Alignment

The Six Core Strategies© are evidence-informed methods proven to be effective in minimizing instances of seclusion and restraint. This comprehensive approach was initially formulated in the United States by the Medical Directors Council of the National Association of State Mental Health Program Directors (NASMHPD).

Strategy 1 | Leadership Toward Organizational Change

The primary approach to reduce instances of seclusion and restraint (S/R), known as "Leadership toward Organizational Change," involves the active participation of senior facility leadership, including the CEO, CNO, and COO. This strategy entails defining a vision for S/R reduction, implementing a targeted performance improvement plan, and ensuring continuous oversight through a public health prevention approach and a multi-disciplinary performance improvement team.

To support this strategy, evidence-based tools include the Six Core Strategies© checklist for leadership and the Reflective Guide for Senior Leaders. These tools offer a structured framework for leaders to follow and assess their progress in implementing the strategy.

Evidence-based tools to support Strategy 1:

- Six Core Strategies© Checklist for Leadership
- Reflective Guide for Senior Leaders

Strategy 2 | Use of Data to Inform Practice

To achieve a successful reduction in seclusion and restraint (S/R), it is essential to gather data at the individual unit level. This approach includes the following steps: establishing baseline data, consistently monitoring facility usage, tracking demographics, involuntary medication use, and injuries associated with S/R events. Moreover, it involves setting improvement goals for comparative monitoring over time. This strategy aims to comprehensively assess and address factors contributing to S/R instances.

Evidence-based tools to support Strategy 2:

- AVADE® 4-Step Debriefing Tool
- Six Core Strategies for Reducing Seclusion and Restraint Use© Planning Tool

Strategy 3 | Workforce Development

The strategy revolves around establishing a treatment environment founded on recovery principles and trauma-informed care to proactively prevent coercion and conflicts. Implementation entails thorough staff training, education, and human resource development. This includes incorporating training on the application of seclusion and restraint (S/R), choice-oriented treatment activities, and individualized person-centered treatment planning. To ensure effectiveness, there is a focus on maintaining consistent communication and supervision. This approach aims to equip staff with the necessary knowledge and skills for the reduction of S/R incidents.

Evidence-based tools to support Strategy 3:

- Staff and Patient Development Support Plan

Strategy 4 | Use of S/R Prevention Tools

The strategy encompasses the integration of tools and assessments into facility policies and individual consumer recovery plans, with a focus on promoting individualized treatment to reduce instances of seclusion and restraint (S/R). Implementation involves the utilization of assessment tools, universal trauma assessments, de-escalation surveys, person-first language, environmental changes, and sensory modulation interventions. These measures aim to teach emotional self-management skills and create a personalized approach to treatment.

Evidence-based tools to support Strategy 4:

- Six Core Strategies for Reducing Seclusion and Restraint Use© Planning Tool

Strategy 5 | Consumer Roles in Inpatient Settings

The strategy actively engages consumers, children, families, and external advocates at all organizational levels to minimize instances of seclusion and restraint. Implementation encompasses their participation in event oversight, monitoring, debriefing interviews, peer support services, and significant roles in key facility committees. Additionally, there is elevated supervision by executive staff, with a focus on addressing ADA (Americans with Disabilities Act) issues in job descriptions, expectations, work hours, and communication. This approach aims to include diverse perspectives and ensure a collaborative effort in reducing seclusion and restraint.

Evidence-based tools to support Strategy 5:

- Staff and Patient Development Support Plan

Strategy 6 | Debriefing Techniques

The strategy places a strong emphasis on conducting a comprehensive analysis of each seclusion and restraint (S/R) event to shape policies and proactively prevent future occurrences. It recommends debriefing activities, including immediate post-event analysis and formal problem analysis using root cause analysis (RCA) steps. The approach acknowledges the need for flexibility in facilities treating children and frequently using holds. This analytical process aims to provide valuable insights that inform policies and contribute to a continuous improvement approach in minimizing S/R incidents.

Evidence-based tools to support Strategy 6:

- Six Core Strategies© Checklist for Leadership
- AVADE® 4-Step Debriefing Tool
- Psychological First Aid, John Hopkins Method (recommended by SAMHSA)

AVADE® Behavioral Health Crisis and De-Escalation Intervention
Level I Modules and Objectives

AVADE® Behavioral Health Crisis and De-Escalation Intervention is a modular-based training program that can be taught in one-day or two-day sessions or presented modularly during safety or departmental meetings throughout a 12-month period.

1 | TRAUMA-INFORMED CARE

The learner will understand trauma-informed care principles, recognize trauma signs and effects, and apply strategies to provide compassionate, safe, and effective care, avoiding re-traumatization and improving patient outcomes.

2 | INTERPERSONAL COMMUNICATION

The learner will understand and apply effective interpersonal communication skills, including active listening, assertiveness, empathy, and nonverbal communication. They will learn to recognize and respond appropriately to verbal and nonverbal cues to reduce conflict, build trust, and improve interactions in personal and professional settings.

3 | THE ASSAULT CYCLE

The learner will understand the five stages of the assault cycle, recognize the warning signs at each stage, and apply appropriate de-escalation techniques to manage and defuse potentially violent situations, ensuring safety for all involved.

4 | DE-ESCALATION TACTICS AND TECHNIQUES

The learner will understand and apply effective de-escalation tactics and techniques to calm agitated individuals, prevent escalation, and manage potentially violent situations, ensuring the safety of all involved.

5 | ANXIETY DISORDER

The learner will understand the characteristics, causes, and symptoms of anxiety disorders. They will be able to identify the signs of anxiety, implement effective crisis interventions and de-escalation strategies, and apply appropriate support measures to help individuals manage anxiety disorders and improve their quality of life.

6 | DEPRESSION DISORDER

The learner will be able to identify and understand the signs, symptoms, and causes of depression disorder. They will be equipped with effective crisis and de-escalation interventions, emphasizing trauma-informed care, empathy, and active listening, to support individuals experiencing a depression disorder crisis and ensure their safety and well-being.

7 | BIPOLAR DISORDER

The learner will be able to identify and understand the symptoms, types, and causes of bipolar disorder, including its manic and depressive episodes. They will also be able to apply crisis and de-escalation interventions to manage and support individuals experiencing a bipolar disorder crisis effectively.

8 | SCHIZOPHRENIA AND OTHER PSYCHOTIC DISORDERS

The learner will be able to identify and understand the signs, symptoms, and types of schizophrenia and other psychotic disorders. They will also learn effective crisis and de-escalation interventions to support individuals experiencing a psychotic episode, ensuring their safety and providing appropriate care.

9 | OBSESSIVE-COMPULSIVE DISORDER

The learner will be able to identify and understand the signs, symptoms, causes, and types of obsessive-compulsive disorder (OCD). They will also learn effective crisis and de-escalation interventions to support individuals experiencing OCD symptoms, ensuring their safety and providing appropriate care.

10 | PTSD (POST-TRAUMATIC STRESS DISORDER)

The learner will be able to identify and understand the signs, symptoms, causes, and risk factors associated with Post-Traumatic Stress Disorder (PTSD). They will also learn effective crisis and de-escalation interventions to support individuals experiencing PTSD symptoms, ensuring their safety and providing appropriate care.

11 | SUBSTANCE USE DISORDERS (SUD)

The learner will be able to identify and understand the signs, symptoms, causes, and risk factors associated with substance use disorder (SUD). They will also learn effective crisis and de-escalation interventions to support individuals experiencing SUD symptoms, ensuring their safety and providing appropriate care.

12 | CO-OCCURRING DISORDERS

The learner will be able to identify and understand the signs, symptoms, causes, and risk factors associated with co-occurring disorders. They will also learn effective crisis and de-escalation interventions to support individuals experiencing symptoms of co-occurring disorders, ensure their safety, and provide appropriate care.

13 | NEUROCOGNITIVE DISORDERS (NCDS), A.K.A. DEMENTIA, ALZHEIMER'S, ETC.

The learner will be able to identify and understand the signs, symptoms, and causes of neurocognitive disorders, as well as differentiate between various subtypes such as Alzheimer's disease, vascular dementia, and traumatic brain injury. They will gain knowledge on the progression of these disorders, effective crisis and de-escalation interventions, and the importance of creating a safe and supportive environment for individuals affected.

14 | BORDERLINE PERSONALITY DISORDER

The learner will be able to identify and understand the signs, symptoms, causes, and types of Borderline Personality Disorder (BPD). They will also learn effective crisis and de-escalation interventions to support individuals experiencing BPD symptoms, ensuring their safety and providing appropriate care.

15 | AUTISM SPECTRUM DISORDER (ASD)

The learner will identify and apply strategies for effectively managing and de-escalating crises in individuals with Autism Spectrum Disorder (ASD) using a trauma-informed approach.

16 | SUICIDE PREVENTION

The learner will be able to identify and understand the warning signs, risk factors, and methods associated with suicidal behavior in both adults and youth. They will gain knowledge on effective crisis intervention and de-escalation strategies, including how to engage in empathetic communication, develop safety plans, and mobilize support networks.

17 | POST-INCIDENT RESPONSE, DEBRIEFING, AND DOCUMENTATION

The learner will be able to comprehend the importance of post-incident response, debriefing, and post-incident documentation. They will also understand the components of writing an accurate and articulate incident report.

Workplace violence is, unfortunately, on the rise. By learning and studying the AVADE® strategies, integrating them, teaching them, and modeling them to your co-workers, you can lessen your chances of being a victim of workplace violence. Integrate the AVADE® safety principles into your workplace/life-place for defusing tense situations. Learn to identify the signs and symptoms of potential violence. Above all, learn to trust your instincts and listen to your intuition.

Remember: your best tools for keeping yourself safe are your own mind and personal safety habits.

AVADE® Self-Defense Tactics and Techniques
Level II Modules and Objectives

AVADE® Level II training is designed for agencies to mitigate the potential of injury and liability risk when using lawful defenses or controlling an aggressive individual. The tactics and techniques in this training curriculum are for incidents where the aggressor is physically combative, resistive, and unarmed.

THE GOAL OF SELF-DEFENSE

The learner will understand, acknowledge, and articulate that the best self-defense is not to be there when the attack occurs. They will also acknowledge that this is not always possible and self-defense is a proactive measure for their personal safety.

1 | FUNDAMENTALS OF DEFENSE

The learner will be able to understand and perform the fundamentals of self-defense. They will also be able to articulate that the fundamentals are a foundation to build upon regarding self-defense.

2 | DEFENSIVE BLOCKING TECHNIQUES

The learner will be able to understand and perform defensive blocking techniques. They will also be able to articulate the importance of blocking and how physically violent individuals attack the human body.

3 | SELF DEFENSE TACTICS AND TECHNIQUES

The learner will be able to understand and perform self-defense techniques from both frontal and rear assaults on themselves or another person and articulate the justification for using any of the personal defense techniques.

4 | POST-INCIDENT RESPONSE, DEBRIEFING, AND DOCUMENTATION

The learner will be able to comprehend the importance of post-incident response, debriefing, and post-incident documentation. They will also understand the components of writing an accurate and articulate incident report.

AVADE® Defensive Control Tactics and Techniques
Level III Modules and Objectives

AVADE® Level III training is designed for agencies to mitigate the potential of injury and liability risk when using lawful defenses or controlling an aggressive individual. The tactics and techniques in this training curriculum are for incidents where the aggressor is physically combative, resistive, and unarmed.

INTRODUCTION TO DEFENSIVE CONTROL

The learner will understand, acknowledge, and articulate the need to be able to control someone who is out of control if there is no option to avoid this behavior. They will also acknowledge that avoidance is not always possible and control tactics are a proactive measure for their personal safety and the safety of others.

1 | FUNDAMENTALS OF DEFENSE

The learner will be able to understand and perform the fundamentals of self-defense. They will also be able to articulate that the fundamentals are a foundation to build upon regarding self-defense.

2 | CONTACT AND COVER POSITIONING

The learner will be able to understand and perform the team tactics for defensive control. They will also be able to articulate the importance of having a team to control someone who is out of control.

3 | ESCORT STRATEGIES AND TECHNIQUES

The learner will be able to understand and perform two escort techniques. They will also be able to incorporate team tactics for escorting an individual.

4 | CONTROL AND DECENTRALIZATION TECHNIQUES

The learner will be able to understand and perform control techniques for a situation where an individual is physically combative. They will also be able to articulate the justification for using any of the control and decentralization techniques.

5 | POST-INCIDENT RESPONSE, DEBRIEFING, AND DOCUMENTATION

The learner will be able to comprehend the importance of post-incident response, debriefing, and post-incident documentation. They will also understand the components of writing an accurate and articulate incident report.

6 | HEALTHCARE RESTRAINT TECHNIQUES

The learner will be able to understand and perform healthcare restraint techniques safely and effectively. They will learn the principles and guidelines for applying restraints, ensuring the safety and dignity of individuals while complying with relevant healthcare regulations and policies.

Creating an Effective Workplace Violence Prevention Plan

Workplace violence is a significant issue that often goes unreported despite its prevalence, with approximately two million victims annually in the U.S. and substantial financial losses for businesses. Many organizations lack comprehensive prevention plans, leading to increased incidents, legal liabilities, and decreased employee morale. Developing an effective workplace violence prevention plan involves creating and refining policies and procedures, providing behavioral training, and implementing environmental measures to ensure a safe work environment. The AVADE® framework—Awareness, Vigilance, Avoidance, Defense, and Escape—serves as a foundation for these efforts, promoting proactive risk management, improved employee morale, reduced absenteeism, and an enhanced organizational reputation. By following a structured approach and integrating these components, organizations can significantly mitigate the risks of workplace violence and ensure the safety and well-being of their employees and stakeholders.

The PLAN: Building a Safe Workspace
A Comprehensive Guide to Creating Your Agency's Workplace Violence Prevention Plan

Download your free copy at
avadetraining.com/AVADE_The_Plan_E-Book.pdf

Proactive Response Planning

Prevention and interventions are essential to eliminating and mitigating security risks in the workplace. Employers now recognize the importance of being proactive in their implementation of workplace violence policies and procedures, conducting worksite audits/analyses, tracking and trending incidents, training and educating staff, as well as other proactive measures to reduce the risk of violence to guests, staff, clients, patients, and visitors. A well-thought-out plan for the prevention of workplace violence takes a proactive approach versus an after-the-fact, reactive-driven response.

Personal Safety Habits

> **Your personal safety is your responsibility— it always has been.**

Personal safety involves maintaining a balance and awareness in all areas of your life while creating habits: mentally, physically, spiritually, and for all of your environments.

What is a habit?

Habits are our acquired patterns of behavior that occur automatically without thought, things we repeatedly do over and over. They can be either good or bad.

We are creatures of habit! You get up in the morning in a certain way and get ready for your day. You brush your teeth, comb your hair, put on your clothes, etc., the same way every day. You don't even think about it; you just do it. The way you answer the phone, greet people, shake hands, gesture, smile, or don't smile are also all your habits.

Habits are ingrained in you and stamped into your unconscious mind. Habits are powerful factors in our lives. They are consistent, unconscious patterns that constantly and daily express our character and produce our effectiveness or ineffectiveness. Habits determine your future—and your safety!

General personal safety measures involve maintaining a balance in all areas of one's life. The four areas of your personal safety involve mental, physical, spiritual, and environmental awareness.

How do you rate your personal safety habits?

> We are what we repeatedly do; therefore, personal safety is not an act, it is a habit.

Developing Personal Safety Habits

> A habit is something that we repeatedly do over and over, an acquired pattern or behavior that occurs automatically without thought.

Identify your limiting personal safety habits
Do you have habits that leave you unsafe? Such as leaving your car unlocked or working late, and cutting through unlit areas? Take a hard look at your daily habits and see what little things you can do to ensure your own safety. Once identified, you can begin to change and improve them.

The 21 Rule
This is the process of making small adjustments in your behavior—twenty-one days of repeatedly doing what you intend to do to create a new habit. The 21 Rule does not apply to a habit that we have had for an extended time. Long-term habits have roots like trees and run very deep. Changing or eliminating long-term habits could take as long as a year or more to develop or break.

Creating new habits

Write out your new personal safety habits. Once you identify your limiting and successful habits, you can clearly decide to change them or make new, more productive, and empowering personal safety habits. Having a clear, defined personal safety goal is the first powerful step to creating a new habit.

Take action with visualization

Written words are powerful—but only when you look at them and make an effort and a commitment to follow through. Focus on your new personal safety habits often; focus on the benefits of your new habits. Use the process of visualization to add more repetitions to your successful new habit.

The no retreat, no surrender policy

The no-retreat, no-surrender policy means that you will do whatever it takes to change or accomplish your personal safety goal. This policy is about doing it even when you don't feel like it—when you're tired, sick, hungry, or stressed. You do it no matter what; you make the commitment!

Evaluate yourself and ask for help

Ask yourself, could I do more to improve my general personal safety and overall sense of safety? Ask for help, and get more training. A good trainer will gladly let you know the areas that you could improve upon. Look to improve in all the areas in which you received negative feedback, too. Negative feedback is not necessarily "bad." Consider negative feedback as a way to add safety and self-improvement to your personal life. It's about taking responsibility for yourself and your circumstances.

COMMITMENT EXERCISE

If you change or add one new, empowering habit every other month. In five years, you will have thirty new habits. Remember, habits are something we unconsciously do; once they're ingrained, you don't even have to think about them.

Commit to developing at least one habit for each workplace violence prevention module. Write it down in your AVADE® Behavioral Health Crisis and De-Escalation Manual. Focus on it often.

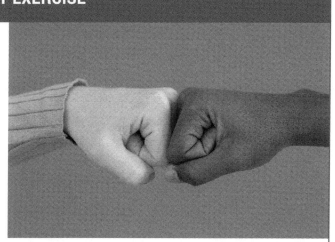

MODULE	HABIT TO DEVELOP	MODULE	HABIT TO DEVELOP
1		10	
2		11	
3		12	
4		13	
5		14	
6		15	
7		16	
8		17	
9			

Benefits of AVADE® Workplace Violence Prevention Training

After going through an AVADE® Behavioral Health Crisis and De-Escalation Intervention Training Program, refer back to your textbook, *AVADE® Behavioral Health Crisis and De-Escalation Intervention Training*, as your personal refresher course.

The AVADE® manuals and student guides on workplace violence prevention will help remind you how to recognize emerging situations, how to deal with someone before they become violent, how to survive and escape a violent attack, and much, much more. Read and study carefully. Integrate the lessons you learn here. Unfortunately, one day you may be responsible for saving your own life—and the lives of your co-workers.

SPATIAL EMPATHY EXERCISE, PART ONE (TO THE FRONT)

"Spatial empathy" is an informal term used to describe our awareness of the proximity, activities, and comfort of the people around us. Having spatial empathy means that you are aware of your personal zones and the personal zones of other people. It's important to realize that being in other people's personal zones may make them uncomfortable. Being aware of that allows you to better help them and to be safer yourself.

1. Form two lines (use blue tape) with participants facing each other at approximately 10' apart.
2. **Line A** approaches **Line B** at a casual pace. **Line B** will stop **Line A** by using the universal hand signal for stop.
3. What are **Line B**'s personal spaces to the front? What is the average? Are there differences?
4. **Line A** will extend their right arm, seeing if they can touch **Line B**'s shoulder.
5. **Line A** will step forward into **Line B**, invading their personal space. How did that make you feel **Line B**?
6. Back up and reverse the roles (steps 1-3).

> Note: Approaching people to the front can be confrontational when a person is in crisis. (e.g.,, stressed, angered, intoxicated, or physically combative)

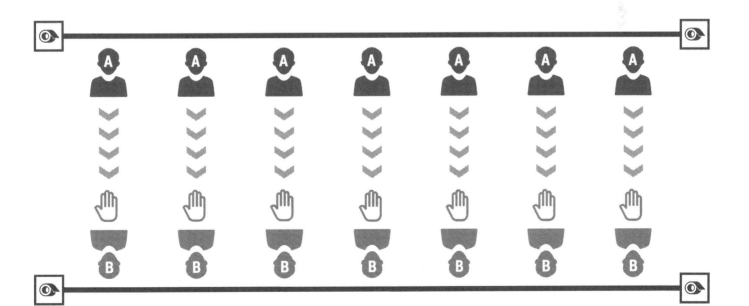

SPATIAL EMPATHY EXERCISE, PART TWO (TO THE SIDE)

1. Form two lines and have participants turn and face the same direction at approximately 10' apart.
2. Line B approaches Line A with a side step. One at a time.
3. As Line B approaches Line A, ask Line A how they feel in regard to their space to the side.
4. Have Line B approach up to the point where they are shoulder to shoulder with Line A.
5. How does that feel? Then have them go face-to-face. How does that feel? Go back side to side.

> Note: When approaching people who are in crisis (e.g.,, stressed, angered, intoxicated, or physically combative) we recommend you approach them at a 45° angle. This exercise illustrates that we feel more comfortable to have someone beside us, versus face to face.

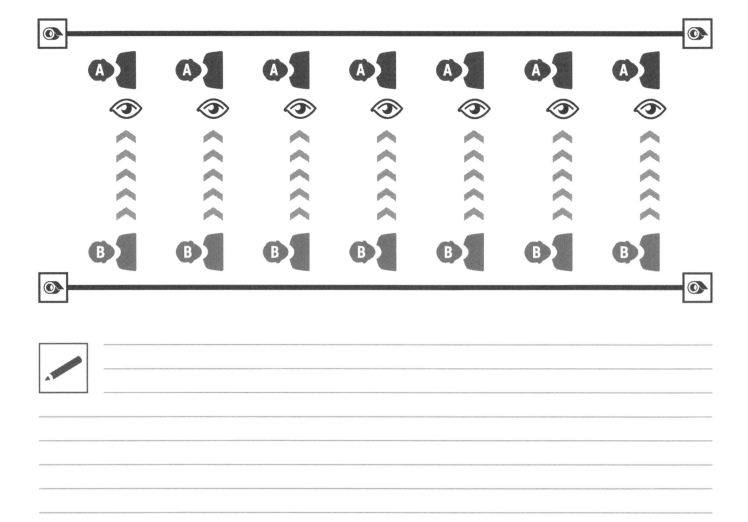

SPATIAL EMPATHY EXERCISE, PART THREE (TO THE REAR)

1. Form two lines with **Line B** facing the opposite direction as **Line A** at approximately 10' apart.
2. **Line B** turns their head to see their partner in **Line A** behind them.
3. Make sure **Line B** keeps their eyes forward and motion to **Line A** to quietly move in behind their partner in **Line B**.
4. Ask **Line B**, did you feel anything?
5. Now have **Line B** turn their head to see that their **Line A** partner is right behind them.

> Note: Most people do not like others directly behind them. It gives people a feeling of discomfort and uneasiness.

IF YOU OR SOMEONE YOU KNOW IS IN CRISIS AND CONSIDERING SELF-HARM OR SUICIDE:

- Call 911 for emergency services.
- Visit the nearest hospital emergency room.
- Call or text 988 to connect with the 988 Suicide and Crisis Lifeline, offering 24-hour, confidential support. *Para ayuda en español, llame al 988.*
- Support is also available via live chat at 988lifeline.org. *AVADE® does not monitor this website for crisis messages, provide medical advice, or make referrals.*

PSTI LEGAL DISCLAIMER

The information in this training book is a supplement, not a substitute, for the expertise of qualified healthcare professionals. The content on AVADE® Behavioral Health, sourced from reliable information, does not constitute medical or professional healthcare advice, diagnosis, or treatment. It is crucial to consult healthcare providers for specific guidelines related to medical or behavioral health conditions. This material does not guarantee that any technique or strategy is safe or effective for any specific needs. Personal Safety Training, Inc., does not dictate policies or procedures for behavioral health violence prevention, self-defense tactics, or any physical interventions. Agencies are responsible for developing their own policies and evaluating the recommendations based on their circumstances.

The author and publisher do not guarantee the completeness or accuracy of the information and assume no risk for its use. Any implied warranty are expressly disavowed.

AVADE® Behavioral Health
LEVEL I

Crisis and De-Escalation Intervention Training

MODULE 1

Trauma-Informed Care

Providing care that recognizes and responds to experiences of trauma

Module 1:
Trauma-Informed Care

Trauma-Informed Care Defined

Trauma-informed care is an approach to providing care that recognizes and responds to trauma experiences. It acknowledges that trauma is widely experienced and often stigmatized. Trauma-informed care helps staff and clients understand the diverse ways that trauma can impact an individual. It can help survivors begin to rebuild a sense of personal safety and empowerment.

When we understand that many people have had some form of trauma, we can communicate in ways that are less likely to re-traumatize them and escalate the situation.

What is Trauma? What Do We Mean by Trauma?

> "Trauma" is typically understood to be caused by an event (or a series of events) that an individual experiences as physically or emotionally harmful or life-threatening and that has lasting adverse effects on the individual's functioning and mental, physical, social, emotional, or spiritual well-being.

Trauma is widespread. For example, 84% or more of adult mental health clients have histories of trauma and yet the topic of trauma has often been ignored—a source of shame and denial. However, it is now increasingly accepted that trauma should be addressed in health care and social service settings, particularly (but not only) when serving patients who have behavioral health disorders.[1]

It generally overwhelms an individual's or community's resources to cope, and it often ignites the "fight, flight, or freeze" reaction at the time of the event(s). It frequently produces a sense of fear, vulnerability, and helplessness.

Examples of trauma include, but are not limited to:

---

1 Center for Substance Abuse Treatment (US). Trauma-Informed Care in Behavioral Health Services. Rockville (MD): Substance Abuse and Mental Health Services Administration (US); 2014. (Treatment Improvement Protocol (TIP) Series, No. 57.) Chapter 1, Trauma-Informed Care: A Sociocultural Perspective. Available from: https://www.ncbi.nlm.nih.gov/books/NBK207195/

- Childhood neglect
- Experiencing or observing physical, sexual, and emotional abuse
- Having a family member with a mental health or substance use disorder
- Experiencing or witnessing violence in the community or while serving in the military
- Poverty and systemic discrimination

Adverse Childhood Experiences (ACE)[2]

Exposure to abuse, neglect, discrimination, violence, and other adverse experiences can significantly increase the risk of serious health problems and health-risk behaviors throughout a person's life, as documented by the Adverse Childhood Experiences (ACE) study. The research study explored the impact of childhood trauma and adversity on long-term health and well-being. The study identified ten types of adverse experiences, including physical abuse, emotional abuse, sexual abuse, neglect, household substance abuse, household mental illness, domestic violence, parental separation or divorce, incarcerated household member, and emotional neglect.

The ACE study found that individuals who experienced a higher number of adverse childhood experiences were more likely to suffer from various health issues later in life, such as chronic diseases, mental health disorders, substance abuse, and even early mortality. The study has had a profound impact on public health and healthcare policies, emphasizing the importance of trauma-informed care and interventions to address childhood trauma and its long-term effects.

Due to the findings of the ACE study and subsequent research, healthcare policymakers and providers recognize the long-term health risks associated with traumatic childhood events.

As awareness of trauma's impact grows, healthcare providers are adopting trauma-informed care approaches. This approach emphasizes understanding a patient's life experiences to deliver effective care, potentially improving patient engagement, treatment adherence, health outcomes, and wellness of providers and staff. Emerging organizational competencies and clinical guidelines aim to improve treatment for patients with trauma histories, though further development is needed for a comprehensive approach, including trauma screening and quality outcome measurement.

What Are Some of the Short and Long-Term Effects of Trauma?

Trauma has wide-ranging physical, emotional, psychological, and behavioral effects. It affects the brain—especially the developing brain. It adversely affects both short-term and long-term well-being and overall functioning and has been associated with mental health disorders, addiction, and other impairments that affect an individual's physical and mental health. Trauma can make it hard for someone to cope with future distress and to form healthy relationships.

Triggers

Trauma can also produce "triggers," situations that remind trauma survivors of the events that originally harmed them. These triggers can cause someone to essentially "relive" the traumatic event and become highly distressed, which can pose a safety hazard to that person and to others. The person may start to have a strong negative emotional, physical, or behavioral reaction.

---

[2] https://nhttac.acf.hhs.gov/soar/eguide/stop/adverse_childhood_experiences

Experiencing trauma, particularly during childhood, significantly heightens the risk of developing serious health problems later in life, such as chronic lung, heart, and liver diseases, depression, sexually transmitted diseases, and substance abuse. Childhood trauma also correlates with increased social service costs.

Adopting trauma-informed care approaches can help healthcare providers engage more effectively with patients, improving outcomes and reducing avoidable healthcare and social service costs. This approach shifts the focus from asking "What's wrong with you?" to "What happened to you?"

Key Elements for Providing Trauma-Informed Care

- **Realize the widespread impact of trauma and understanding potential paths for recovery.** Recognize that trauma is prevalent and affects many individuals, and identify ways to support recovery.

- **Recognize the signs and symptoms of trauma in clients, families, staff, and others.** Develop the ability to identify indicators of trauma in various individuals within the healthcare setting.

- **Respond by integrating knowledge about trauma into policies, procedures, and practices.** Ensure that the understanding of trauma informs all aspects of organizational operations and clinical practice.

- **Seek to actively resist re-traumatization.** Make concerted efforts to avoid practices and policies that could trigger trauma responses or re-traumatize individuals.

Six Principles for Trauma-Informed Care

- **Safety**: Organizations can strive to create environments where staff and clients feel safe, both physically and psychologically.

- **Trustworthy and transparent**: Decisions should be made in a transparent way, with the goal of building trust with and between clients and staff.

- **Peer support**: Trauma survivors can support one another to build a climate of safety, recovery, and hope.

- **Collaboration and mutuality**: By attending to power imbalances in an organization or between staff and clients, we recognize the importance of shared decision making and that everyone has a role to play on the path to healing.

- **Empowerment, voice, and choice**: Recognize the unique strengths of trauma survivors and believe in the possibility of recovery. Support client's participation in goal-setting and self-advocacy.

- **Cultural, historical, and gender issues**: Recognize/address cultural biases and stereotypes, as well as historical trauma. Be attentive to the needs of different people based on their gender identity, sexual orientation, age, race, ethnicity, or backgrounds.

These attributes form the core principles of a trauma-informed organization and may necessitate modifications to mission statements, changes to human resource policies, amendments to bylaws, allocation of resources, and updates to clinical manuals. The following sections outline key strategies for implementing these principles at both the organization-wide and clinical levels.

Key Ingredients of Trauma-Informed Organizational Practices

Leading and communicating about the transformation process

Becoming a trauma-informed organization involves gaining steady support from senior leaders and empowering the workforce to participate in the transformation process. Key strategies include crafting a clear plan, communicating the rationale and benefits of changes to both staff and patients, and adapting communication strategies based on the organization's size and structure. Successful transformation often requires significant investments in staff training, consultants, and facility modifications, with senior leaders responsible for securing resources and balancing financial considerations related to training time versus billable clinical activities.

Engaging patients in organizational planning

To engage patients in organizational planning for trauma-informed care, health care organizations should form a stakeholder committee that includes individuals who have experienced trauma. This committee will oversee the process and provide valuable first-hand perspectives to inform organizational changes. Patients can serve alongside staff, patient advisory boards, and boards of trustees. It's important to compensate patients and community members for their time, similar to other highly valued consultants, to ensure their contributions are recognized and valued.

Training clinical, as well as non-clinical, staff

Providing trauma training is essential for both clinical and non-clinical employees within a healthcare organization. Clinical staff must learn to create a safe and trusting environment during patient interactions, while non-clinical staff such as front-desk workers, security personnel, and drivers also play crucial roles in patient engagement and setting a supportive tone. For example, a warm greeting from front-desk staff can foster feelings of safety and encourage patients to engage in treatment. Therefore, comprehensive trauma training for all staff members is key to ensuring a healing and supportive environment for patients.

Creating a safe environment

Creating a safe environment is crucial for effectively engaging patients who have experienced trauma, as feeling physically, socially, or emotionally unsafe can trigger extreme anxiety and potentially re-traumatize individuals. Examples of creating a safe environment include ensuring well-lit parking lots and common areas, monitoring building entrances and exits, using welcoming language in signage, and maintaining low noise levels in waiting rooms. Additionally, the social-emotional environment should prioritize welcoming and respectful interactions, healthy boundaries among staff, consistent communication, and awareness of cultural differences in perceptions of safety and privacy.

Preventing secondary traumatic stress in staff

Working with patients who have experienced trauma can lead to secondary traumatic stress for both clinical and non-clinical staff. This stress, characterized by emotional distress resulting from hearing about others' trauma experiences, can manifest as chronic fatigue, disturbing thoughts, poor concentration, emotional detachment, exhaustion, avoidance, absenteeism, and physical illness. Staff experiencing these symptoms may struggle to provide high-quality care, leading to burnout and staff turnover, creating a negative cycle that affects remaining employees.

Many in helping professions, including healthcare, may have their own trauma histories, which can be exacerbated by working with trauma survivors. This is also true for non-clinical staff, especially in communities with high rates of adversity and trauma, such as poverty, violence, and discrimination, where staff members may live in the same neighborhood as patients and have their own trauma experiences. Addressing secondary traumatic stress is crucial to maintaining staff well-being and ensuring high-quality care for patients.

Preventing secondary traumatic stress can increase staff morale, allow staff to function optimally, and reduce the expense of frequently hiring and training new employees. Strategies to prevent secondary traumatic stress in staff include:

- Providing training that raises awareness of secondary traumatic stress
- Offering opportunities for staff to explore their own trauma histories
- Supporting reflective supervision, in which a service provider and supervisor meet regularly to address feelings regarding patient interactions
- Encouraging and incentivizing physical activity and mindfulness practices
- Allowing "mental health days" for staff

Best Practices of Trauma-Informed Care[3]

Here are some strategies for creating a trauma-informed environment:

- Provide a calm environment and take your time with interactions.
- Avoid rushing into services and maintain a relaxed demeanor.
- Screen for trauma and be sensitive to potential triggers.
- Respond empathetically and validate individuals' experiences with brief, supportive responses.
- Encourage open communication and invite questions or concerns.
- Normalize concerns and reassure individuals that their feelings are understandable.
- Explain procedures before carrying them out to reduce anxiety.
- Offer choices and empower individuals to make decisions about their care.
- Respect individuals' autonomy by informing them of their options, including the ability to decline participation.

3 https://www.samhsa.gov/nctic/trauma-interventions

- Educate individuals about self-care practices.
- Reflect on your own triggers and biases to better understand how they may impact your interactions.

Trauma-informed care awareness and vigilance

Implementing public education campaigns similar to seat belt use can help raise awareness and vigilance in trauma-informed care. These campaigns should highlight the long-lasting effects of trauma on physical, mental, and social well-being, aiming to reduce stigma surrounding trauma-informed services. Healthcare organizations should develop clear educational materials for patients and providers, utilize social media campaigns, and create public service announcements.

This shift requires a change in the healthcare culture, acknowledging the significance of trauma and the value of trauma-informed care. Early cross-disciplinary training in trauma-informed approaches is crucial for healthcare providers, including those in medical, public health, nursing, social work, and residency/fellowship programs. Offering continuing education credits focused on trauma-informed training can further enhance awareness and vigilance among current healthcare workers.

Trauma-Informed Care Educational Videos

What is Trauma-Informed Care?
youtube.com/watch?v=fWken5DsJcw&t=13s

Trauma-Informed Practice
youtube.com/watch?v=ml5-P3P7IXo

What is Trauma-Informed Care?
youtube.com/watch?v=AnBEROaeiak

Adverse Childhood Experiences (ACE) Overview
youtube.com/watch?v=OtXd19s9i8k

IF YOU OR SOMEONE YOU KNOW IS IN CRISIS AND CONSIDERING SELF-HARM OR SUICIDE:

- Call 911 for emergency services.
- Visit the nearest hospital emergency room.
- Call or text 988 to connect with the 988 Suicide and Crisis Lifeline, offering 24-hour, confidential support. *Para ayuda en español, llame al 988.*
- Support is also available via live chat at 988lifeline.org. *AVADE® does not monitor this website for crisis messages, provide medical advice, or make referrals.*

PSTI LEGAL DISCLAIMER

The information in this training book is a supplement, not a substitute, for the expertise of qualified healthcare professionals. The content on AVADE® Behavioral Health, sourced from reliable information, does not constitute medical or professional healthcare advice, diagnosis, or treatment. It is crucial to consult healthcare providers for specific guidelines related to medical or behavioral health conditions. This material does not guarantee that any technique or strategy is safe or effective for any specific needs. Personal Safety Training, Inc., does not dictate policies or procedures for behavioral health violence prevention, self-defense tactics, or any physical interventions. Agencies are responsible for developing their own policies and evaluating the recommendations based on their circumstances.

The author and publisher do not guarantee the completeness or accuracy of the information and assume no risk for its use. Any implied warranty are expressly disavowed.

MODULE 2

Interpersonal Communication

Sharing ideas and feelings by simultaneously sending and receiving messages

Module 2: Interpersonal Communication

Interpersonal Communication (IPC)

Interpersonal Communication (IPC) is a transactional process through which people share their ideas and feelings by simultaneously sending and receiving messages.

It's a complex and dynamic process in which individuals interact with one another, usually face-to-face. Messages may be exchanged verbally or nonverbally and sent intentionally or unintentionally.

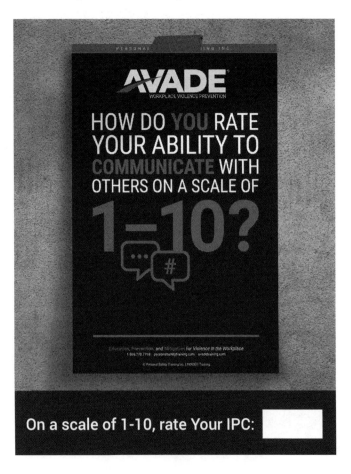

Interpersonal Communication Fundamentals

Our ability to communicate with others can significantly reduce the potential for escalation. Interpersonal communications skills involve the following:

Active Listening

Active listening is a structured way of listening and responding to others. It focuses attention on the other person. Active listening is, arguably, the most important communication skill of all because, without it, no other technique, theory, or principle will work.

- Webster defines **active** as: "involving action or participation."
- Webster defines **listen** (verb) as: "to hear something with thoughtful attention, give consideration."

> *When we use active listening, we are actively involved in hearing and paying attention to what the other person is saying.*

Active listening helps build trust and rapport, ensures mutual understanding, and can lead to more effective problem-solving and conflict resolution.

When using active listening, you should:

- Pay attention to the inflection of the person's words.
- Pay attention to the context of what they are saying.

- Use supportive body language and eye communication (shows you are interested).
- Avoid rolling your eyes.
- Avoid repeatedly rubbing your neck.
- Avoid looking away often.
- Avoid unconsciously shaking your head back and forth (this says "no").
- Avoid shuffling your feet.
- Avoid crossing arms, tapping fingers, biting lip, etc.
- Avoid checking your cell phone, writing notes, texting, etc.

Asserting

Asserting is stating or expressing positively one's rights, beliefs, or positions. The caveat to this communication skill is that our rights and beliefs should not affect another person's rights and beliefs. When we are assertive, we state our position in a strong, definite, professional way. There are times (not all the time!) in our communication when we must be assertive.

Influencing

Influence is our power to affect people, actions, and events. The ability to influence others is more than just using words; it involves our body language and our para-language (tone and inflection).

Persuading

To persuade is to succeed in causing a person to do, or consent to do, something. We are all in the sales business. We are either selling an idea, a product, or a service. In some cases, we are selling all three. Your ability to communicate through persuasion helps you accomplish your goal of serving others, getting your idea across, or selling your product. To be persuasive, one must believe in what one is doing, selling, or providing.

> It's not what you do, it's how you do it, that influences and persuades others.

Empathizing

To empathize is to sense and understand someone else's feelings as if they were your own. In other words, you are putting yourself in another person's shoes. This can be difficult at times, as some situations make it extremely difficult to imagine being in that person's shoes. However, the key to these situations is to *try* to put yourself in their shoes. When we try, it comes across in our verbal and non-verbal communication, and people recognize our empathy. Using empathy fulfills a person's need for psychological survival. We all need to feel understood.
Caution: Do not confuse "sympathy" with "empathy."

Empathy is the capacity to understand or feel what another being is experiencing from within the other person's frame of reference.

Compassion

Compassion is a relational process that involves noticing another person's pain, experiencing an emotional reaction to it, and acting in some way to help ease or alleviate the pain. *Compassion fatigue is a major concern.* It is a condition characterized by emotional and physical exhaustion leading to a diminished ability to empathize or feel compassion for others, often described as the negative cost of caring.

What are three effective self-care practices you incorporate into your routine?

1. _____

2. _____

3. _____

Sensitivity

Sensitivity is being cognizant of emotional feelings (of self and others). A person who is not sensitive in their communication comes across as callous and not caring. Being sensitive when communicating with others demonstrates that you truly care for them. Sensitivity is expressed in our words, tone, inflection, and body language.

Diplomacy

Diplomacy is having tact and skill in dealing with people in an effective way. Not having diplomacy in our communications is communicating ineffectually. A person who has tact and diplomatic skill will *not* always say what's on their mind. The opposite of this is a person who has no filter and says whatever's on their mind. Being mindful of what we say is the key to diplomacy. In relationships, business deals, and in situations where we deal with difficult people, diplomacy is absolutely necessary.

Maslow's Hierarchy of Needs[1]

Maslow's hierarchy of needs is often portrayed in the shape of a pyramid with the largest, most fundamental needs at the bottom and the need for self-actualization and self-transcendence at the top.

The most fundamental and basic needs that an individual has are primarily: physiological, safety, love and belonging, and self-esteem. If these needs are not met, the individual will feel anxious and tense. Maslow's theory suggests that the most basic level of needs must be met before the individual will strongly desire (or focus motivation upon) the secondary or higher-level needs of self-actualization and self-transcendence.

---

1 Maslow, A.H. (1943). "A theory of human motivation." *Psychological Review.* 50 (4): 370–96. doi:10.1037/h0054346. Via psychclassics.yorku.ca.

Maslow's research stated that a certain need "dominates" the human organism. Thus Maslow acknowledged the likelihood that the different levels of motivation could occur at any time in the human mind, but he focused on identifying the basic types of motivation and the order in which they would tend to be met. This understanding helps us recognize, communicate, and de-escalate individuals who are upset/aggressive because their perception is their needs are not being met.

Physiological (physical) needs

Physiological needs are the physical requirements for human survival. If these requirements are not met, the human body cannot function properly and will ultimately fail. Physiological needs are thought to be the most important; they should be met first. This is the first and basic need for the hierarchy of needs. Without them, the other needs cannot follow up.

> Physiological needs include: breathing, water, food, sleep, clothing, shelter, sex, and safety.

Safety needs

Once a person's physiological needs are relatively satisfied, their safety needs take precedence and dominate behavior. Safety and security needs are about keeping us safe from harm. These include shelter, job security, health, and safe environments. If a person does not feel safe in an environment, they will seek to find safety before they attempt to meet any higher level of survival, but the need for safety is not as important as basic physiological needs.

> Safety and security needs include personal security, emotional security, financial security, health, and well-being.

Love and belonging needs (interpersonal)

After physiological and safety needs are fulfilled, the third level of human needs is interpersonal and involves feelings of belongingness. This need is especially strong in childhood, and it can override the need for safety, as witnessed in children who cling to abusive parents.

> Social belonging needs include friendships, intimacy, and family.

Esteem needs

Esteem needs are ego needs, or status needs to develop a concern with getting recognition, status, importance, and respect from others. All humans have a need to feel respected; this includes the need to have self-esteem and self-respect. Esteem presents the typical human desire to be accepted and valued by others.

Self-actualization needs

The term "self-actualization" refers to focusing on becoming the best person that one can possibly strive for in the service of both the self and others. Maslow's term of self-actualization might not properly portray the full extent of this level; quite often, when a person is at the level of self-actualization, much of what they accomplish in general may benefit others or "the greater good."

Self-transcendence needs

Abraham Maslow explored a further dimension of needs while criticizing his own vision on self-actualization. By this later theory, the self only finds its actualization in giving itself to some higher outside goal, in altruism and spirituality. He equated this with the desire to reach the infinite. "Transcendence refers to the very highest and most inclusive or holistic levels of human consciousness, behaving and relating, as ends rather than means, to oneself, to significant others, to human beings in general, to other species, to nature, and to the cosmos."

> By understanding a person's needs, we can better communicate with them and ultimately de-escalate conflicts.

Understanding Interpersonal Communication Skills

Communication skills involve much more than just speaking well. Albert Mehrabian was a pioneer researcher of body language. In his book, *Nonverbal Communication*, he explained that most of our communication in a face-to-face encounter is nonverbal.

Our attitudes and emotions are continuously revealed on our faces—and most of us are completely unaware of it. Most people form 60% to 80% of their initial opinion about a new person in just a few minutes or less. To communicate effectively, you need to understand the 93% of communication that isn't verbal. Know what message you're sending—and accurately read the message being sent to you.

COMMUNICATION IS 93% NONVERBAL

55%	38%	7%
NONVERBAL	VOCAL tone | inflection	VERBAL words only

It's well known that good **communication** is the foundation of any successful relationship, be it personal or professional. It's important to recognize, though, that it's our **nonverbal communication**—our facial expressions, gestures, eye contact, posture, and tone of voice—that speak the loudest.

> Actions speak louder than words.
>
> It's not what you say, but how you say it.

- Over 90% of our communication is non-verbal.
- Most people are unconscious of their non-verbal communication.
- When reading another person's non-verbal communication, look for clusters.
- When individuals are stressed, angered, intoxicated, or combative, they will focus more on your non-verbal communication and less on your spoken words.
- Failure to pick up on incongruent verbal and non-verbal messages can be tragic.

Facial Expressions

Smiling and laughing are universally considered to be signals that show a person is happy. Smiling serves much the same purpose as it does with other primates:

it tells another person you are non-threatening and asks them to accept you on a personal level.

Genuine smiles are controlled by two sets of muscles, the zygomatic major muscles, which run down the sides of the face and connect to the corners of the mouth, and the orbicularis oculi, which pull the eyes back. Among humans, smiling is an expression denoting pleasure, sociability, happiness, joy, or amusement. It is distinct from a similar but usually involuntary expression of anxiety known as a grimace. Cross-cultural studies have shown that smiling is a means of communication throughout the world.[2]

Eye Communication

The Three I's of Eye Communication

- Intimate (signals interest in a person)
- Intimidating (a person will stare to intimidate or dominate another)
- Interested (recommended for appropriate interpersonal communications)

Give the amount of eye contact that makes others feel comfortable and that you are interested in them. When talking, we maintain 40% to 60% eye contact, with an average of 80% when listening. To build a good rapport with people, your eye contact should meet theirs about two-thirds of the time. (The exception to this is Japanese and some other Asian and South American cultures where extended eye contact can be seen as aggressive or disrespectful.)

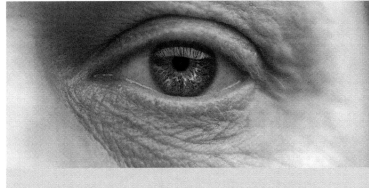

Reading Eye Communications

We have all heard that the eyes are the window to the soul. But what does this really tell us?

- **Looking up:** indicates a person is thinking.
- **Looking down:** a signal of submission.
- **Looking sideways:** can indicate distraction, showing interest in something, or irritation.
  - **Side-to-side:** shiftiness, lying, or looking for an escape route.
- **Glancing:** may indicate a person wants something.
  - **Target glance:** indicates a person is looking at the striking area.
- **Staring:** may indicate shock, disbelief, aggressiveness, or derangement.
- **Tears:** indicates sadness, extreme fear, or tears of joy.
- **Blinking:** blinking a lot can indicate significant stress—non-blinking can indicate attack.
- **Pupil size:** the pupils are affected by light and can also be affected by intoxication.
  - **Dilated:** may indicate use of cocaine, crack, meth, hallucinogens, and other stimulants
  - **Constricted:** may indicated use of heroin, depressants, and opioids

---

2 Izard, Carroll E. (1971). *The Face of Emotion*. New York: Appleton-Century-Croft. ISBN 0-390-47831-8.

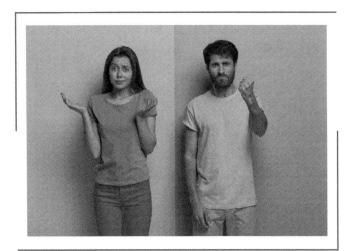

Body Language, Postures, and Gestures

> Body language is an outward reflection of a person's emotional condition. Stand up straight when talking and lean slightly forward when listening.

Crossed arms
When a person has a nervous, negative, or defensive attitude, it is very likely they will fold their arms firmly on their chest, displaying that they feel threatened. Crossed arms on the chest are universally perceived as defensive or negative.

Head nod
Nodding the head is almost universally used to indicate "yes" or agreement. Using a triple nod can be a persuasion tool. Research shows that people will talk three to four times more than usual when the listener nods their head at regular intervals.

Gestures
Be expressive, but don't overdo it. Keep your fingers closed when you gesture, hands below chin level, and avoid arm or feet crossing.

Hand Positions (Universal Signals)

The hands have been the most important tools in human evolution. **There are more connections between the brain and the hands than between any other body part.** Throughout history, the open palm has been associated with truth, honesty, allegiance, and submission. Hidden palms may give a person an intuitive feeling that the person they are communicating with is untruthful.

UNIVERSAL HAND SIGNALS

PALMS UP — Open

BLADED HANDS — Defensive

PALMS DOWN — Authority

CLENCHED HANDS — Aggressive

PALMS OUT — Stop

POINTING HANDS — Insulting

Developing and Improving Your Interpersonal Communication Skills

Some things to keep in mind when communicating:

1. **Be clear and concise when speaking.** Avoid using slang and jargon when speaking to people. It helps avoid confusion, misdirection, complaints, and poor interpersonal relations.
2. **Play the part of the scene you are in.** "All the world is indeed a stage, and we are merely players." As the stage changes, play the appropriate part to keep yourself and others safe.
3. **The Golden Rule** (treating others as you would like to be treated). Treating and speaking to people with respect is a universally accepted standard of treating people. "Do unto others as you would have them do unto you."
4. **Platinum Rule.** Treat others the way *they* want to be treated.
5. **Use common courtesies** consistently and repeatedly with all people, all the time.

    - Please.
    - Thank you.
    - Yes, please.
    - My pleasure.
    - You're welcome.
    - I am sorry to disturb you, but I need to speak with you for a moment.

6. **People watch and pay attention.** Watch and learn as you view the stage that others are on. Pay attention to what works and doesn't work for you and other people.
7. **Learn from your experiences and the experiences of others.** Experience is a great teacher! Knowledge, training, and experiences are the keys to understanding and de-escalating situations that are threatening, aggressive, and unsafe.

THE MIRACLE EXERCISE

1. Pair up facing one another.
2. One of you will be Partner A, and the other person will be Partner B.
3. If you are Partner A, while looking at Partner B, raise the corners of your mouth up one inch, take a deep breath, and hold it for 10 seconds.
    - Partner A: you are smiling.
4. More than likely Partner B will start smiling too.
5. Partner A now releases their breath in short exhalations. Partner A: you are now laughing.
    - Unless Partner B is a curmudgeon (grump), they'll probably start laughing too.
6. Repeat the process by reversing your roles.

Make a habit of smiling at others and see what happens. More than likely it will have a positive effect on both of you. Smiles attract smiles, and smiles make people feel good.

The Law of Reciprocation

The remarkable thing about a smile is that when you give it to someone, it causes them to reciprocate by returning the smile, even when you are both using fake smiles. This is why smiling is important to have as part of your customer service presence repertoire, even when you don't feel like it, because smiling directly influences other people's attitudes and how they respond to you.

Dr. Paul Ekman found that one of the reasons we are attracted to smiling and laughing faces is because they can actually affect our autonomic nervous system. We smile when we see a smiling face and this releases endorphins into our system.

Studies prove that when you make a point of regularly smiling, most customer encounters will run more smoothly, last longer, have more positive outcomes, and dramatically improve relationships.

■ Smiles produce a positive reaction in others.

Interpersonal Communication (IPC) involves sharing ideas and feelings through verbal and nonverbal messages. Key skills include active listening, assertiveness, influencing, persuading, empathizing, and demonstrating compassion. Nonverbal communication, such as facial expressions and body language, is crucial, making up 93% of communication. Effective IPC reduces conflict and builds understanding. Developing these skills involves clarity, respect, and learning from experiences. Smiling plays a significant role in fostering positive interactions and reciprocation.

Interpersonal Communication Videos

How Empathy Works - and Sympathy Can't
youtube.com/watch?v=1f0eSejlzLo

Elements that Impact your Communication
youtube.com/watch?v=f__g25cVPeU

The 7 - 38 - 55% Rule in Communication
youtube.com/watch?v=oeVRLSpu8uk

IF YOU OR SOMEONE YOU KNOW IS IN CRISIS AND CONSIDERING SELF-HARM OR SUICIDE:

- Call 911 for emergency services.
- Visit the nearest hospital emergency room.
- Call or text 988 to connect with the 988 Suicide and Crisis Lifeline, offering 24-hour, confidential support. *Para ayuda en español, llame al 988.*
- Support is also available via live chat at 988lifeline.org. *AVADE® does not monitor this website for crisis messages, provide medical advice, or make referrals.*

PSTI LEGAL DISCLAIMER

The information in this training book is a supplement, not a substitute, for the expertise of qualified healthcare professionals. The content on AVADE® Behavioral Health, sourced from reliable information, does not constitute medical or professional healthcare advice, diagnosis, or treatment. It is crucial to consult healthcare providers for specific guidelines related to medical or behavioral health conditions. This material does not guarantee that any technique or strategy is safe or effective for any specific needs. Personal Safety Training, Inc., does not dictate policies or procedures for behavioral health violence prevention, self-defense tactics, or any physical interventions. Agencies are responsible for developing their own policies and evaluating the recommendations based on their circumstances.

The author and publisher do not guarantee the completeness or accuracy of the information and assume no risk for its use. Any implied warranty are expressly disavowed.

MODULE 3

The Assault Cycle

The understanding of how aggressive incidents happen over a period of time

Module 3:
The Assault Cycle

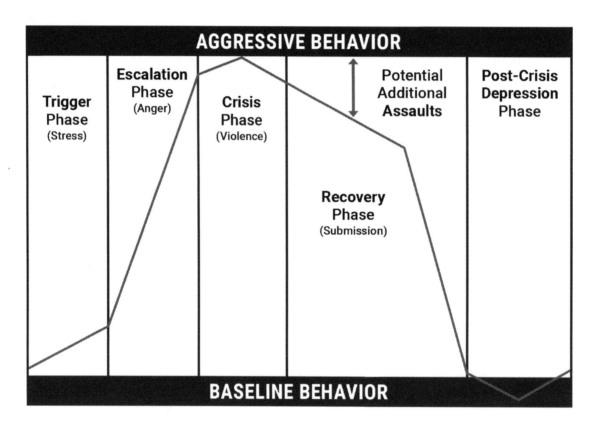

The Assault Cycle Defined

The Assault Cycle is a theory that describes how aggressive incidents happen over a period of time, developing through five specific stages or phases. This concept reminds us that violent events rarely happen without any warning signs, and it helps us to understand and manage people who have the potential to become violent. It highlights, in particular, the important role played by de-escalation techniques in preventing aggressive incidents from spiraling into violence.

Understanding the Assault Cycle and its phases are crucial to knowing how to de-escalate and defuse a potentially dangerous situation in order to break the cycle before violence occurs or escalates. The Assault Cycle is the predictable behavior that leads to violence. It includes individuals who are stressed, intoxicated, angry, physically combative, and submissive.

> Use caution when dealing with these behaviors as they can be violence-predicting factors.

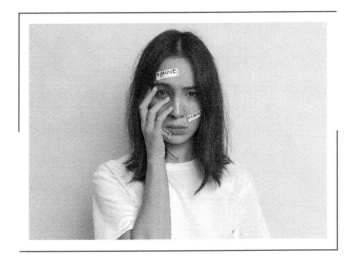

The Five Stages of the Assault Cycle

1. The Triggering Event (Stressors)
This is the initial stage where an event or situation triggers the individual's stress response. Triggers can be internal or external, such as frustration, fear, or environmental stressors. The individual perceives the event as very threatening, causing feelings of extreme fear or frustration. This phase begins when the individual feels there is a threat to their personal well-being, leading to frustration and a sense of deprivation or being ignored. Observable signs of distress might include reacting to arguments, disturbing phone calls, or loss of privileges, while non-observable threats could stem from delusions, hallucinations, or substance reactions. The individual may show signs of feeling a loss of control during this phase.

2. Escalation Phase (Anger)
During the Escalation Phase, the individual's behavior becomes more agitated and aggressive. Warning signs include increased verbal aggression, physical agitation, and nonverbal cues like clenched fists or a tense posture. The person becomes increasingly tense and ready to fight, displaying behaviors such as yelling, banging, pacing, kicking walls, and throwing objects. They may verbally challenge those associated with the perceived threat.

If verbal and nonverbal techniques fail to de-escalate the behavior, chemical or physical restraints might be necessary to prevent progression to the Crisis Phase. It is crucial to inform the individual of the consequences of their current behavior and the benefits of changing it. Maintaining a non-threatening and calm demeanor is essential to avoid further escalating the situation.

3. Crisis Phase (Violence)
This is the peak of the Assault Cycle where the individual may become violent, losing control over their actions and posing a risk to themselves and others. They might hit, kick, throw objects, or engage in other forms of physical assault, attacking the perceived threat. Generally, this phase is brief, as the individual cannot sustain the high energy required to continue the attack for long. Immediate intervention is crucial to ensure the safety of all involved.

4. Recovery Phase (Submission)
After the crisis, the individual begins to regain control and their aggression decreases. They may feel relief, embarrassment, or remorse as their body and mind start to relax and recover. The combative behavior appears to have ended, though it might only be temporary. During this phase, the individual slows down and seems more relaxed but has not yet returned to their baseline state. If another perceived threat occurs, another attack could happen. This phase is critical for monitoring and providing support to ensure the individual continues to de-escalate.

5. Post-Crisis Depression Phase
Following the recovery, the individual might experience feelings of guilt, depression, or fatigue. This phase is crucial for reflection and understanding the events that led to the crisis. The aggressor feels the emotional and physical toll of their actions and may exhibit signs of fatigue, depression, and/or guilt. They might cry, try to hide, or lie down.

This phase offers an opportunity for intervention and support to help the individual process their emotions and prevent future incidents.

Intervention strategies can be applied at each phase to prevent escalation and manage the situation effectively, emphasizing de-escalation techniques and ensuring the safety of everyone involved.

THE ASSAULT CYCLE = PREDICTABLE BEHAVIOR

The Assault Cycle is the predictable behavior pattern that may lead to violence. Understanding this cycle is crucial for de-escalating and defusing potentially dangerous situations, allowing intervention before violence occurs or escalates. The components of the assault cycle can involve any perpetrators of violence, including strangers, clients, patients, colleagues, or domestic individuals. Key factors include individuals who are stressed, intoxicated, angry, or physically combative.

The Assault Cycle describes the predictable stages leading to violence. It begins with a triggering event that causes stress and frustration. This is followed by the escalation phase, where behavior becomes increasingly agitated and aggressive. The crisis phase marks the peak of violence, posing significant risks. In the recovery phase, aggression decreases, but the threat may still linger. Finally, the post-crisis depression phase involves feelings of guilt and fatigue. Understanding these stages is crucial for de-escalating and managing potentially violent situations, ensuring safety, and preventing re-escalation. Constant vigilance is necessary, as individuals can disguise recovery to launch another attack.

Example of the Aggression Cycle
youtube.com/watch?v=98mxWhFnr4o

REACTIONARY GAP EXERCISE

> The "Reactionary Gap" is 4–6 feet: The distance between and you and an aggressor in which your ability to react/respond is impaired due to the close proximity of the aggressor.

When we are approaching individuals who are in the Assault Cycle (stressed, intoxicated, angry, escalated), we should approach them at a 45-degree angle versus approaching them head-on. We then proceed with our 5 Habits and maintain the appropriate distance from them.

- Action beats reaction within the Reactionary Gap.
- When we are too close to an individual, it can cause them anxiety and escalate them.
- When we lean in, we appear to be closer than we really are.
- A minimum distance of 4–6 feet is always recommended.
- Avoid using statements that can escalate a person.

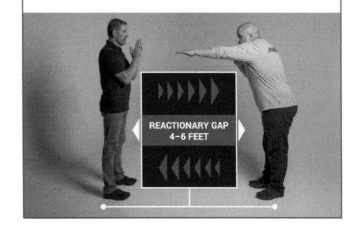

REACTIONARY GAP EXERCISE (PT. 1)

"Reactionary Gap" is the distance between and individual and an aggressor in which the ability to react is impaired due to the close proximity of the aggressor.

1. Form two lines with participants facing each other at approximately 10' apart.
2. Have **Line A** approach Line B until they are arm's length away from them and able to touch their shoulder.
3. Have both **Line A** and Line B place their hands in the prayer position.
4. **Line A** will begin by quickly touching Line B's shoulder with either hand. (Always come back to the prayer position. The touching of the shoulder is simulating an unarmed attack.)
5. Line B will try to defend against the shoulder attack by blocking with either hand or moving out of the way.
6. Reverse the roles of attacker and defender.
7. How did it go? Who didn't get hit?

> "Action beats reaction within the Reactionary Gap"

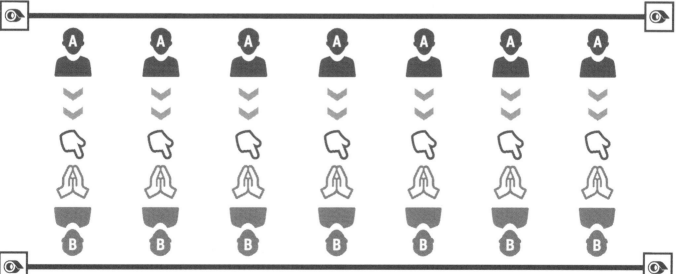

REACTIONARY GAP EXERCISE (PT. 2)

"Reactionary Gap" is the distance between and individual and an aggressor in which the ability to react is impaired due to the close proximity of the aggressor.

1. Form two lines with participants facing each other at approximately 10' apart.
2. Now instruct **Line B** to stop **Line A** as they approach with 4–6' of distance away from them.
3. **Line A** will again attack **Line B**'s shoulder from this new distance (4–6'). Notice that **Line A** must lunge in, in order to reach **Line B**'s shoulder.
4. **Line B**, again will defend by blocking with either hand or moving out of the way.
5. How did it go, **Line B**?
6. Reverse the roles of attacker and defender.

> **The minimum distance needed in order to react to an unarmed attack is 4–6' away from the attacker.**

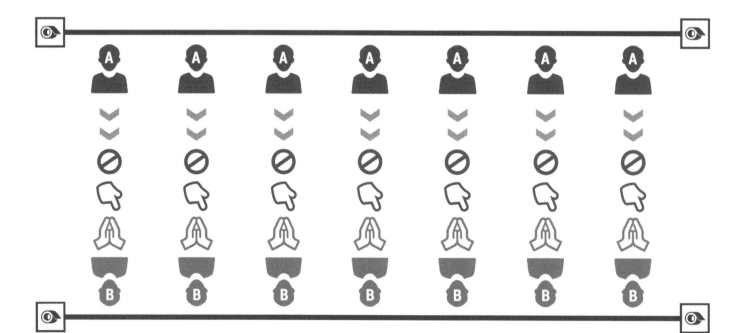

IF YOU OR SOMEONE YOU KNOW IS IN CRISIS AND CONSIDERING SELF-HARM OR SUICIDE:

- Call 911 for emergency services.
- Visit the nearest hospital emergency room.
- Call or text 988 to connect with the 988 Suicide and Crisis Lifeline, offering 24-hour, confidential support. *Para ayuda en español, llame al 988.*
- Support is also available via live chat at 988lifeline.org. *AVADE® does not monitor this website for crisis messages, provide medical advice, or make referrals.*

PSTI LEGAL DISCLAIMER

The information in this training book is a supplement, not a substitute, for the expertise of qualified healthcare professionals. The content on AVADE® Behavioral Health, sourced from reliable information, does not constitute medical or professional healthcare advice, diagnosis, or treatment. It is crucial to consult healthcare providers for specific guidelines related to medical or behavioral health conditions. This material does not guarantee that any technique or strategy is safe or effective for any specific needs. Personal Safety Training, Inc., does not dictate policies or procedures for behavioral health violence prevention, self-defense tactics, or any physical interventions. Agencies are responsible for developing their own policies and evaluating the recommendations based on their circumstances.

The author and publisher do not guarantee the completeness or accuracy of the information and assume no risk for its use. Any implied warranty are expressly disavowed.

MODULE 4

De-Escalation Tactics and Techniques

Effective strategies for calming conflicts and preventing violence

Module 4:
De-Escalation Tactics and Techniques

De-escalation is a strategy for reducing the intensity of a conflict or potentially violent situation. It involves techniques and communication methods for calming an agitated person and preventing further escalation.

Have You Encountered an Escalated Individual?

Have you ever . . .

- been harassed by someone?
- been intimidated by someone?
- been threatened by someone?
- been challenged by someone?
- been cursed at by someone?
- had someone verbally assault you?
- had someone verbally threaten you?
- had someone not respond to your communication?
- had someone push your buttons?
- been in conflict with someone?

If you answered **yes** to any of the above questions, you have witnessed or experienced escalated behavior. Escalation is a result of conflict!

De-Escalation and Escalation Defined

Escalation is the process of increasing or rising, derived from the concept of an escalator.

De-escalation refers to behavior that is intended to escape the escalations of conflicts. It may also refer to approaches in conflict resolution.

What is Conflict?

> Webster's definition of conflict:
>
> 1. fight, battle, war, and armed conflict
>
> 2. a: competitive or opposing action of incompatibles: antagonistic state or action (as of divergent ideas, interests, or persons) a conflict of principles
>
>   b: mental struggle resulting from incompatible or opposing needs, drives, wishes, or external or internal demands his conscience was in conflict with his duty.
>
> 3. the opposition of persons or forces that gives rise to the dramatic action in a drama or fiction. The conflict in the play is between the king and the archbishop.

Webster states it well. We have conflict because we are incompatible with each other; we have different needs, consciences, drives, wishes with internal and external demands. When these aren't met, we fight, battle, and arm ourselves for the conflict.

Conflict can be the result of unmet expectations.

All people will face conflict in their lives. Nations have conflicts with other nations; workers have conflicts with their fellow employees and customers; husbands and wives have conflicts with each other and with their children. One absolute in life is that we will not always agree with each other, as our expectations can be completely different from one another. Does that make the other person wrong? Does that make us right? No, it just makes us different.

Conflict can lead to escalation.

People don't automatically get aggressive and violent; there is an escalation process. While we may not always see the escalation, it is always present. Picture the escalator at the mall: you start at the bottom, and it brings you up to the top, or you start at the top, and it brings you down to the bottom. This analogy helps us understand that it is much easier to de-escalate a person at the bottom of the escalator before they reach the top. Conversely, it is more challenging to bring them down once they are at the top. Simply stated, the goal of this training is to intervene early with de-escalation skills and techniques to help prevent and mitigate escalating behavior, effectively turning the escalator down or off.

Escalation can lead to violence.

We live in a world filled with escalation and violence. Not a day goes by without hearing of an atrocity happening in our cities, streets, neighborhoods, and workplaces. De-escalation is a crucial tool that helps prevent people from escalating into violence, promoting safety and peace in our communities.

De-Escalation Ingredients

Specific uses of the term in reference to aggressive behavior include:[1]

Valuing the client
Providing genuine acknowledgement that the client's concerns are valid, important, and will be addressed in a meaningful way.

Reducing fear
Listen actively to the client and offers genuine empathy while suggesting that the client's situation has the potential for positive future change.

Inquiring about the client's queries and anxiety
Can communicate a thorough understanding of the client's concerns and works to uncover the root of the issue.

Providing guidance to the client
Suggests multiple ways to help the client with their current concerns and recommends preventative measures.

Working out possible agreements
Takes responsibility for the client's care and concludes the encounter with an agreed-upon short-term solution and a long-term action plan.

Remaining calm
Maintains a calm tone of voice and a steady pace that is appropriate to the client's feelings and behavior.

Spatial Risks
Maintains a moderate distance from the client to ensure safety but does not appear guarded and fearful.

---

[1] Mavandadi, V.; Bieling, P. J.; Madsen, V. (2016-08-01). "Effective ingredients of verbal de-escalation: validating an English modified version of the 'De-Escalating Aggressive Behaviour Scale.'" *Journal of Psychiatric and Mental Health Nursing.* 23 (6-7): 357–368.

The Aim of De-Escalation: Calm, Empathic Communication

De-escalation is aimed at calmly communicating with an agitated or escalated individual to understand, manage, and resolve their concerns. These actions help reduce the individual's agitation and potential for future aggression or violence. Inadequate or delayed intervention may force staff to resort to physical measures to manage an aggressive or violent individual. Physical measures, such as defensive tactics, subject control techniques, restraint, and seclusion, should always be *a last resort* and based on agency policies and procedures.

> Conflict/crisis: When individuals are in conflict/crisis, you are either de-escalating or escalating the person's behavior.

Response vs. Reaction

When we are trained, we can proactively respond. When we are not trained, we tend to react. The problem with reacting . . . there are two. One is called *overreacting*, and the other is *underreacting*. Neither is suitable for de-escalation. Response-able individuals are proactive versus reactive.

It is best explained in a simple equation:

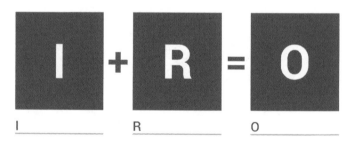

I + R = O

If an individual is aggressive and escalating (incident), knowing how to respond (response) to the situation can lead to a non-violent outcome. You can increase your personal safety by taking responsibility for all the incidents you are in and by making conscious, informed choices and decisions about the people you are dealing with.

This training will illustrate de-escalation responses to a variety of incidents and behaviors. There are no guarantees that we can de-escalate everyone, as some individuals may be intent on being violent. However, the AVADE® mission, vision, and philosophy holds that with proper knowledge and understanding of how people communicate, you can successfully intervene and de-escalate most situations. **The common denominator in the equation (I+R=O) is you.** If you are involved with a person who is upset and escalating, you are part of the equation. Your responses can either de-escalate or escalate the incident.

React = DIE (Denial, Ignorance, and Emotions)

Denial, ignorance, and emotions are not proper responses to people in crisis or conflict. They are also ineffective when dealing with individuals who are upset, stressed, angry, intoxicated, in a mental health crisis, or violent. Denial, ignorance, and emotions spell out the word "DIE." Believing that you will not encounter people in conflict is denial. Ignoring people in conflict can escalate the incident. Emotions can cause us to be reactive rather than proactive. Proper responses to situations or incidents make us response-able (responsible). AVADE® Behavioral Health Training focuses on properly responding to escalated individuals.

De-escalation responses

This de-escalation training is intended to equip you (the reader) for incidents in your workplace and personal life. The strategies and techniques in this training program have been utilized by thousands of individuals in workplaces throughout North America. Our clients in healthcare, private corporations, gaming/casinos, private security, and law enforcement encounter people daily who are escalating in behavior.

The 5 Habits of De-Escalation and Making a Positive Impression

Making a first impression refers to the initial perception that others form about you when they meet you for the first time. This impression is based on a combination of factors, including your appearance, body language, demeanor, and the way you communicate. First impressions are formed quickly, often within the first few seconds of meeting someone, and can have a lasting impact on how you are perceived in the future.

The saying "You only get one chance to make a first impression" emphasizes the importance of creating a positive initial impression because you typically have only one opportunity to do so. First impressions are formed quickly and can be difficult to change, so it's crucial to present yourself in the best possible way from the start. This adage highlights the lasting impact that first interactions can have on relationships and perceptions.

THE 5 HABITS OF DE-ESCALATION EXERCISE

Habit I
360° View of Awareness and Plan "E"scape

Habit II
Approach 45° and blade your body 45° (relaxed 45° with at least 4-6 feet away)

Habit III
Hands open (palms up—this approach is less threatening to people)

Habit IV
Introduce yourself and get the individual's name (use your name, seek their name, and use their name when explaining why you are there)

Habit V
QTIP – Quit taking it personally

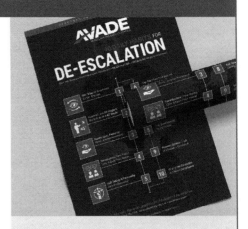

When approaching individuals who are in the assault cycle (stressed, intoxicated, angry, escalated), approach them at a 45-degree angle versus approaching them head-on. This type of approach reduces tension and is a lot safer.

"Good morning /afternoon /evening, "I am (name and job title) with (state your agency), and you are?"

"I am here (use their name) because (explain why you are there)."

De-Escalation for the Triggering Phase (upset/stressed individuals)

The following information can assist you in recognizing that an individual has been triggered and is now upset or stressed, and has the potential to escalate.

Signs/symptoms of an individual being triggered:

- **Emotional:** agitated, frustrated, moody, feeling overwhelmed, difficulty relaxing or quieting the mind, low self-esteem, feeling depressed, avoiding others, etc.
- **Physical:** change in facial expression, change in eye contact, low energy, medical symptoms (headache, upset stomach, etc.), nervousness, dry mouth, clenched jaw, grinding teeth, shallow breathing, etc.
- **Cognitive:** constant worrying, racing thoughts, inability to focus, poor judgment, pessimism, acting distracted or confused, etc.
- **Behavioral:** change in appetite, change in speech, procrastinating and avoiding responsibilities, increased use of alcohol and drugs, nail biting, fidgeting, pacing, etc.

Triggering Phase De-Escalation Techniques

Use these verbal and physical maneuvers and interventions to defuse and de-escalate and to avoid escalation and violent behavior:

- **Habit I:** 360° view of awareness and plan "E"scape
- **Habit II:** Approach at 45° and blade your body 45° (relaxed 45°, 4–6 ft. away)
  - Blade your body so the other person does not feel threatened. When dealing with people who are stressed, angered, intoxicated, or escalated, always *blade* your body. The bladed stance is done by simply turning your body slightly to the side. This stance protects your vulnerable line (nose to groin) as you are now in an angled position. This position is less threatening to others and provides less of a target to an aggressor if the situation escalates. The bladed position can also be done from a seated position.
  - Assess the area and space you're in and *stay at least 4–6' away*. Know your escape routes. Getting too close to people can escalate them.
- **Habit III:** Hands open (palms up—this approach is less threatening to people)
  - Assess your body language: What signals are you sending? Avoid being rigid. Staying relaxed will encourage the other person to relax.
  - Remember, over 90% of communication is non-verbal.
- **Habit IV:** Introduce yourself and get the individual's name.
  - Use your voice and a slow, quiet, confident tone.
  - Use names (the individual's and yours). Introduce yourself and ask the individual his or her name.

Personalizing a situation can reduce tension and establish a bond.

- **Habit V:** QTIP (Quit Taking It Personally)
  - Control your behavior. If you get upset or agitated, you will escalate the situation. Do not get sucked into the issue.
  - Remember **I + R = O**, and be a professional.
- **Do not touch the individual.** Touching a person may escalate the situation.
- **Break eye contact to remain non-threatening.** Use your interested eye contact when you do look the person in the eye.
- **Use attentive listening.** Make sure the individual feels like he/she is being listened to (use paraphrasing).
- **Do not make promises that you cannot keep.** Medications and service times are particularly relevant triggers in regard to promises.
- **Clarify communications and ask for specific responses.**
  - "You want _____, is that correct?"
  - "What can I do to help you?"
  - "I sense you are upset?"
  - "Do you have any questions for me?"
  - "Are you understanding everything?"
- **Express your intention to help.**
  - "I am here to help."
  - "Is there anything I can get you?"
- **Redirect environment.** We redirect environments by getting people to move to a new location or area. Moving a person to another location allows them to "save face" (respect) if there are friends and family near. It may also provide you a safer location to deal with them.
- **Redirect thoughts.** We redirect thoughts by asking questions, and questions are powerful. Properly asked questions can enable the person posing them to de-escalate the entire situation. A redirected thought could be facilitated by a randomly asked question (RAQ).

De-Escalation for the Escalation Phase (angry/aggressive individuals)

The following information can assist you in recognizing that an individual has escalated, is now angry and aggressive, and has the potential to further escalate into a crisis.

Signs/symptoms of an individual who has escalated:

- Loud voice
- Challenging statements
- Foul language
- Verbal threats
- Veiled threats: "What do you mean by?"
- Physically acting out (pacing and tense)

- Personal history of violence (knowledge of a person's background and history can be extremely important as it can be a pre-incident indicator of escalation to violence)
- Exaggerated movements (stomping, hitting objects, posturing)
- Demanding expressions (finger-pointing, lips pressed or pushed forward, nose wrinkled, and posturing)
- Demanding (unnecessary services, unnecessary attention, entitlement)
- Acting disgruntled (may be passive aggression)
- Attempting to intimidate (by invading a person's personal space)

Escalation Phase De-Escalation Techniques

Use these verbal and physical maneuvers and interventions to defuse and de-escalate and to avoid escalation and violent behavior:

- **Habit I:** 360° view of awareness and plan "E"scape
- **Habit II:** Approach at 45° and blade your body 45° (relaxed 45°, 4–6 ft. away)
  - Blade your body so the other person does not feel threatened. When dealing with people who are stressed, angered, intoxicated, or escalated, always *blade* your body. The bladed stance is done by simply turning your body slightly to the side. This stance protects your vulnerable line (nose to groin) as you are now in an angled position. This position is less threatening to others and provides less of a target to an aggressor if the situation escalates. The bladed position can also be done from a seated position.
  - Assess the area and space you're in and *stay at least 4–6' away*. Know your escape routes. Getting too close to people can escalate them.
- **Habit III:** Hands open (palms up—this approach is less threatening to people)
  - Assess your body language: What signals are you sending? Avoid being rigid. Staying relaxed will encourage the other person to relax.
  - Remember, over 90% of communication is non-verbal.
- **Habit IV:** Introduce yourself and get the individual's name.
  - Use your voice and a slow, quiet, confident tone.
  - Use names (the individual's and yours). Introduce yourself and ask the individual his or her name. Personalizing a situation can reduce tension and establish a bond.
- **Habit V:** QTIP (Quit Taking It Personally)
  - Control your behavior. If you get upset or agitated, you will escalate the situation. Do not get sucked into the issue.
  - Remember **I + R = O**, and be a professional.
- **Walk away if possible.** Yes, just walk away (tap out and remove yourself from the situation).
- **Avoid arguing.** No one ever really wins an argument. So avoid arguing and telling someone they are wrong. Instead, use this powerful phrase: "If I were in your shoes, I would probably feel the same way." With the information received, you may be able to offer a resolution (fix) to the problem.
- **Don't interrupt.** Allow them to vent. Interrupting a person is the quickest and surest way to tell them that you are not listening and that your thoughts and ideas are more important than theirs.

- **Display sincerity.** Sincerity means freedom from deceit, hypocrisy, or duplicity. The ancient word "sincere" means without wax. When we are sincere, we are real. People know when individuals are fake. Be sincere!
- **Seek to agree.** And get them to say "yes." When we agree with another person or get them to agree with us, it builds a bond. (Example: "You're right; this place is a bummer." "Yeah, it is overcrowded in here.")
- **Use a collaborative approach.** Using "we" and "us" gives a person a feeling of belonging. (Example: "Why don't we sit down and talk about this." "Between us, we will come up with something." "Why don't we go outside and talk about this.")
- **Identify the problem.** Ask them, "I sense you are angry/upset?" Using this technique gets right to the heart of the problem versus dancing around the issue. There may be a simple solution or a way to fix it for the person who is angry. People who are asked the question ("I sense you are angry/upset") will generally tell you why they are angry/upset. With the information received, you may be able to offer a resolution (fix) to the problem.
- **Ask questions rather than give orders!** What are the most common problems that you face in your workplace? Identify them. And instead of ordering a person to stop what they're doing, ask a question. Examples:
  - **Order**: "You need to take your meds."
    Question: "Did you know that it is time for meds?"
  - **Order**: "You can't be in this area."
    Question: "Did you know this area is for staff only?"
  - **Order**: "You need to get back in your room."
    Question: "Did you know it is quiet time for all residents in their rooms?"

> Asking a question versus giving an order gives a person an out. It allows them to save face, develops a rapport with them, and provides the compliance that you are looking for.

- **Give options.** People don't like absolutes; they prefer options. Always offer the best option first and less desirable options after. It puts the "ball in their court," so to speak.
- **Resist being defensive (do not make threats and ignore challenges).** When we are defensive or make threats and challenges, we become the aggressive individual. Remember QTIP, and don't go down in the mud with the individual. If you feel like you are getting sucked into the situation, remove yourself.
- **Set and enforce boundaries.** But only set ones you can enforce. Initially, we allow people to vent. But when people vent, and vent, and continue to vent, you may need to intervene and set boundaries. If you say you are going to do something, you need to be able to back it up. .

REMEMBER: THE GOAL OF DE-ESCALATION IS COMPLIANCE AND COOPERATION

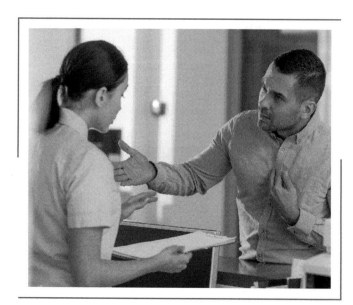

Avoidance for the Crisis Phase (physically combative/violent individuals)

When staff are physically assaulted in an incident, it is primarily because they miss the signs and symptoms of imminent assault. Most of these signs and symptoms are non-verbal, which will be covered extensively in the following information. Another primary reason staff are physically assaulted is that they are too close to the aggressor/attacker. Action beats reaction within the 4-6 foot reactionary gap, so maintaining distance may give time to avoid and escape a combative situation. Staff can also become victims of assault because they are compromised in their environment, lacking an escape plan or route, and do not have control (owning) of the door. Lastly, staff can be physically assaulted while responding to an emergency situation where they need to defend others or control an individual who is out of control and a threat to themselves and others.

The following information can assist you in recognizing that an individual has escalated, is now angry and aggressive, and has the potential to further escalate into a crisis.

Signs/symptoms of an individual who is in the Assault Cycle of crisis:

- Changes in posture—dropping into a fighting stance (pugilistic stance)
- Preparatory signals—rolls sleeves up, takes the coat off, etc., or stands up suddenly
- Scanning area by moving head side to side
- Non- or slow-blinking pattern ("thousand-yard stare")
- Flanking positioning (finding a suitable position to attack)
- Telegraphing intentions—arm swings or gets cocked before a punch is thrown
- Looks at striking area—an assailant will almost always look at the area they intend to strike before the attack (target glance)
- Exaggerated movements (lunging in)
- Changes in verbalization—either talking a lot more or suddenly talking less
- Bracing effect—as though bracing to hit or be hit
- Tightening of body and/or fists (clenching)
- Trying to distract you

Strategies to Avoid Physical Harm from the Assault Cycle of Crisis

- **Escape immediately.** That is the most important thing you can do. Once someone has reached the state of combative aggression, your number one priority is to get away. The best self-defense is not to be there! Escape-Escape-Escape!
- **Defensive presence.** Show that you're ready to defend yourself by blading your body and hands. A defensive presence demonstrates that you are trained and ready to defend yourself if needed. A defensive presence should only be used in a combative situation; otherwise, it could escalate a situation by sending a message that you are aggressive.
- **Loud scream/yell so you can attract attention.** Yelling, "Stop!" can also arrest someone's attack. Yelling or screaming loudly will alert others, create witnesses, establish your authority, keep you breathing, distract the aggressor, provide direction to the aggressor, and reduce liability risk to you and your agency.
- **Use distractions to interrupt their focus/intent.** Distractions buy us time to escape, defend or control. Distractions interrupt one or more of the

five senses, giving you time to act. Distractions are sounds, movements, lights, and psychological interruptions. Always use distractions!

- **Stay aware—avoid tunnel vision.** When your heart rate exceeds 145 beats per minute, your vision narrows, causing what is called "tunnel vision." Knowing this, you can avoid it by physically turning your head from side to side.

- **Watch to see what they are planning to do next.** Awareness is always the key component in dealing with combative individuals. Anticipating what the combatant will do next gives us time. And time is precious.

- **Get help: Alert others by motioning or verbalizing.** There is safety in numbers! Many agencies have "emergency codes" for combative persons. Know your codes and how to initiate them.

- **Last resort: Defend or control if escape is impossible!** If you cannot get away, you are left with only two options, defend yourself and/or control the out-of-control individual. Being a victim is not an option!

Security/Code Team Responses to Workplace Violence Incidents

- Ensure that you know how to contact security in an emergency. Memorize their number and extension.
- Security can assist law enforcement with contact, directions, and proper documentation.
- Security should be notified of all incidents of workplace violence.

The Recovery Phase: Submission

Just as important as knowing the phases of triggering, escalation, and crisis (components of the assault cycle) is knowing the signs of submission (recovery phase). Submission is displayed through a significant cluster of body movements that signal fear and readiness to submit. This behavior is common in both humans and animals. Many animals avoid fighting amongst themselves (which could maim or kill them) by displaying either aggression or submission.

Signs/Symptoms of an individual who is recovering (submission):

- **Body positions.** In fearful stances, the body is generally closed in on itself and may also exhibit other signs of fearfulness.

- **Self-protection.** Hunching inwards reduces the size of the body, limiting the potential of being hit and protecting vital areas—for example, hands covering the crotch or chin pushed down to protect the neck. In a natural setting, being small may also reduce the chance of being seen. Arms are held in. A crouching position may be taken, with knees slightly bent. This posture approaches the curled-up, regressive fetal position.

- **Lowering.** Putting the body in a lower position shows the other person that you are not a physical threat. This can include hunching down, bowing, kneeling, or even prostration. It is no surprise that these are typically used in formal greetings of a superior person. Even in sitting, a submissive person will choose a lower chair or slump in order to be lower than others are.

- **Motionlessness.** In a natural setting, staying still reduces the chance of being seen (which is why many animals freeze when they are fearful). If exposed, it also reduces the chance of accidentally sending signals that may be interpreted as aggressive. Staying still signals submission, that you are ready to be struck and will not fight back..

- **Head down.** Turning the chin and head down protects the vulnerable neck from attack. You also avoid looking at the other person in the face (since staring is a sign of aggression).

- **Eyes down.** Widening the eyes makes you look more like a baby and hence signals your vulnerability. Looking attentively at the other person shows that you are hanging on to their every word.

- **Mouth (smile).** Submissive people smile more at dominant people. However, they often smile with the mouth but not with the eyes.

- **Submissive gestures.** The many gestures that show submission communicate that there is no intent to harm the other person. Hands out and palms up show that no weapons are held and are a common pleading gesture. Other gestures and actions that indicate tension may reveal a state of fear. This includes hair tugging, face touching, and jerky movement. There may also be signs such as losing color in the face and sweating.

- **Small gestures.** When the submissive person must move, they often make small gestures. These may be slow to avoid alarming the other person, although tension may make them jerky.

- **Submissive verbalization.** Common verbalizations will be:
  - "I'm sorry,"
  - "I shouldn't have...,"
  - "I didn't mean to,"
  - "I apologize,"
  - "What can I do?"
  - "You're right; I'm wrong," etc.

- **Wanting to shake your hand.** An individual may want to shake your hand as an expression of their submission. Caution! When shaking a person's hand, we are within the reactionary gap (4-foot zone) and may be vulnerable to an attack. This tactic could be a ploy to lead you into the attack zone.

Dealing with people who are stressed, angry, intoxicated, or physically combative can be a frightening experience. For some, it is part of daily experience at their workplace. No matter what you do, your interpersonal communications/de-escalation can help you recognize and defuse a potentially violent situation.

Post-Crisis Phase

Following recovery, the individual might experience feelings of guilt, depression, or fatigue, reflecting on the events that led to the crisis. They may exhibit signs such as crying, hiding, or lying down, indicating the emotional and physical toll of their actions. Intervention/support is necessary for an individual to process their emotions and prevent future incidents.

IF YOU OR SOMEONE YOU KNOW IS IN CRISIS AND CONSIDERING SELF-HARM OR SUICIDE:

- Call 911 for emergency services.
- Visit the nearest hospital emergency room.
- Call or text 988 to connect with the 988 Suicide and Crisis Lifeline, offering 24-hour, confidential support. *Para ayuda en español, llame al 988.*
- Support is also available via live chat at 988lifeline.org. AVADE® does not monitor this website for crisis messages, provide medical advice, or make referrals.

PSTI LEGAL DISCLAIMER

The information in this training book is a supplement, not a substitute, for the expertise of qualified healthcare professionals. The content on AVADE® Behavioral Health, sourced from reliable information, does not constitute medical or professional healthcare advice, diagnosis, or treatment. It is crucial to consult healthcare providers for specific guidelines related to medical or behavioral health conditions. This material does not guarantee that any technique or strategy is safe or effective for any specific needs. Personal Safety Training, Inc., does not dictate policies or procedures for behavioral health violence prevention, self-defense tactics, or any physical interventions. Agencies are responsible for developing their own policies and evaluating the recommendations based on their circumstances.

The author and publisher do not guarantee the completeness or accuracy of the information and assume no risk for its use. Any implied warranty are expressly disavowed.

Anxiety Disorder

MODULE 5

Excessive, persistent worry and fear that interferes with daily activities

Module 5: Anxiety Disorder

Anxiety Disorder Defined

> Anxiety disorder is a mental health condition characterized by excessive and persistent worry, fear, or nervousness that is disproportionate to the actual threat or situation. Unlike normal anxiety, which is a temporary and often rational response to stress or danger, anxiety disorder involves chronic anxiety that interferes with daily activities and functioning.

Anxiety is a feeling of fear, dread, and uneasiness. It might cause you to sweat, feel restless and tense, and have a rapid heartbeat. It can be a normal reaction to stress. For example, you might feel anxious when faced with a difficult problem at work, before taking a test, or before making an important decision. It can help you to cope. The anxiety may give you a boost of energy or help you focus. But for people with anxiety disorders, the fear is not temporary and can be overwhelming.

Anxiety disorders are conditions in which you have anxiety that does not go away and can get worse over time. The symptoms can interfere with daily activities such as job performance, schoolwork, and relationships.

Anxiety Disorder Facts and Statistics

- Almost 20% of adults in the U.S. suffer from anxiety disorders.
- Anxiety disorders are highly treatable, yet only 1/3 of those suffering receive treatment.
- People with an anxiety disorder are 3-5x more likely to go to the doctor and 3x more likely to be hospitalized for psychiatric disorders than those who do not suffer from anxiety disorders.[1]
- Almost 3% of Americans experience panic disorder in a given year and it is twice as common in women than in men.
- 1/3 of youth (ages 13-18) suffer from anxiety disorder.[2] Research shows that untreated children with anxiety disorders are at higher risk of performing poorly in school, missing out on important social experiences, and engaging in substance abuse.

---

1 https://adaa.org/understanding-anxiety/facts-statistics#-Facts%20and%20Statistics

2 https://mhanational.org/sites/default/files/B2S%202018%20Fact%20Sheet%20-%20Recognizing%20Anxiety.pdf

- Generalized anxiety disorder (GAD) affects over 3% of the U.S. population, in any given year.[3]
- Social anxiety disorder affects approximately 15 million American adults and is the second most commonly diagnosed anxiety disorder following specific phobia.[4]
- Specific phobias affect almost 10% of the U.S. population.
- It's not uncommon for someone with an anxiety disorder to also suffer from depression or vice versa. Nearly one-half of those diagnosed with depression are also diagnosed with an anxiety disorder.

Signs and Symptoms of Anxiety

Anxiety disorders are a group of related conditions, each having unique symptoms. However, all anxiety disorders have one thing in common: persistent, excessive fear or worry in situations that are not threatening. People typically experience one or more of the following symptoms:

Emotional symptoms
- Feelings of apprehension or dread
- Feeling tense or jumpy
- Restlessness or irritability
- Anticipating the worst and being watchful for signs of danger

Physical symptoms
- Pounding or racing heart and shortness of breath
- Sweating, tremors and twitches
- Headaches, fatigue and insomnia
- Upset stomach, frequent urination or diarrhea

[3] https://adaa.org/understanding-anxiety/generalized-anxiety-disorder-gad

[4] https://adaa.org/understanding-anxiety/social-anxiety-disorder

Anxiety Causes

The causes of anxiety disorders aren't fully understood. Life experiences such as traumatic events appear to trigger anxiety disorders in people who are already prone to anxiety. Inherited traits also can be a factor. For some people, anxiety may be linked to an underlying health issue.

In some cases, anxiety signs and symptoms are the first indicators of a medical illness. If your doctor suspects your anxiety may have a medical cause, he or she may order tests to look for signs of a problem.

Examples of medical problems that can be linked to anxiety include: heart disease, diabetes, thyroid problems, respiratory disorders, such as chronic obstructive pulmonary disease (COPD) and asthma, drug misuse or withdrawal, withdrawal from alcohol, anti-anxiety medications (benzodiazepines) or other medications, chronic pain or irritable bowel syndrome, and rare tumors that produce certain fight-or-flight hormones.

Anxiety Risk Factors

These factors may increase your risk of developing an anxiety disorder:

- **Trauma.** Children who endured abuse or trauma or witnessed traumatic events are at higher risk of developing an anxiety disorder at some point in life. Adults who experience a traumatic event also can develop anxiety disorders.
- **Stress due to an illness.** Having a health condition or serious illness can cause significant worry about issues such as your treatment and your future.
- **Stress buildup.** A big event or a buildup of smaller stressful life situations may trigger excessive anxiety — for example, a death in the family, work stress or ongoing worry about finances.

- **Personality.** People with certain personality types are more prone to anxiety disorders than others.
- **Other mental health disorders.** People with other mental health disorders, such as depression, often also have an anxiety disorder.
- **Having blood relatives with an anxiety disorder.** Anxiety disorders can run in families.
- **Drugs or alcohol.** Drug or alcohol use/misuse or withdrawal can cause or worsen anxiety.

Types of Anxiety Disorders

Anxiety disorders can vary in symptoms and triggers, but they can all interfere with daily activities. Some common types of anxiety disorders include:

- **Generalized anxiety disorder (GAD):** Persistent and excessive worry that interferes with daily activities.
- **Panic disorder:** Can cause severe bouts of elevated anxiety, chest pains, racing heartbeat, and difficulty breathing.
- **Phobias:** Intense fear of or aversion to specific objects or situations, such as agoraphobia (fear of public places) or claustrophobia (fear of closed-in spaces)
- **Social anxiety disorder:** Previously called social phobia; a condition marked by an intense fear of being judged by others, significantly impacting daily activities and social interactions.

Anxiety Disorder Crisis

> An anxiety disorder crisis typically refers to a severe and overwhelming episode of anxiety symptoms that significantly impair a person's ability to function. An anxiety crisis can be an intense and persistent form of anxiety that lasts for a prolonged period of time, such as an anxiety attack. Anxiety attacks can last from several minutes to weeks.

People with anxiety disorders frequently have intense, excessive, and persistent worry and fear about everyday situations. An anxiety disorder crisis can involve severe symptoms that may escalate to an emergency situation.

This can include the following:

- **Panic attacks:** People with panic disorder may experience panic attacks characterized by intense fear and physical symptoms such as chest pain, shortness of breath, and dizziness. In some instances, these symptoms can mimic those of a heart attack, leading the person to seek emergency medical attention.
- **Suicidal thoughts:** Severe anxiety can sometimes lead to suicidal thoughts or behaviors, especially if the person feels overwhelmed and unable to cope with their symptoms. Suicidal ideation is a serious emergency that requires immediate intervention by mental health professionals.
- **Self-harm:** Some individuals with anxiety disorders may resort to self-harming behaviors as a way to cope with overwhelming emotions. This can lead to serious physical injuries and may require urgent medical treatment.
- **Substance abuse:** In an attempt to alleviate anxiety symptoms, some individuals may turn to substance

abuse, such as alcohol or drugs. This can lead to addiction, overdose, or other medical emergencies.

- **Severe impairment:** If anxiety symptoms become so severe that the person is unable to take care of themselves or engage in daily activities, it can result in a crisis situation requiring immediate intervention and support.

If someone with an Anxiety Disorder is exhibiting these crisis symptoms, it's crucial to seek immediate help from mental health professionals, crisis intervention services, or emergency services to ensure their safety and provide appropriate care.

Crisis and De-Escalation Interventions for Anxiety Disorder

- Use a trauma-informed approach.
- Use positive interpersonal communication skills.
- Use the daily habits of de-escalation.
- Guidelines for Anxiety Disorder crisis and de-escalation strategies:
  - **Contact crisis intervention teams.** Contact mental health crisis intervention teams if the situation escalates and professional intervention is needed.
  - **Contact the Suicide and Crisis Lifeline.** If you or someone you know is struggling or having thoughts of suicide, call or text the 988 Suicide & Crisis Lifeline at 988 or chat at 988lifeline.org. In life-threatening situations, call 911.
  - **Ensure safety.** Assess the environment to remove any potentially harmful objects and maintain physical distance to avoid escalating the situation.
  - **Stay calm yourself.** It's essential to remain calm and composed when interacting with someone in an anxiety crisis. Your calm demeanor can help the person feel more secure and less overwhelmed.
  - **Use calming language.** Speak in a soothing and reassuring tone. Avoid using harsh or commanding language. Use phrases like "I'm here to help" or "You're safe" to convey support.
  - **Acknowledge their feelings.** Validate the person's emotions and let them know that it's okay to feel anxious. Avoid minimizing their feelings or dismissing their concerns.
  - **Encourage slow breathing.** Breathing exercises can help reduce anxiety symptoms. Encourage the person to take slow, deep breaths. You can model the breathing technique for them to follow.
  - **Create a safe space.** If possible, move to a quiet and comfortable environment away from crowds or loud noises. Provide a safe space where the person can sit or lie down if needed.
  - **Offer distraction.** Engage the person in calming activities or distractions, such as listening to soothing music, focusing on a relaxing object, or practicing mindfulness exercises.
  - **Respect personal boundaries.** Respect the person's personal space and boundaries.
  - **Use visual cues.** Visual cues, such as hand gestures or written instructions, can be helpful for communication if the person is having difficulty verbalizing their needs.
- **Guidelines to avoid anxiety crisis escalation:**
  - **Avoid stressful environments.** High-stress environments, such as crowded spaces, noisy settings, or chaotic situations, can trigger anxiety in susceptible individuals.
  - **Avoid conflict or confrontation.** Interpersonal conflicts, arguments, or confrontational situations can escalate anxiety, especially for individuals with social anxiety disorder or generalized anxiety disorder.

- **Avoid impatience or frustration.** Rushing their recovery with remarks like "snap out of it" or expressing irritation can make them feel pressured, misunderstood, and more anxious or sad.
- **Avoid traumatic events or triggers.** Exposure to traumatic events, triggers related to past traumas, or reminders of distressing experiences can significantly escalate anxiety symptoms.
- **Avoid health concerns.** Physical health issues, chronic illnesses, or concerns about one's health can trigger health anxiety and lead to increased anxiety levels.
- **Avoid financial problems.** Financial difficulties, job insecurity, or economic stressors can contribute to anxiety, particularly for individuals prone to worry and stress about the future.
- **Avoid sleep disturbances.** Lack of adequate sleep, insomnia, or disruptions in sleep patterns can impair emotional regulation and increase susceptibility to anxiety triggers.
- **Avoid isolation or loneliness.** Feelings of isolation, loneliness, or a lack of social support can intensify anxiety symptoms and contribute to a sense of vulnerability.

- Build a trusting relationship and work in an open, engaging, and non-judgmental manner.
- Be aware that stigma and discrimination can be associated with a diagnosis of anxiety.
- Work as a multidisciplinary team and offer guidance and support (family, caregivers).
- Encourage them to meet their ADL's (Activities of Daily Living).
- Show environmental awareness (safely remove any objects that the person could use to harm themselves).
- Seek immediate suicide intervention when needed (see Module 16).

Effective de-escalation and crisis intervention for anxiety disorder requires a combination of compassion, empathy, active listening, and practical actions to ensure immediate safety and long-term support. By creating a safe and supportive environment, engaging appropriate resources, and following up with continuous care, individuals experiencing a crisis can be guided toward stability and recovery.

It's important to recognize that triggers can vary from person to person, and what may escalate one individual's anxiety may not affect another in the same way. Understanding personal triggers and developing coping strategies tailored to individual needs can be instrumental in managing anxiety effectively.

Addressing the risks associated with an anxiety disorder crisis requires a proactive and compassionate approach. By implementing training, support systems, and clear protocols and promoting a supportive workplace culture, organizations can effectively manage these risks and ensure the safety and well-being of all staff members. Mental health is a crucial aspect of overall health, and taking steps to support it benefits both individuals and the organization as a whole.

Anxiety Disorder Treatments[5]

> **Disclaimer:** Personal Safety Training Inc. makes no claim as to what type of treatment is needed for any mental health disorder.

Treatment for anxiety disorders typically involves a combination of therapy, medication, lifestyle changes, and self-care strategies:

- **Therapy:** Cognitive Behavioral Therapy (CBT) addresses negative thoughts and behaviors, exposure therapy gradually desensitizes anxiety triggers, and mindfulness practices increase awareness to manage anxiety.
- **Medication:** SSRIs and SNRIs balance neurotransmitters, benzodiazepines provide short-term relief but have dependence risks, and beta-blockers address physical symptoms like rapid heartbeat.
- **Lifestyle changes:** Regular exercise, a healthy diet, adequate sleep, and stress management techniques such as deep breathing and stretching help reduce anxiety.
- **Self-care strategies:** Engaging in self-care activities, avoiding anxiety triggers, and setting realistic goals to improve well-being.
- **Support groups:** Joining support or therapy groups provides community, validation, and shared experiences.

It's essential for individuals with anxiety disorders to work closely with mental health professionals to develop a personalized treatment plan that addresses their specific needs and preferences. Combination approaches often yield the best results in managing anxiety symptoms effectively.

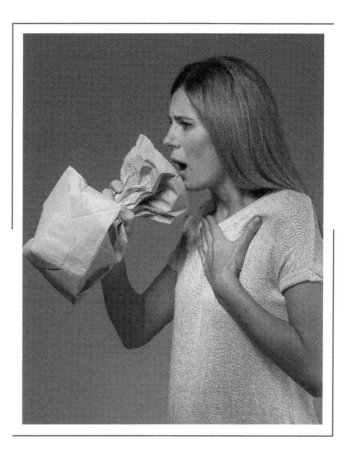

Panic Attack Assessment and Monitoring

A panic attack is a sudden episode of intense fear that triggers severe physical reactions when there is no real danger or apparent cause. Panic attacks can be very frightening. When panic attacks occur, you might think you're losing control, having a heart attack, or even dying.

Many people have just one or two panic attacks in their lifetimes, and the problem goes away, perhaps when a stressful situation ends. But if you've had recurrent, unexpected panic attacks and spent long periods in constant fear of another attack, you may have a condition called panic disorder.[6] Panic Disorder affects almost 3% of the U.S. population.

---

5 https://www.nami.org/about-mental-illness/mental-health-conditions/anxiety-disorders/?tab=treatment

6 https://www.mayoclinic.org/diseases-conditions/panic-attacks/symptoms-causes/syc-20376021

Helping Someone During a Panic Attack

If someone you know has a panic attack, they may become very anxious and not think clearly.

You can help the person by doing the following:

- Stay with the person and keep calm.
- Don't make assumptions about what the person needs. Ask.
- Speak to the person in short, simple sentences.
- Be predictable. Avoid surprises.
- Help slow a person's breathing by breathing with them / counting slowly to 10.

It can be helpful to say things such as:

- "You can get through this."
- "I am proud of you. Good job."
- "Tell me what you need now."
- "Concentrate on your breathing. Stay in the present."
- "It's not the place that is bothering you; it's the thought."
- "What you are feeling is scary, but it is not dangerous."

By following these simple guidelines, you can:

- Reduce the amount of stress in this very stressful situation.
- Prevent the situation from getting worse.
- Help put some control in a confusing situation.
- You can offer ongoing help as the person tries to recover from panic disorder:
- Allow the person to proceed in therapy at his or her own pace.
- Be patient and praise all efforts toward recovery
- Do not agree to help the person avoid things or situations that cause anxiety.
- Do not panic when the person panics.
- Remember that it is all right to be concerned and anxious yourself.

LEVEL I · MODULE 5

IF YOU OR SOMEONE YOU KNOW IS IN CRISIS AND CONSIDERING SELF-HARM OR SUICIDE:

- Call 911 for emergency services.
- Visit the nearest hospital emergency room.
- Call or text 988 to connect with the 988 Suicide and Crisis Lifeline, offering 24-hour, confidential support. *Para ayuda en español, llame al 988.*
- Support is also available via live chat at 988lifeline.org. *AVADE® does not monitor this website for crisis messages, provide medical advice, or make referrals.*

PSTI LEGAL DISCLAIMER

The information in this training book is a supplement, not a substitute, for the expertise of qualified healthcare professionals. The content on AVADE® Behavioral Health, sourced from reliable information, does not constitute medical or professional healthcare advice, diagnosis, or treatment. It is crucial to consult healthcare providers for specific guidelines related to medical or behavioral health conditions. This material does not guarantee that any technique or strategy is safe or effective for any specific needs. Personal Safety Training, Inc., does not dictate policies or procedures for behavioral health violence prevention, self-defense tactics, or any physical interventions. Agencies are responsible for developing their own policies and evaluating the recommendations based on their circumstances.

The author and publisher do not guarantee the completeness or accuracy of the information and assume no risk for its use. Any implied warranty are expressly disavowed.

References for Module 5

https://988lifeline.org/

https://www.apa.org/

https://www.cdc.gov/

https://mhanational.org/

https://www.nami.org/

https://www.nimh.nih.gov/

https://www.psychiatry.org/

https://www.samhsa.gov/

Video: What is Anxiety?
youtube.com/watch?v=JOKS9Bx8-Sw&t=38s

Video: What is an Anxiety Disorder?
youtube.com/watch?v=vtUdHOx494E

Video: Anxiety Disorders in Adults
youtube.com/watch?v=odg02IGrDKo

American Psychiatric Association. *Diagnostic and Statistical Manual of Mental Disorders Fifth Edition DSM-5®*. American Psychiatric Association Publishing. Washington, DC 2013

Boland, Robert, MD, Marcia L. Verduin, MD, Pedro Ruiz, MD. *Kaplan & Saddock's Synopsis of Psychiatry 12th Edition*. Philadelphia, PA. Wolters Kluwer, 2022

Brown, Catana, PhD., Virginia C. Stoffel PhD, and Jaime Muñoz PhD. *Occupational Therapy in Mental Health, A Vision for Participation*. Philadelphia, PA. F.A Davis Company, 2015.

Buser, Steven, MD. *DSM-5® Insanely Simplified, Unlocking the Spectrums within DSM_5 and ICD-10*. Asheville, NC. Chiron Publications, 2014

Duckworth, Ken, MD. *You Are Not Alone, The NAMI Guide to Navigating Mental Health*. New York, NY. Zando, 2022

Glick, Rachel Lipson, MD, Scott L. Zeller, MD, Jon S. Berlin, MD. *Emergency Psychiatry Principles and Practice. 2nd Edition*. Philadelphia, PA. Wolters Kluwer, 2021

Mental Health America. *Where to Start, A Survival Guide To Anxiety, Depression, and Other Mental Health Challenges*. New York, NY. Penguin Random House LLC, 2023

Morrissey, Jean and Patrick Callaghan. *Communication Skills for Mental Health Nurses*. Berkshire, England. McGraw-Hill Education, Maiden, 2011

Morrison, James. *DSM-5® Made Easy, The Clinicians Guide to Diagnosis*. New York, NY. The Guilford Press, 2014

Townsend, Mary C. *Psychiatric Mental Health Nursing, Concepts of Care in Evidenced Based Practice 8th Edition*. Philadelphia, PA. F.A Davis Company, 2015.

MODULE 6

Depression Disorder

Persistent sadness, hopelessness, and lack of interest in most activities

Module 6:
Depression Disorder

Depression Disorder Defined

> Depressive disorder, commonly referred to as depression, is a mental health condition characterized by persistent feelings of sadness, hopelessness, and a lack of interest or pleasure in most activities. It can significantly impact a person's daily life, affecting how they think, feel, and handle daily activities such as sleeping, eating, or working.

Depression is a mood disorder that causes a persistent feeling of sadness and loss of interest. Also called major depressive disorder or clinical depression, it affects how you feel, think, and behave and can lead to a variety of emotional and physical problems.[1]

Depression is likely the oldest and still one of the most frequently diagnosed psychiatric illnesses. Symptoms of depression have been described almost as far back as there is evidence of written documentation.

Depression Disorder Facts and Statistics

- Almost 10% of adults in the U.S. suffer from Major Depressive Disorder (MDD)
- Almost half of adults with MDD are not receiving treatment.
- MDD is more prevalent in women than in men.
- Over 10% of women will have depression at some in their lives.
- 1/3 of all hospitalizations are from mood disorders, which include depression.
- Almost 20% of youth (ages 12-17) suffer from major depression.[2]
- Almost 15% of youth suffer from severe depression.
- Over half of adolescents with a major depressive episode did not get treatment.
- Major depression is one of the most common mental illnesses.
- Depression is the leading cause of disability worldwide as measured by years lived with disability.

---

1 https://www.mayoclinic.org/diseases-conditions/depression/symptoms-causes/syc-20356007

2 https://mhanational.org/mentalhealthfacts

- Almost 3/4 of people with mental disorders remain untreated in developing countries with almost one million people taking their lives each year.[3]
- It is not uncommon for someone with clinical depression to have another mental health condition or a physical health condition, or both.[4]

Signs and Symptoms of Depression[5]

- Continued feelings of sadness, hopelessness, pessimism, emptiness
- Fatigue, lack of energy
- Insomnia or other sleep issues, such as waking up very early or sleeping too much
- Anxiety, irritability, restlessness
- Feeling worthless or guilty
- Lack of interest or joy in hobbies and activities
- Changes in appetite, leading to weight loss or weight gain
- Moving, talking, or thinking more slowly or feeling extra fidgety
- Forgetfulness
- Thoughts of not wanting to live, death or suicide, suicide attempts, or self-harm behaviors

Depression Causes and Risk Factors

Depression does not have a single cause. It can be triggered by a life crisis, physical illness, or something else—but it can also occur spontaneously. Scientists believe several factors can contribute to depression:

---

3 https://adaa.org/understanding-anxiety/depression/facts-statistics

4 https://www.bridgestorecovery.com/depression/depression-facts-and-statistics/

5 https://www.samhsa.gov/mental-health/depression

- **Trauma.** When people experience trauma at an early age, it can cause long-term changes in how their brains respond to fear and stress. These changes may lead to depression.
- **Genetics.** Mood disorders, such as depression, tend to run in families.
- **Life circumstances.** Marital status, relationship changes, financial standing, and where a person lives influence whether a person develops depression.
- **Brain changes.** Imaging studies have shown that the frontal lobe of the brain becomes less active when a person is depressed. Depression is also associated with changes in how the pituitary gland and hypothalamus respond to hormone stimulation.
- **Other medical conditions.** People who have a history of sleep disturbances, medical illness, chronic pain, anxiety, and attention-deficit hyperactivity disorder (ADHD) are more likely to develop depression. Some medical syndromes (like hypothyroidism) can mimic depressive disorder. Some medications can also cause symptoms of depression.
- **Drug and alcohol misuse.** Co-occurring disorders require coordinated treatment for both conditions, as alcohol can worsen depressive symptoms.

Types of Depression Disorders

Major depressive disorder and persistent depressive disorder are two of the most common types of depression that people experience, however, there are many types of depression.

Major Depressive Disorder (MDD)

People who have major depressive disorder have had at least one major depressive episode (five or more symptoms for at least a two-week period). For some people, this disorder is recurrent, which means they may experience episodes once a month, once a year, or several times throughout their lives. People with recurrent episodes of major depression are sometimes said to have unipolar depression (or what used to be called "clinical depression") because they only experience periods of low or depressed mood.

Persistent Depressive Disorder

Persistent depressive disorder (formerly dysthymia) is a continuous long-term, chronic state of low-level depressed mood. The depressed state of persistent depressive disorder is not as severe as with major depression but can be just as disabling.

Postpartum Depression

Postpartum depression is characterized by feelings of sadness, indifference, exhaustion, and anxiety that a woman may experience after the birth of her baby. It affects one in every nine women who have had a child and can affect any woman, regardless of her age, race, or economic background.

Bipolar Depression

People diagnosed with bipolar disorder have mood swings involving both lows (bipolar depression) and highs (called mania if severe or hypomania if mild). When people experience the lows of bipolar disorder (bipolar depression), their symptoms are very similar to those that someone with unipolar depression might experience.

Seasonal Affective Disorder

Seasonal Affective Disorder (SAD) typically starts in the late fall and early winter and dissipates during the spring and summer. Depressive episodes linked to the summer can occur but are much less common than winter episodes of SAD.

Psychotic Depression

Psychotic depression occurs when psychotic features such as hallucinations and delusions are accompanied by a major depressive episode, though psychotic symptoms generally have a depressive theme such as guilt, worthlessness, and death.

Depression Disorder Crisis

> A depression disorder crisis is a severe episode of depression that significantly impairs an individual's ability to function and may escalate into an emergency situation. A depression disorder crisis can involve severe symptoms that may escalate to an emergency situation.

This can include:

- **Suicidal thoughts or attempts:** A person in crisis might express a desire to harm themselves or make an actual attempt.
- **Non-suicidal self-injury:** Engaging in self-injurious behaviors such as cutting, burning, or hitting oneself.
- **Severe emotional distress:** Intense feelings of sadness, hopelessness, or anxiety that impair daily functioning.
- **Behavioral changes:** Increased irritability, withdrawal from social interactions, or unusual behaviors.
- **Physical symptoms:** Changes in sleep, appetite, or physical health that become overwhelming.
- **Increased agitation or aggression:** Sudden outbursts of anger or aggression, which may indicate severe inner turmoil. Sudden and severe changes in behavior, mood, or personality.

If someone with Depression Disorder is exhibiting these crisis symptoms, it's crucial to seek immediate help from mental health professionals, crisis intervention services, or emergency services to ensure their safety and provide appropriate care.

Crisis and De-Escalation Interventions for Depression Disorder

- Use a trauma-informed approach.
- Use positive interpersonal communication skills.
- Use the daily habits of de-escalation.
- **Guidelines for depression crisis and de-escalation strategies:**
  - **Contact crisis intervention teams.** Contact mental health crisis intervention teams if the situation escalates and professional intervention is needed.
  - **Contact the Suicide and Crisis Lifeline.** If you or someone you know is struggling or having thoughts of suicide, call or text the 988 Suicide & Crisis Lifeline at 988 or chat at 988lifeline.org. In life-threatening situations, call 911.
  - **Ensure safety.** Assess the environment to remove any potentially harmful objects and maintain physical distance to avoid escalating the situation.
  - **Practice active and attentive listening** by showing full engagement in the conversation through eye contact, nodding, and using verbal acknowledgments like "I hear you," or "Go on." Additionally, reflect and paraphrase what the person has said in your own words to demonstrate understanding, such as "It sounds like you're feeling overwhelmed because…"
  - **Encourage open communication** by asking open-ended questions that invite them to share their feelings and thoughts more fully, avoiding yes/no questions. Examples include, "Can you tell me more about what's been going on?" or "How have you been feeling lately?"
  - **Show empathy and validation** by acknowledging their feelings without judgment, using phrases like "It's okay to feel this way" or "I can see why you'd feel this way." Additionally, express empathy by showing that you care and understand their pain through statements such as "I'm here for you" or "That sounds really tough."
  - **Maintain a calm and composed demeanor** to soothe the person, speaking in a soft, gentle tone. Avoid escalating the situation; if they become agitated, respond with measured and calm reactions instead of anger or frustration.
  - **Create a safe space** by providing a comfortable and private environment for conversation, ensuring they feel safe and secure. Respect their boundaries by giving them space and not pressuring them to talk if they're not ready.
  - **Offer practical support** by asking how you can assist with immediate needs, as simple tasks or chores can be overwhelming during depression.
  - **Practice patience** by allowing time for healing, recognizing that recovery from depression is a gradual process.
  - **Encourage small steps** by assisting them in setting manageable goals and celebrating small victories along the way.

- **Promote self-care** by encouraging activities such as exercise, healthy eating, and adequate sleep to help improve their mood.

- **Guidelines to avoid depression crisis escalation:**
  - **Avoid dismissing their feelings** by saying things like "Just snap out of it" or "Others have it worse," and refrain from offering simplistic solutions such as "Just think positive" or "Just cheer up," as these can be invalidating and unhelpful for someone experiencing depression.
  - **Avoid judgmental or critical attitudes**, such as blaming them for their condition with remarks like "You just need to try harder" or "You're being lazy," and criticizing their behavior, as these actions can exacerbate feelings of guilt, worthlessness, and failure.
  - **Avoid impatience or frustration**, as rushing their recovery with remarks like "snap out of it" or expressing irritation can make them feel pressured, misunderstood, and more anxious or sad.
  - **Avoid being emotionally detached** or failing to acknowledge their pain and emotional state, as this can make them feel unimportant, unsupported, and invisible.
  - **Avoid invasive or controlling behavior**, such as trying to control their actions or decisions.
  - **Avoid arguing or being confrontational**, as disputing their feelings or experiences can escalate their emotional state, and challenging their thoughts or feelings aggressively can make them defensive and more distressed.
  - **Avoid insensitive comments or behavior**, such as making jokes about their condition, which can be hurtful and damaging, and avoid insensitive comparisons that invalidate their experiences, such as comparing their situation to others' or suggesting that others have it worse.
  - **Avoid neglecting their need for support** by being available when they seek help, which can prevent feelings of abandonment and isolation, and by following through on promises or offers to help to maintain trust and reduce feelings of worthlessness.
  - **Avoid pressuring for information or action** by refraining from demanding explanations about their feelings or justifications for their depression, as this can be overwhelming and counterproductive. Additionally, avoid forcing them to take action, such as insisting on certain activities or decisions, as this can increase their stress and anxiety.

- Build a trusting relationship and work in an open, engaging, and non-judgmental manner.
- Be aware that stigma and discrimination can be associated with a diagnosis of depression.
- Work as a multidisciplinary team and offer guidance and support (family, caregivers).
- Encourage them to meet their ADL's (Activities of Daily Living).
- Show environmental awareness (safely remove any objects that the person could use to harm themselves).
- Seek immediate suicide intervention when needed (see Module 16).

Effective de-escalation and crisis intervention for depression disorder requires a combination of compassion, empathy, active listening, and practical actions to ensure immediate safety and long-term support. By creating a safe and supportive environment, engaging appropriate resources, and following up with continuous care, individuals experiencing a crisis can be guided toward stability and recovery.

Addressing the risks associated with a depression disorder crisis requires a proactive and compassionate approach. By implementing training, support systems, and clear protocols and promoting a supportive workplace culture, organizations can effectively manage these risks and ensure the safety and well-being of all staff members. Mental health is a crucial aspect of overall health, and taking steps to support it benefits both individuals and the organization as a whole.

Depression Disorder Treatments

> Disclaimer: Personal Safety Training Inc. makes no claim as to what type of treatment is needed for any mental health disorder.

Depressive disorder, while often devastating, can respond well to treatment with a specific evaluation and treatment plan. Safety planning is crucial for those with suicidal thoughts. After ruling out other causes, a patient-centered treatment plan may include:

- **Psychotherapy:** Cognitive behavioral therapy, family-focused therapy, and interpersonal therapy.
- **Medications:** Antidepressants, mood stabilizers, and antipsychotic medications.
- **Exercise:** Helpful for prevention and mild-to-moderate symptoms.
- **Light Therapy:** Uses a light box to regulate melatonin.
- **Alternative Approaches:** Acupuncture, meditation, faith, and nutrition as part of a comprehensive plan.

Collaborating with mental health professionals to develop a personalized treatment plan is essential for effective management.

IF YOU OR SOMEONE YOU KNOW IS IN CRISIS AND CONSIDERING SELF-HARM OR SUICIDE:

- Call 911 for emergency services.
- Visit the nearest hospital emergency room.
- Call or text 988 to connect with the 988 Suicide and Crisis Lifeline, offering 24-hour, confidential support. *Para ayuda en español, llame al 988.*
- Support is also available via live chat at 988lifeline.org. *AVADE® does not monitor this website for crisis messages, provide medical advice, or make referrals.*

PSTI LEGAL DISCLAIMER

The information in this training book is a supplement, not a substitute, for the expertise of qualified healthcare professionals. The content on AVADE® Behavioral Health, sourced from reliable information, does not constitute medical or professional healthcare advice, diagnosis, or treatment. It is crucial to consult healthcare providers for specific guidelines related to medical or behavioral health conditions. This material does not guarantee that any technique or strategy is safe or effective for any specific needs. Personal Safety Training, Inc., does not dictate policies or procedures for behavioral health violence prevention, self-defense tactics, or any physical interventions. Agencies are responsible for developing their own policies and evaluating the recommendations based on their circumstances.

The author and publisher do not guarantee the completeness or accuracy of the information and assume no risk for its use. Any implied warranty are expressly disavowed.

References for Module 6

https://988lifeline.org/

https://www.apa.org/

https://www.cdc.gov/

https://mhanational.org/

https://www.nami.org/

https://www.nimh.nih.gov/

https://www.psychiatry.org/

https://www.samhsa.gov/

Video: What is Depression?
youtube.com/watch?v=CTXkyFbGqEg

Video: What is Depression?
youtube.com/watch?v=18qcsQqC9bQ

Video: What is Major Depressive Disorder (MDD)?
youtube.com/watch?v=m9hZnT-9wek

American Psychiatric Association. *Diagnostic and Statistical Manual of Mental Disorders Fifth Edition DSM-5®*. American Psychiatric Association Publishing. Washington, DC 2013

Boland, Robert, MD, Marcia L. Verduin, MD, Pedro Ruiz, MD. *Kaplan & Saddock's Synopsis of Psychiatry 12th Edition*. Philadelphia, PA. Wolters Kluwer, 2022

Brown, Catana, PhD., Virginia C. Stoffel PhD, and Jaime Muñoz PhD. *Occupational Therapy in Mental Health, A Vision for Participation*. Philadelphia, PA. F.A Davis Company, 2015.

Buser, Steven, MD. *DSM-5® Insanely Simplified, Unlocking the Spectrums within DSM_5 and ICD-10*. Asheville, NC. Chiron Publications, 2014

Duckworth, Ken, MD. *You Are Not Alone, The NAMI Guide to Navigating Mental Health*. New York, NY. Zando, 2022

Glick, Rachel Lipson, MD, Scott L. Zeller, MD, Jon S. Berlin, MD. *Emergency Psychiatry Principles and Practice. 2nd Edition*. Philadelphia, PA. Wolters Kluwer, 2021

Mental Health America. *Where to Start, A Survival Guide To Anxiety, Depression, and Other Mental Health Challenges*. New York, NY. Penguin Random House LLC, 2023

Morrissey, Jean and Patrick Callaghan. *Communication Skills for Mental Health Nurses*. Berkshire, England. McGraw-Hill Education, Maiden, 2011

Morrison, James. *DSM-5® Made Easy, The Clinicians Guide to Diagnosis*. New York, NY. The Guilford Press, 2014

Townsend, Mary C. *Psychiatric Mental Health Nursing, Concepts of Care in Evidenced Based Practice 8th Edition*. Philadelphia, PA. F.A Davis Company, 2015.

MODULE 7

Bipolar Disorder

Extreme mood swings that include emotional highs and lows

Module 7:
Bipolar Disorder

Bipolar Disorder Defined

> Bipolar disorder (formerly called manic-depressive illness or manic depression) is a mental health condition characterized by extreme mood swings, including emotional highs (mania or hypomania) and lows (depression). These shifts can affect sleep, energy levels, behavior, concentration, and the ability to think clearly, making it difficult to carry out day-to-day tasks.

There are several types of bipolar disorder. The most common are: Bipolar I Disorder, Bipolar II Disorder, and Cyclothymic Disorder. All types involve changes in mood, energy, and activity levels, ranging from manic episodes (extremely elevated or irritable behavior) to depressive episodes (very sad or hopeless periods). Hypomanic episodes are less severe manic periods.[1]

---

1 https://www.nimh.nih.gov/health/topics/bipolar-disorder

What is Mania?

Mania is more than just having extra energy to burn. It's a mood disturbance that makes you abnormally energized, both physically and mentally. Mania can be severe enough to require you to be hospitalized.

Mania occurs in people with bipolar I disorder. In many cases of bipolar I, manic episodes alternate with periods of depression. However, people with bipolar I don't always have depressive episodes.

What is Hypomania?

Hypomania is a milder form of mania. If you're experiencing hypomania, your energy level is higher than normal, but it's not as extreme as in mania. Other people will notice if you have hypomania. It causes problems in your life, but not to the extent that mania can. If you have hypomania, you may not need to be hospitalized for it.

- People with Bipolar II Disorder may experience hypomania that alternates with depression.
- The main difference between mania and hypomania is the intensity of the symptoms. Symptoms of mania are much more intense than those of hypomania.

Mania and hypomania are integral to the diagnosis of bipolar disorder, with mania being associated with Bipolar I Disorder and hypomania with Bipolar II Disorder and Cyclothymic Disorder.

Bipolar Facts and Statistics

- Almost 3% of adults in the U.S. had a bipolar episode in the past year.
- Bipolar disorder is left untreated in half of the diagnosed individuals in any given year.
- Over 4% of U.S. adults will experience a bipolar disorder in their lifetime.[2]
- Of all mood disorders, those with a diagnosis of bipolar disorder were found to have the highest likelihood of being classified with "severe" impairment (over 80%)[3].
- The average age of bipolar onset is 25 years old.
- People ages 18 to 29 years old have the highest rate of bipolar disorder.
- On average, bipolar disorder results in a 9.2-year reduction in expected lifespan.
- The risk of suicide is high in people with bipolar disorder with over 15% committing suicide.

- Over half of all people with any mental health disorder, including bipolar disorder, develop substance use disorders.
- Of those with bipolar disorder, many report co-occurring health conditions, which are most commonly migraine, asthma, and high cholesterol. High blood pressure, thyroid disease, and osteoarthritis were also identified as high probability of co-occurring health problems.
- People with bipolar disorder are more likely to experience other mental health conditions, including anxiety, post-traumatic stress disorder (PTSD), substance use disorder, attention deficit hyperactivity disorder (ADHD), obsessive-compulsive disorder (OCD), eating disorders, and autism spectrum disorder (ASD).[4]

Signs and Symptoms of Bipolar Disorder (Mania/Hypomania)

While they vary in intensity, most of the symptoms of mania and hypomania are the same. The key symptoms include:

- Incredibly disorganized
- Feeling very up, high, elated, euphoric, or extremely irritable or touchy
- Feeling jumpy or wired, more active than usual
- Having a decreased need for sleep
- Talking fast about a lot of different things ("flight of ideas")
- Racing thoughts/poor judgment
- Engaging in risky behavior: gambling with life savings, spending sprees, giving money and possessions away

2 https://www.nimh.nih.gov/health/statistics/bipolar-disorder

3 https://www.singlecare.com/blog/news/bipolar-disorder-statistics/

4 https://www.medicalnewstoday.com/articles/bipolar-disorder-facts#complications

- Feeling able to do many things at once without getting tired
- Having an excessive appetite for food, drinking, sex, or other pleasurable activities
- Feeling unusually important, talented, grandiosity, or powerful

Signs and symptoms of bipolar I and bipolar II disorders may include other features, such as anxious distress, melancholy, psychosis or others. The timing of symptoms may include diagnostic labels such as mixed or rapid cycling. In addition, bipolar symptoms may occur during pregnancy or change with the seasons.

Individuals may experience both manic and depressive symptoms simultaneously, known as an episode with mixed features. Bipolar disorder can present with less extreme symptoms, such as in bipolar II disorder, where hypomania occurs. During hypomanic episodes, individuals may feel productive and well, though others might notice changes. Without treatment, hypomania can escalate to severe mania or depression.

Mixed Episodes in Bipolar Disorder

During a mixed episode in bipolar disorder, individuals experience simultaneous manic and depressive symptoms. This includes elevated mood, increased energy, and impulsivity alongside feelings of sadness, fatigue, and negative thoughts. Treatment typically involves a combination of mood stabilizers, antipsychotic medications, therapy, and support to manage these complex and challenging emotional states effectively.

The more severe symptoms of mania

Unlike hypomanic episodes, manic episodes can lead to serious consequences. When the mania subsides, you may be left with remorse or depression for things you've done during the episode.

With mania, a person may also have a break from reality. Psychotic symptoms can include:

- visual or auditory hallucinations
- delusional thoughts
- paranoid thoughts

Anosognosia

Anosognosia (*uh-naa-suh-now-zhuh*) is a neurological condition that makes it difficult for people to recognize or understand their own health conditions. It's also known as "lack of insight" or "denial of deficit". Anosognosia can make it hard for people to seek or follow treatment, which can be frustrating for caregivers.

Anosognosia is associated with mental illness, dementia, and structural brain lesions. It's a common symptom of certain mental illnesses, such as schizophrenia and bipolar disorder, and it's estimated that 40–90% of people with these conditions experience it. Anosognosia can occur when the brain's frontal lobe is damaged, which prevents it from properly updating a person's self-image. This can cause people to partially lose their ability to see themselves clearly, or it can come and go.

Bipolar Causes/Risk Factors[5]

The exact cause of bipolar disorder is unknown, but several factors may be involved, such as:

- **Biological differences.** People with bipolar disorder appear to have physical changes in their brains. The significance of these changes is still uncertain but may eventually help pinpoint causes.
- **Genetics.** Bipolar disorder is more common in people who have a first-degree relative, such as a

---

5 https://www.mayoclinic.org/diseases-conditions/bipolar-disorder/symptoms-causes/syc-20355955

sibling or parent, with the condition. Researchers are trying to find genes that may be involved in causing bipolar disorder.

Factors that may increase the risk of developing bipolar disorder or act as a trigger for the first episode include:

- Having a first-degree relative, such as a parent or sibling, with bipolar disorder
- Periods of high stress, such as the death of a loved one or other traumatic event
- Drug or alcohol abuse

Types of Bipolar Disorder

The types of bipolar disorder include:

- **Bipolar I Disorder** is defined by manic episodes that last for at least 7 days (nearly every day for most of the day) or by manic symptoms that are so severe that the person needs immediate medical care. Usually, depressive episodes occur as well, typically lasting at least two weeks. Episodes of depression with mixed features (having depressive symptoms and manic symptoms at the same time) are also possible. Experiencing four or more episodes of mania or depression within one year is called "rapid cycling."
- **Bipolar II Disorder** is defined by a pattern of depressive episodes and hypomanic episodes. The hypomanic episodes are less severe than the manic episodes in bipolar I disorder.
- **Cyclothymic Disorder (Cyclothymia)** is defined by recurring hypomanic and depressive symptoms that are not intense enough or do not last long enough to qualify as hypomanic or depressive episodes.

Sometimes a person might experience symptoms of bipolar disorder that do not match the three categories listed above, and this is referred to as "other specified and unspecified bipolar and related disorders."

Bipolar disorder is often diagnosed during late adolescence (teen years) or early adulthood. Sometimes, bipolar symptoms can appear in children. Although the symptoms may vary over time, bipolar disorder usually requires lifelong treatment. Following a prescribed treatment plan can help people manage their symptoms and improve their quality of life.

Bipolar Complications

Left untreated, bipolar disorder can result in serious problems that affect every area of your life, such as:

- Problems related to drug and alcohol use
- Suicide or suicide attempts
- Legal or financial problems
- Damaged relationships
- Poor work or school performance

Bipolar Disorder Crisis

> A bipolar disorder crisis is a severe and acute phase of the condition characterized by extreme mood swings that significantly impair a person's ability to function and may require immediate medical or psychiatric intervention.

- Extreme mood swings between manic episodes and depressive episodes
- Manic episodes characterized by high energy, risk-taking behavior, and racing thoughts
- Depressive episodes marked by sadness, hopelessness, and lack of energy
- Impulsivity and irritability
- Difficulty concentrating
- Changes in sleep patterns
- Thoughts of self-harm or suicide
- Psychosis, including hallucinations or delusions

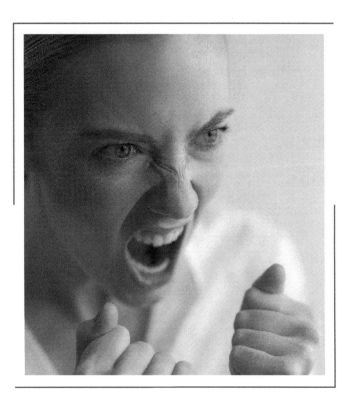

If someone with Bipolar Disorder is exhibiting these crisis symptoms, it's crucial to seek immediate help from mental health professionals, crisis intervention services, or emergency services to ensure their safety and provide appropriate care.

Crisis and De-Escalation Interventions for Bipolar Disorder

- Use a trauma-informed approach.
- Use positive interpersonal communication skills.
- Use the daily habits of de-escalation.
- **Guidelines for bipolar crisis and de-escalation strategies:**
  - **Contact crisis intervention teams.** Contact mental health crisis intervention teams if the situation escalates and professional intervention is needed.
  - **Contact the Suicide and Crisis Lifeline.** If you or someone you know is struggling or having thoughts of suicide, call or text the 988 Suicide & Crisis Lifeline at 988 or chat at 988lifeline.org. In life-threatening situations, call 911.
  - **Ensure safety.** Assess the environment to remove any potentially harmful objects and maintain physical distance to avoid escalating the situation.
  - **Active listening and empathy** involve fully engaging and showing understanding with verbal cues like "I'm here for you," and validating their feelings by acknowledging their emotions without judgment, such as saying, "I can see this is really tough for you."
  - **Stay calm and composed** by maintaining a soothing presence and speaking gently, while managing your own emotions even if they become agitated.

- **Create a safe environment** by removing potentially harmful objects and providing a calm, quiet space to reduce stimulation during manic episodes.
- **Set boundaries and limits** by clearly and respectfully communicating acceptable behaviors and applying these limits consistently to prevent confusion and frustration.
- **Use distraction techniques** by redirecting their focus to less stressful activities and suggesting calming activities like listening to music, drawing, or taking a walk.
- **Use clear and simple communication** by giving straightforward instructions and repeating information if needed, especially if the person seems confused or distracted.
- **Respect their autonomy** by involving them in decision-making about their care, empowering their choices, and giving them space if needed without forcing interactions.
- **When dealing with manic episodes**, prioritize reducing environmental stimuli and maintaining calm, structured interactions to avoid overstimulation. Focus on ensuring safety for the individual and others, particularly if risky behaviors are present.

- **Guidelines to avoid bipolar crisis escalation:**
  - **Avoid ignoring or downplaying someone's mood swings**, as it can make them feel invalidated and misunderstood, escalating their feelings of frustration and isolation. Instead, foster understanding and support by acknowledging their emotions and experiences without minimizing them.
  - **Avoid inconsistency in responses and refrain from changing rules or boundaries**—this is crucial as it prevents confusion and frustration, providing clarity and stability in the individual's environment.
  - **Avoid responding with equal intensity during a manic episode**, as this can escalate their behavior. Also, refrain from reacting with anger or frustration, as it may exacerbate their emotional state.
  - **Avoid being judgmental** by refraining from blaming, criticizing, or making assumptions about their mood swings or behavior. Such actions can escalate conflict and worsen their feelings of distress.
  - **Avoid invalidating someone's experiences** by refraining from dismissing their feelings as "just a phase" or comparing their struggles to others, as this can increase their sense of isolation. Instead, acknowledge and validate their emotions without minimizing them.
  - **Avoid pressuring for immediate solutions**, such as demanding immediate change or forcing medication compliance, as this can be overwhelming and unproductive, leading to resistance and exacerbating the situation. Instead, approach solutions with understanding and patience.
  - **Avoid using confrontational language**, such as arguing or debating about their symptoms, or using threatening language like ultimatums, as this can escalate tension and increase anxiety and distress. It's important to communicate in a calm and supportive manner.
  - **Avoid neglecting their need for support** by being unavailable or not following through on promises, as this can make them feel abandoned and increase distress. Instead, prioritize being present and reliable in providing the support they need to foster trust and well-being.

- **Avoid overreacting to manic behavior with fear or panic**, as this can intensify their emotions. Similarly, avoid reacting strongly to depressive symptoms with frustration or disappointment, as it can worsen their self-esteem. Instead, respond calmly and supportively to their behavior.
- **Avoid downplaying the importance of treatment or ignoring warning signs** of a potential crisis, as this can be harmful and lead to dangerous situations. Instead, recognize the importance of seeking professional help when needed and respond promptly to warning signs.

- Build a trusting relationship and work in an open, engaging, and non-judgmental manner.
- Be aware that stigma and discrimination can be associated with a diagnosis of bipolar.
- Work as a multidisciplinary team and offer guidance and support (family, caregivers).
- Encourage them to meet their ADL's (Activities of Daily Living).
- Show environmental awareness (safely remove any objects that the person could use to harm themselves).
- Seek immediate suicide intervention when needed (see Module 16).

Effective de-escalation and crisis intervention for bipolar disorder requires a combination of compassion, empathy, active listening, and practical actions to ensure immediate safety and long-term support. By creating a safe and supportive environment, engaging appropriate resources, and following up with continuous care, individuals experiencing a crisis can be guided toward stability and recovery.

Addressing the risks associated with a bipolar disorder crisis requires a proactive and compassionate approach. By implementing training, support systems, and clear protocols and promoting a supportive workplace culture, organizations can effectively manage these risks and ensure the safety and well-being of all staff members. Mental health is a crucial aspect of overall health, and taking steps to support it benefits both individuals and the organization as a whole.

Bipolar Treatments

> **Disclaimer: Personal Safety Training Inc. makes no claim as to what type of treatment is needed for any mental health disorder.**

Bipolar disorder is treated and managed through various approaches:

- **Psychotherapy:** Includes cognitive behavioral therapy and family-focused therapy.
- **Medications:** Such as mood stabilizers, antipsychotic medications, and sometimes antidepressants.
- **Self-management strategies:** Involves education and recognition of early symptoms.
- **Complementary health approaches:** Activities like aerobic exercise, meditation, faith, and prayer can support but not replace treatment.

For individuals with bipolar disorder, collaborating closely with mental health professionals to develop a personalized treatment plan is essential, as combination approaches often yield the best results in managing symptoms effectively.

IF YOU OR SOMEONE YOU KNOW IS IN CRISIS AND CONSIDERING SELF-HARM OR SUICIDE:

- Call 911 for emergency services.
- Visit the nearest hospital emergency room.
- Call or text 988 to connect with the 988 Suicide and Crisis Lifeline, offering 24-hour, confidential support. *Para ayuda en español, llame al 988.*
- Support is also available via live chat at 988lifeline.org. *AVADE® does not monitor this website for crisis messages, provide medical advice, or make referrals.*

PSTI LEGAL DISCLAIMER

The information in this training book is a supplement, not a substitute, for the expertise of qualified healthcare professionals. The content on AVADE® Behavioral Health, sourced from reliable information, does not constitute medical or professional healthcare advice, diagnosis, or treatment. It is crucial to consult healthcare providers for specific guidelines related to medical or behavioral health conditions. This material does not guarantee that any technique or strategy is safe or effective for any specific needs. Personal Safety Training, Inc., does not dictate policies or procedures for behavioral health violence prevention, self-defense tactics, or any physical interventions. Agencies are responsible for developing their own policies and evaluating the recommendations based on their circumstances.

The author and publisher do not guarantee the completeness or accuracy of the information and assume no risk for its use. Any implied warranty are expressly disavowed.

References for Module 7

https://988lifeline.org/

https://www.apa.org/

https://www.cdc.gov/

https://mhanational.org/

https://www.nami.org/

https://www.nimh.nih.gov/

https://www.psychiatry.org/

https://www.samhsa.gov/

Video: Tell Me About Bipolar Disorder
youtube.com/watch?v=XQ2PbPr2AH4&t=6s

Video: Signs of Bipolar Disorder
youtube.com/watch?v=wrkMjgQs9rs&t=29s

Video: What is Bipolar Disorder?
youtube.com/watch?v=G9vkGCo7Gtg

American Psychiatric Association. *Diagnostic and Statistical Manual of Mental Disorders Fifth Edition DSM-5®*. American Psychiatric Association Publishing. Washington, DC 2013

Boland, Robert, MD, Marcia L. Verduin, MD, Pedro Ruiz, MD. *Kaplan & Saddock's Synopsis of Psychiatry 12th Edition*. Philadelphia, PA. Wolters Kluwer, 2022

Brown, Catana, PhD., Virginia C. Stoffel PhD, and Jaime Muñoz PhD. *Occupational Therapy in Mental Health, A Vision for Participation*. Philadelphia, PA. F.A Davis Company, 2015.

Buser, Steven, MD. *DSM-5® Insanely Simplified, Unlocking the Spectrums within DSM_5 and ICD-10*. Asheville, NC. Chiron Publications, 2014

Duckworth, Ken, MD. *You Are Not Alone, The NAMI Guide to Navigating Mental Health*. New York, NY. Zando, 2022

Glick, Rachel Lipson, MD, Scott L. Zeller, MD, Jon S. Berlin, MD. *Emergency Psychiatry Principles and Practice. 2nd Edition*. Philadelphia, PA. Wolters Kluwer, 2021

Mental Health America. *Where to Start, A Survival Guide To Anxiety, Depression, and Other Mental Health Challenges*. New York, NY. Penguin Random House LLC, 2023

Morrissey, Jean and Patrick Callaghan. *Communication Skills for Mental Health Nurses*. Berkshire, England. McGraw-Hill Education, Maiden, 2011

Morrison, James. *DSM-5® Made Easy, The Clinicians Guide to Diagnosis*. New York, NY. The Guilford Press, 2014

Townsend, Mary C. *Psychiatric Mental Health Nursing, Concepts of Care in Evidenced Based Practice 8th Edition*. Philadelphia, PA. F.A Davis Company, 2015.

MODULE 8

Schizophrenia Disorder

Distorted thinking, perceptions, emotions, language, sense of self, and behavior

Module 8:
Schizophrenia Disorder

Schizophrenia Disorder Defined

> Schizophrenia is a serious brain disorder that causes people to interpret reality abnormally, often experiencing delusions, hallucinations, and disorganized thinking, which can lead to paranoia and hearing voices. This condition can severely disrupt daily life, but with consistent treatment involving medication, therapy, and social support, individuals can manage the disease and lead fulfilling lives.

Schizophrenia usually involves delusions (false beliefs), hallucinations (seeing or hearing things that don't exist), unusual physical behavior, and disorganized thinking and speech. It is common for people with schizophrenia to have paranoid thoughts or hear voices. For example, they may believe that someone is controlling their mind or going to cause them harm. These psychotic episodes are often frightening, confusing, and isolating.

Schizophrenia can be extremely disruptive to a person's life, making it hard to go to school or work, keep a schedule, socialize, complete daily tasks, or take care of oneself. However, with consistent treatment—a combination of medication, therapy, and social support—people with schizophrenia can manage the disease and lead fulfilling lives.[1]

People with schizophrenia usually are diagnosed in the late teen years to early 30s. In men, schizophrenia symptoms usually start in the late teens to early 20s. In women, symptoms usually begin in the late 20s to early 30s. There also is a group of people—usually women—who are diagnosed later in life. It isn't common for children to be diagnosed with schizophrenia.

Schizophrenia/Psychotic Disorders Facts and Statistics

- Around 1.5 million U.S. adults have been diagnosed with schizophrenia.
- Less than 1% of adults in the U.S. suffer from Schizophrenia.
- Schizophrenia is one of the top 15 leading causes of disability worldwide.
- Individuals with schizophrenia have an increased risk of premature mortality (death at a younger age than the general population).

---

1 https://www.samhsa.gov/mental-health/schizophrenia

- Almost 5% of people with schizophrenia die by suicide, a rate that is far greater than the general population, with the highest risk in the early stages of illness.

- Approximately half of individuals with schizophrenia have co-occurring mental and/or behavioral health disorders.[2]

- Studies estimate that between 15-100 people out of 100,000 develop psychosis each year.[3]

- Psychosis often begins in young adulthood when a person is in their late teens to mid-20s.

- Every year, about 100,000 teenagers and young adults in the United States experience their first psychotic episode.

Signs and Symptoms of Schizophrenia Disorder

It's important to recognize the symptoms of schizophrenia and seek help as early as possible. People with schizophrenia are usually diagnosed between the ages of 16 and 30, after the first episode of psychosis. Starting treatment as soon as possible following the first episode of psychosis is an important step toward recovery. However, research shows that gradual changes in thinking, mood, and social functioning often appear before the first episode of psychosis. Schizophrenia is rare in younger children.

Schizophrenia symptoms can differ from person to person, but they generally fall into three main categories: positive, negative, and cognitive.

Positive symptoms

Positive symptoms include changes in the way a person thinks, acts, and experiences the world. A person experiencing psychotic symptoms often has disrupted thoughts and perceptions, and they may have difficulty recognizing what is real and what is not. Positive symptoms include:

- **Hallucinations:** When a person sees, hears, smells, tastes, or feels things that are not actually there. Hearing voices is common for people with schizophrenia. People who hear voices may hear them for a long time before family or friends notice a problem.

- **Delusions:** When a person has strong beliefs that are not true and may seem irrational to others. For example, individuals experiencing delusions may believe that people on the radio and television are sending special messages that require a certain response, or they may believe that they are in danger or that others are trying to hurt them.

- **Thought disorder:** When a person has ways of thinking that are unusual or illogical. People with thought disorders may have trouble organizing their thoughts and speech. Sometimes a person will stop talking in the middle of a thought, jump from topic to topic, or make up words that have no meaning.

Negative symptoms

Negative symptoms include loss of motivation, loss of interest or enjoyment in daily activities, withdrawal from

---

2 https://www.nimh.nih.gov/health/statistics/schizophrenia

3 https://www.nimh.nih.gov/health/publications/understanding-psychosis

social life, difficulty showing emotions, and difficulty functioning normally.

- Having trouble planning and sticking with activities, such as grocery shopping
- Having trouble anticipating and being motivated by pleasure in everyday life
- Talking in a dull voice and showing limited facial expression
- Avoiding social interaction or interacting in socially awkward ways
- Having very low energy and spending a lot of time in passive activities. In extreme cases, a person might stop moving or talking for a while, which is a rare condition called catatonia.

These symptoms are sometimes mistaken for symptoms of depression or other mental illnesses.

Cognitive symptoms

Cognitive symptoms include problems in attention, concentration, and memory. These symptoms can make it hard to follow a conversation, learn new things, or remember appointments. A person's level of cognitive functioning is one of the best predictors of their day-to-day functioning. Healthcare providers evaluate cognitive functioning using specific tests.

- Having trouble processing information to make decisions
- Having trouble using information immediately after learning it
- Having trouble focusing or paying attention

Symptoms in teenagers

Schizophrenia symptoms in teenagers are like those in adults, but the condition may be harder to pinpoint. That's because some early symptoms of schizophrenia—those that occur before hallucinations, delusions, and disorganization—are commonly seen in many teens, such as:

- Withdrawing from friends and family
- Not doing well in school
- Having trouble sleeping
- Feeling irritable or depressed
- Lacking motivation

Risk of violence

Most people with schizophrenia are not violent. Overall, people with schizophrenia are more likely than those without the illness to be harmed by others. For people with schizophrenia, the risk of self-harm and of violence to others is greatest when the illness is untreated or co-occurs with alcohol or substance misuse. It is important to help people who are showing symptoms to get treatment as quickly as possible.

What is the difference between schizophrenia and psychosis?

Schizophrenia is a mental health condition that affects how a person behaves, thinks, and feels. *Psychosis* refers to a collection of symptoms that affect the mind and cause a loss of grasp on reality. Psychosis is a common symptom of schizophrenia.

Schizophrenia Disorder Causes

The exact causes of schizophrenia are unknown. Research suggests a combination of physical, genetic, psychological, and environmental factors can make a person more likely to develop the condition. Some people may be prone to schizophrenia, and a stressful or emotional life event might trigger a psychotic episode.

Although the cause of schizophrenia is not known, these factors seem to make schizophrenia more likely:

- A family history of schizophrenia.
- Life experiences, such as living in poverty, stress or danger.
- Some pregnancy and birth issues, such as not getting enough nutrition before or after birth, low birth weight, or exposure to toxins or viruses before birth that may affect brain development.
- Taking mind-altering, also called psychoactive or psychotropic, drugs as a teen or young adult.

Types of Schizophrenia and Other Psychotic Disorders

Psychotic disorders are a group of serious illnesses that affect the mind. They make it hard for someone to think clearly, make good judgments, respond emotionally, communicate effectively, understand reality, and behave appropriately.

There are different types of psychotic disorders, including:

- **Schizophrenia:** People with this illness have changes in behavior and other symptoms—such as delusions and hallucinations—that last longer than 6 months. It usually affects them at work or school, as well as their relationships. Know the early warning signs of schizophrenia.
- **Schizoaffective disorder:** People have symptoms of both schizophrenia and a mood disorder, such as depression or bipolar disorder.
- **Schizophreniform disorder:** This includes symptoms of schizophrenia, but the symptoms last for a shorter time: between 1 and 6 months.
- **Brief psychotic disorder:** People with this illness have a sudden, short period of psychotic behavior, often in response to a very stressful event, such as a death in the family. Recovery is often quick—usually less than a month.
- **Delusional disorder:** The key symptom is having a delusion (a false, fixed belief) involving a real-life situation that could be true but isn't, such as being followed, being plotted against, or having a disease. The delusion lasts for at least 1 month.
- **Shared psychotic disorder (also called folie à deux):** This illness happens when one person in a relationship has a delusion and the other person in the relationship adopts it, too.
- **Substance-induced psychotic disorder:** This condition is caused by the use of or withdrawal from drugs, such as hallucinogens and crack cocaine, that cause hallucinations, delusions, or confused speech.
- **Psychotic disorder due to another medical condition:** Hallucinations, delusions, or other symptoms may happen because of another illness that affects brain function, such as a head injury or brain tumor.
- **Paraphrenia:** This condition has symptoms similar to schizophrenia or a delusional disorder and is not formally recognized in the DSM V. It starts late in life when people are elderly, and may be related to neurological problems.

Schizophrenia/Psychotic Disorders Crisis

> A schizophrenia/psychotic disorder crisis is a severe mental health emergency marked by hallucinations, delusions, disorganized thinking, and extreme agitation. Individuals may become highly fearful, confused, and unable to distinguish reality, leading to potentially dangerous behaviors. Immediate professional intervention is crucial for safety and stabilization.

- **Safety concerns:** If someone's safety is at risk, call 911 and tell the operator it's a mental health emergency. You can ask for police officers who are trained to assist with a crisis.
- **Suicidal thoughts:** If someone is in danger of suicide or has attempted suicide, stay with them and contact a suicide hotline. In the U.S., you can call or text 988 to reach the 988 Suicide & Crisis Lifeline, which is available 24/7.
- **Other signs** that require immediate attention include:
  - Attempts or threats to harm or kill
  - Verbal or physical abuse
  - Excessive withdrawal
  - Not sleeping or eating for several days
  - Delusions, hallucinations, command hallucinations
  - Polydipsia
  - Paranoia/catatonia

If someone with Schizophrenia/Psychotic Disorders is exhibiting these crisis symptoms, it's crucial to seek immediate help from mental health professionals, crisis intervention services, or emergency services to ensure their safety and provide appropriate care.

Crisis and De-Escalation Interventions for Schizophrenia/Psychotic Disorders

- Use a trauma-informed approach.
- Use positive interpersonal communication skills.
- Use the daily habits of de-escalation.
- **Guidelines for schizophrenia crisis and de-escalation strategies:**
  - **Contact crisis intervention teams.** Contact mental health crisis intervention teams if the situation escalates and professional intervention is needed.
  - **Contact the Suicide and Crisis Lifeline.** If you or someone you know is struggling or having thoughts of suicide, call or text the 988 Suicide & Crisis Lifeline at 988 or chat at 988lifeline.org. In life-threatening situations, call 911.
  - **Ensure safety.** Assess the environment to remove any potentially harmful objects and maintain physical distance to avoid escalating the situation.
  - **Stay calm and composed.** Use a calm, gentle tone and remain composed, even if the person becomes agitated or aggressive.

- **Use clear and simple communication.** Provide clear, straightforward instructions and be prepared to calmly repeat information if they appear confused or distracted.
- **Validate their experience.** Acknowledge their feelings with empathy, such as saying, "I understand that you're feeling scared right now," and avoid confrontation by not arguing with their beliefs or experiences, gently redirecting the conversation if necessary.
- **Provide reassurance and support.** Offer reassurance by letting them know you are there to help and keep them safe, and be patient, giving them time to process and respond.
- **Use distraction techniques.** Redirect their focus by engaging them in less stressful activities, and suggest calming activities like listening to music, drawing, or taking a walk.
- **Set boundaries and limits.** Clearly and respectfully communicate acceptable behaviors, and apply limits consistently to avoid confusion and frustration.

■ **Guidelines to avoid schizophrenia/psychotic escalation:**

- **Avoid invalidating their experience** by refraining from dismissing hallucinations or delusions as "not real" and minimizing their feelings, as it can increase their sense of isolation and distress.
- **Avoid reacting emotionally by matching their energy or reacting with fear or panic**, as it can escalate the situation and increase their anxiety.
- **Avoid being confrontational or judgmental** with their beliefs or blaming them for symptoms, as it can escalate distress and lead to defensiveness and agitation.
- **Avoid ignoring or dismissing their concerns** by not listening attentively or dismissing what they say, as it can make them feel unheard and invalidated. Also, maintain eye contact to convey attentiveness and care.
- **Avoid pressuring for immediate solutions** by demanding explanations for symptoms or pressuring medication compliance without addressing concerns, as it can be overwhelming and lead to resistance.
- **Avoid being inconsistent in responses or changing rules/boundaries**, as it can confuse and frustrate them. Inconsistent responses to similar situations or sudden changes in expectations or boundaries can lead to confusion and agitation.
- **Avoid overreacting or underreacting to their symptoms.** Overreacting with exaggerated fear or concern can intensify their anxiety, while underreacting by ignoring or downplaying crisis signs can lead to dangerous situations.
- **Avoid neglecting their need for support** by being available when they need it, as not being there can make them feel abandoned and increase distress. Additionally, following through on promises and commitments is crucial to build trust and prevent feelings of mistrust.
- **Avoid using confrontational language**, such as threats or negative labels, as it can increase anxiety and escalate the situation. Instead, use supportive and non-stigmatizing language to communicate effectively.
- **Avoid neglecting safety measures** by addressing safety concerns promptly, such as self-harm or harm to others, to prevent serious consequences. Additionally, ensure environmental safety by removing potential hazards to reduce the risk of accidents.

- Build a trusting relationship and work in an open, engaging, and non-judgmental manner.
- Be aware that stigma and discrimination can be associated with a diagnosis of schizophrenia or a psychotic disorder.
- Work as a multidisciplinary team and offer guidance and support (family, caregivers).
- Encourage them to meet their ADL's (Activities of Daily Living).
- Show environmental awareness (safely remove any objects that the person could use to harm themselves).
- Seek immediate suicide intervention when needed (see Module 16).

Effective de-escalation and crisis intervention for schizophrenia and psychotic disorders requires a combination of compassion, empathy, active listening, and practical actions to ensure immediate safety and long-term support. By creating a safe and supportive environment, engaging appropriate resources, and following up with continuous care, individuals experiencing a crisis can be guided toward stability and recovery.

Addressing the risks associated with a schizophrenia and psychotic disorders crisis requires a proactive and compassionate approach. By implementing training, support systems, and clear protocols and promoting a supportive workplace culture, organizations can effectively manage these risks and ensure the safety and well-being of all staff members. Mental health is a crucial aspect of overall health, and taking steps to support it benefits both individuals and the organization as a whole.

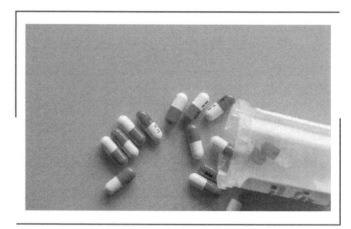

Schizophrenia/Psychotic Disorder Treatments

> Disclaimer: Personal Safety Training Inc. makes no claim as to what type of treatment is needed for any mental health disorder.

Schizophrenia and psychotic disorders are typically treated with a combination of medication and therapy to help manage symptoms and improve daily life. Antipsychotic medications, which affect dopamine in the brain, are commonly prescribed and can be taken daily or as monthly injections. If standard antipsychotics are ineffective, clozapine or other medications like antidepressants, mood stabilizers, or antianxiety drugs may be used. Psychological treatments, such as cognitive behavioral therapy (CBT), can help modify negative thoughts and manage symptoms. Additional support may include community mental health teams, rehabilitation for life-management skills, vocational training, and social skills training. While many people recover from schizophrenia, relapses can occur, but treatment and support can reduce the condition's impact on life.

IF YOU OR SOMEONE YOU KNOW IS IN CRISIS AND CONSIDERING SELF-HARM OR SUICIDE:

- Call 911 for emergency services.
- Visit the nearest hospital emergency room.
- Call or text 988 to connect with the 988 Suicide and Crisis Lifeline, offering 24-hour, confidential support. *Para ayuda en español, llame al 988.*
- Support is also available via live chat at 988lifeline.org. *AVADE® does not monitor this website for crisis messages, provide medical advice, or make referrals.*

PSTI LEGAL DISCLAIMER

The information in this training book is a supplement, not a substitute, for the expertise of qualified healthcare professionals. The content on AVADE® Behavioral Health, sourced from reliable information, does not constitute medical or professional healthcare advice, diagnosis, or treatment. It is crucial to consult healthcare providers for specific guidelines related to medical or behavioral health conditions. This material does not guarantee that any technique or strategy is safe or effective for any specific needs. Personal Safety Training, Inc., does not dictate policies or procedures for behavioral health violence prevention, self-defense tactics, or any physical interventions. Agencies are responsible for developing their own policies and evaluating the recommendations based on their circumstances.

The author and publisher do not guarantee the completeness or accuracy of the information and assume no risk for its use. Any implied warranty are expressly disavowed.

References for Module 8

https://988lifeline.org/

https://www.apa.org/

https://www.cdc.gov/

https://mhanational.org/

https://www.nami.org/

https://www.nimh.nih.gov/

https://www.psychiatry.org/

https://www.samhsa.gov/

Video: What is Schizophrenia?
  youtube.com/watch?v=tYiTznmuSu4

Video: What is Psychosis?
  youtube.com/watch?v=RRGGxK3OpNc

Video: What is Psychosis?
  youtube.com/watch?v=h7pceQWJZRY

American Psychiatric Association. *Diagnostic and Statistical Manual of Mental Disorders Fifth Edition DSM-5®*. American Psychiatric Association Publishing. Washington, DC 2013

Boland, Robert, MD, Marcia L. Verduin, MD, Pedro Ruiz, MD. *Kaplan & Saddock's Synopsis of Psychiatry 12th Edition*. Philadelphia, PA. Wolters Kluwer, 2022

Brown, Catana, PhD., Virginia C. Stoffel PhD, and Jaime Muñoz PhD. *Occupational Therapy in Mental Health, A Vision for Participation*. Philadelphia, PA. F.A Davis Company, 2015.

Buser, Steven, MD. *DSM-5® Insanely Simplified, Unlocking the Spectrums within DSM_5 and ICD-10*. Asheville, NC. Chiron Publications, 2014

Duckworth, Ken, MD. *You Are Not Alone, The NAMI Guide to Navigating Mental Health*. New York, NY. Zando, 2022

Glick, Rachel Lipson, MD, Scott L. Zeller, MD, Jon S. Berlin, MD. *Emergency Psychiatry Principles and Practice. 2nd Edition*. Philadelphia, PA. Wolters Kluwer, 2021

Mental Health America. *Where to Start, A Survival Guide To Anxiety, Depression, and Other Mental Health Challenges*. New York, NY. Penguin Random House LLC, 2023

Morrissey, Jean and Patrick Callaghan. *Communication Skills for Mental Health Nurses*. Berkshire, England. McGraw-Hill Education, Maiden, 2011

Morrison, James. *DSM-5® Made Easy, The Clinicians Guide to Diagnosis*. New York, NY. The Guilford Press, 2014

Townsend, Mary C. *Psychiatric Mental Health Nursing, Concepts of Care in Evidenced Based Practice 8th Edition*. Philadelphia, PA. F.A Davis Company, 2015.

MODULE 9

Obsessive-Compulsive Disorder (OCD)

Recurring, unwanted thoughts and repetitive behaviors

Module 9:
Obsessive-Compulsive Disorder (OCD)

Obsessive-Compulsive Disorder (OCD) Defined

> Obsessive-compulsive disorder is a disorder in which people have recurring, unwanted thoughts, ideas, or sensations (obsessions). To get rid of the thoughts, they feel driven to do something repetitively (compulsions). Repetitive behaviors, such as hand washing, checking things, and mental acts like counting, can significantly interfere with a person's daily activities and social interactions.

Many people without OCD have distressing thoughts or repetitive behaviors. However, these do not typically disrupt daily life. For people with OCD, thoughts are persistent and intrusive, and behaviors are rigid. Not performing the behaviors commonly causes great distress, often attached to a specific fear of dire consequences (to self or loved ones) if the behaviors are not completed. Many people with OCD know or suspect their obsessional thoughts are not realistic; others may think they could be true. Even if they know their intrusive thoughts are not realistic, people with OCD have difficulty disengaging from the obsessive thoughts or stopping the compulsive actions.

A diagnosis of OCD requires the presence of obsessional thoughts and/or compulsions that are time-consuming (more than one hour a day), cause significant distress, and impair work or social functioning. OCD affects 2-3% of people in the United States, and among adults, slightly more women than men are affected. OCD often begins in childhood, adolescence, or early adulthood. Some people may have some symptoms of OCD but not meet full criteria for this disorder.[1]

Obsessive-Compulsive Disorder Facts and Statistics

- Just over 1% of adults in the U.S. suffer from Obsessive-Compulsive Disorder (OCD).[2]
- Females are more likely to suffer from OCD (almost 2% in the U.S.)
- Most adults with OCD typically range from mild to severe impairments.

---

1 https://www.psychiatry.org/patients-families/obsessive-compulsive-disorder/what-is-obsessive-compulsive-disorder

2 https://www.nimh.nih.gov/health/statistics/obsessive-compulsive-disorder-ocd

- 50% of adults with OCD have more serious impairments.
- Genetics play a significant role in OCD, with a 25% chance that an immediate family member will have the disorder if you, your parent, or a sibling have it.
- The average age of onset of OCD is 19.5 years old.
- The majority (90%) of the adults who had OCD at some point in their lives also had at least one other mental disorder.
- Males make up the majority of very early-onset cases. Almost a quarter of males have onsets before age 10. Most females are diagnosed with OCD during adolescence (after age 10).

Signs and Symptoms of Obsessive-Compulsive Disorder

People with OCD may have obsessions, compulsions, or both.

Obsessions

> Obsessions are repeated thoughts, urges, or mental images that are intrusive, unwanted, and make most people anxious.

Obsessions are recurrent and persistent thoughts, impulses, or images that cause distressing emotions such as anxiety, fear, or disgust. Many people with OCD recognize that these are a product of their minds and that they are excessive or unreasonable. However, the distress caused by these intrusive thoughts cannot be resolved by logic or reasoning. Most people with OCD try to ease the distress of obsessional thinking or to undo the perceived threats by using compulsions. They may also try to ignore or suppress the obsessions or distract themselves with other activities.

Common obsessions include:

- Fear of contamination by people or the environment
- Disturbing sexual thoughts or images
- Religious, often blasphemous, thoughts or fears
- Fear of perpetrating aggression or being harmed (self or loved ones)
- Extreme worry something is not complete
- Extreme concern with order, symmetry, or precision
- Fear of losing or discarding something important
- Can also be seemingly meaningless thoughts, images, sounds, words or music

Compulsions

> Compulsions are repetitive behaviors or mental acts that a person feels driven to perform in response to an obsession.

The behaviors typically prevent or reduce a person's distress related to an obsession temporarily, and they are then more likely to do the same in the future. Compulsions may be excessive responses that are directly related to an obsession (such as excessive hand washing due to the fear of contamination) or actions that are completely unrelated to the obsession. In the most severe cases, a constant repetition of rituals may fill the day, making a normal routine impossible.

Common compulsions include:

- Excessive or ritualized hand washing, showering, brushing teeth, or toileting
- Repeated cleaning of household objects
- Ordering or arranging things in a particular way
- Repeatedly checking locks, switches, appliances, doors, etc.
- Constantly seeking approval or reassurance

- Rituals related to numbers, such as counting, repeating, excessively preferencing or avoiding certain numbers
- People with OCD may also avoid certain people, places, or situations that cause them distress and trigger obsessions and/or compulsions. Avoiding these things may further impair their ability to function in life and may be detrimental to other areas of mental or physical health.

Obsessive-Compulsive Disorder Causes

Although the exact causes of OCD are unknown, various risk factors increase the chances of developing the disorder. These risk factors include:

- **Genetics**: Studies have shown that having a first-degree relative (parent or sibling) with OCD is associated with an increased chance of developing the disorder. Scientists have not identified any one gene or set of genes that definitively leads to OCD, but studies exploring the connection between genetics and OCD are ongoing.
- **Biology**: Brain imaging studies have shown that people with OCD often have differences in the frontal cortex and subcortical structures of the brain, areas of the brain that impact the ability to control behavior and emotional responses. Researchers also have found that several brain areas, brain networks, and biological processes play a key role in obsessive thoughts, compulsive behavior, and associated fear and anxiety. Research is underway to better understand the connection between OCD symptoms and parts of the brain. This knowledge can help researchers develop and adapt treatments targeted to specific brain locations.
- **Temperament**: Some research has found that people who exhibit more reserved behaviors, experience negative emotions, and show symptoms of anxiety and depression as children are more likely to develop OCD.
- **Childhood trauma**: Some studies have reported an association between childhood trauma and obsessive-compulsive symptoms. More research is needed to understand this relationship.

Types of Obsessive-Compulsive Disorder

There is no single official way to divide OCD into sub-types. However, many researchers agree that there are certain common themes and symptom clusters among people with OCD.

Checking

One of the most common symptoms of OCD is compulsive checking. People with "checking OCD" may excessively check the following types of things:

- Their appliances are turned off.
- Their doors and windows are locked.
- They haven't lost, damaged, or misplaced something important.

Checking rituals can also be related to excessive doubts, anxiety, and a fear of losing control. There is often the fear of intentionally or unintentionally causing something bad to happen. For example, someone with OCD may not be able to leave the house for over an hour due to repeatedly checking that the stove is off in order to prevent a fire.

Order and symmetry

Many people with OCD experience obsessions and compulsions related to order, symmetry, arranging, and counting. Symmetry-related compulsive rituals may involve:

- Lining things up over and over
- Constantly rearranging furniture to make it look "just right"
- Repeatedly counting items to ensure they're divided into equal groups

Someone with an irrational preference for order may also become overly preoccupied with their body proportions and/or grooming habits, which can lead to disordered eating and poor self-image. Others feel compelled to perform excessive scheduling, planning, time management, and organizing rituals.

Contamination

Fear of contamination is one of the most common obsessive themes among people with OCD. People who fear germs and/or contamination may:

- Clean surfaces over and over
- Wash their hands compulsively
- Worry excessively about ingredients in food or household products
- Avoid touching things others have touched

Some people with OCD also experience a fear of emotional contamination. Someone who fears emotional contamination may go out of their way to avoid people, places, or topics they see as "immoral" or "dirty."

Ruminations or intrusive thoughts

Rumination refers to obsessive, intrusive, and unwanted thoughts around a certain theme. Rumination frequently involves taboo or forbidden topics, such as sexuality, violence, or religion.

Intrusive thoughts can take on many forms. Some include:

- Ruminating about their sexual orientation
- Constantly question their religious identity
- Constantly worry that they will cheat on their partner
- Worry they will hurt themselves or someone else
- Worry they may become sexually predatory, even in the absence of any evidence

Others experience intrusive, graphic sexual or violent mental imagery that they consider inappropriate or disturbing.

Often, rumination is related to an underlying obsession with guilt and excessive responsibility for harm. People who experience intrusive thoughts may perform compulsive rituals in an attempt to "neutralize" the perceived threat. For example, someone who has forbidden thoughts around religion or blasphemy may pray excessively to protect themselves or others spiritually. Someone else may count, tap, or repeat certain movements or phrases because they believe it will save someone they love from harm.

Obsessive-Compulsive Disorder Crisis

> An OCD crisis refers to a severe and acute phase of obsessive-compulsive disorder where the individual's symptoms become overwhelming and significantly impair their ability to function. Immediate intervention from mental health professionals is often necessary to manage the crisis and ensure the individual's safety.

Concerns

- **Safety**: There may be concerns about the individual's safety, especially if their obsessions or compulsions involve harmful behaviors or if they have thoughts of self-harm.
- **Emotional well-being**: The person's emotional well-being may be at risk due to distress caused by obsessive thoughts or compulsive behaviors.
- **Functioning**: OCD symptoms can significantly impair daily functioning, including work, relationships, and self-care.

Signs and warnings

- **Intense anxiety**: The person may experience intense anxiety or panic attacks related to their obsessions or compulsions.
- **Increased rituals**: There may be an escalation in rituals or compulsive behaviors, such as excessive handwashing, checking, or counting.
- **Avoidance**: They might avoid certain situations or places due to obsessive fears or compulsive urges.
- **Time-consuming behaviors**: Spending excessive amounts of time on rituals or repetitive behaviors can be a sign of distress.
- **Mental exhaustion**: Obsessive thoughts can lead to mental exhaustion, affecting concentration, decision-making, and cognitive abilities.
- **Changes in mood**: Mood changes such as irritability, agitation, or depression may be noticeable during a crisis.
- **Physical symptoms**: Stress from OCD symptoms can manifest in physical symptoms like fatigue, tension, or headaches.
- **Isolation**: They may withdraw from social interactions or isolate themselves due to shame or embarrassment about their symptoms.
- **Suicidal thoughts**: In severe cases, there may be signs of suicidal ideation or self-harm behaviors.

If someone with Obsessive-Compulsive Disorder is exhibiting these crisis symptoms, it's crucial to seek immediate help from mental health professionals, crisis intervention services, or emergency services to ensure their safety and provide appropriate care.

Crisis and De-Escalation Interventions for Obsessive-Compulsive Disorder

- Use a trauma-informed approach.
- Use positive interpersonal communication skills.
- Use the daily habits of de-escalation.

- **Guidelines for obsessive-compulsive crisis and de-escalation strategies:**
  - **Contact crisis intervention teams.** Contact mental health crisis intervention teams if the situation escalates and professional intervention is needed.
  - **Contact the Suicide and Crisis Lifeline.** If you or someone you know is struggling or having thoughts of suicide, call or text the 988 Suicide & Crisis Lifeline at 988 or chat at 988lifeline.org. In life-threatening situations, call 911.
  - **Ensure safety.** Assess the environment to remove any potentially harmful objects and maintain physical distance to avoid escalating the situation.
  - **Assess the situation.** Identify specific triggers that are causing distress or exacerbating OCD symptoms and ensure safety for the individual and others.
  - **Provide a safe environment.** Maintain a quiet, calm, and non-threatening environment while minimizing external stimuli to reduce anxiety and distress.
  - **Active listening and empathy.** Show empathy by listening non-judgmentally and acknowledging their feelings without criticism or dismissal, validating their emotions and reassuring them that it's okay to feel distressed.
  - **Use clear and simple communication.** Communicate using clear and straightforward language, avoiding complicated explanations.
  - **Offer reassurance and support.** Provide reassurance that they are safe and that their feelings are valid, using supportive statements such as "We'll work through this together" or "You're doing the best you can."
  - **Use distraction techniques.** Redirect attention from obsessive thoughts by engaging in a different activity or topic. Additionally, suggest calming strategies such as deep breathing or progressive muscle relaxation to promote relaxation.
  - **Set boundaries and limits.** Establish clear boundaries by respectfully communicating limitations, such as not engaging in rituals or compulsions during crisis situations. Encourage healthy coping strategies and self-care practices.

- **Guidelines to avoid obsessive-compulsive escalation:**
  - **Avoid invalidating their experience.** Refrain from dismissing obsessions or compulsions as "irrational" or "silly," and avoid minimizing the impact of OCD on their daily life or mental well-being.
  - **Avoid reacting emotionally** by showing frustration, impatience, or annoyance with their rituals or obsessions, and refrain from expressing disbelief or skepticism about their symptoms.
  - **Avoid being critical or judgmental** towards someone with OCD by refraining from criticizing or blaming them for their symptoms.
  - **Avoid interfering with their coping mechanisms,** such as preventing rituals or compulsions even with good intentions, or belittling and mocking their coping strategies, which can be counterproductive and increase distress.
  - **Avoid increasing pressure or demands** on someone with OCD, such as pressuring them to stop rituals abruptly or demanding explanations for their behavior, as it can be overwhelming and counterproductive.
  - **Avoid disrupting their routine** by intentionally interfering with their rituals or making sudden changes to their environment or schedule without

warning can cause distress and disrupt their coping mechanisms.

- **Avoid ignoring or dismissing their triggers and sources of anxiety**, as well as exposing them to triggers without their consent or preparation, can increase distress and exacerbate OCD symptoms.

- **Avoid using negative reinforcement** by punishing or shaming them for their OCD symptoms or withholding support or reassurance when they are struggling, which can be harmful and worsen their distress.

- **Avoid being inconsistent in providing support or responses to their symptoms**, as well as changing rules or expectations unpredictably, which can confuse and frustrate someone with OCD, leading to increased distress.

- **Avoid overprotecting** by shielding them from anxiety triggers, which can lead to avoidance behaviors, and enabling rituals or compulsions by participating in or facilitating their behavior, can reinforce OCD patterns and hinder progress in managing symptoms.

- **Avoid neglecting their need for support** by being unavailable or dismissive, and failing to acknowledge their efforts or progress in managing OCD, can undermine their well-being. Additionally, introducing unnecessary stressors or pressure that exacerbate anxiety can be detrimental.

- **Avoid being condescending or patronizing** by talking down to them or treating them as incapable of managing their symptoms, or using condescending language or tone when discussing their OCD, which can undermine their confidence and hinder their progress in coping with the disorder.

- **Avoid ignoring boundaries** by disregarding their personal space or privacy during times of distress and invading their privacy or personal rituals without permission can lead to feelings of violation and exacerbate their distress.

- Build a trusting relationship and work in an open, engaging, and non-judgmental manner.

- Be aware that stigma and discrimination can be associated with a diagnosis of obsessive-compulsive disorder.

- Work as a multidisciplinary team and offer guidance and support (family, caregivers).

- Encourage them to meet their ADL's (Activities of Daily Living).

- Show environmental awareness (safely remove any objects that the person could use to harm themselves).

- Seek immediate suicide intervention when needed (see Module 16).

Effective de-escalation and crisis intervention for obsessive-compulsive disorder requires a combination of compassion, empathy, active listening, and practical actions to ensure immediate safety and long-term support. By creating a safe and supportive environment, engaging appropriate resources, and following up with continuous care, individuals experiencing a crisis can be guided toward stability and recovery.

Addressing the risks associated with obsessive-compulsive disorder crisis requires a proactive and compassionate approach. By implementing training, support systems, and clear protocols and promoting a supportive workplace culture, organizations can effectively manage these risks and ensure the safety and well-being of all staff members. Mental health is a crucial aspect of overall health, and taking steps to support it benefits both individuals and the organization as a whole.

Obsessive-Compulsive Disorder Treatments

> Disclaimer: Personal Safety Training Inc. makes no claim as to what type of treatment is needed for any mental health disorder.

Effective treatments for OCD often enhance quality of life and functioning. Key approaches include:

- **Cognitive Behavioral Therapy (CBT).** Exposure and Response Prevention (ERP) helps patients face fears and resist compulsive behaviors, reducing anxiety over time.
- **Medication.** Selective Serotonin Reuptake Inhibitors (SSRIs) are effective, often at higher doses than for depression, with benefits typically seen after six to twelve weeks.
- **Neurosurgical treatments.** Gamma ventral capsulotomy and deep brain stimulation (DBS) are options for treatment-resistant cases, though they are invasive and complex.
- **Self-care.** Maintaining a healthy lifestyle, good sleep, healthy eating, exercise, and relaxation techniques support overall mental health.

IF YOU OR SOMEONE YOU KNOW IS IN CRISIS AND CONSIDERING SELF-HARM OR SUICIDE:

- Call 911 for emergency services.
- Visit the nearest hospital emergency room.
- Call or text 988 to connect with the 988 Suicide and Crisis Lifeline, offering 24-hour, confidential support. *Para ayuda en español, llame al 988.*
- Support is also available via live chat at 988lifeline.org. *AVADE® does not monitor this website for crisis messages, provide medical advice, or make referrals.*

PSTI LEGAL DISCLAIMER

The information in this training book is a supplement, not a substitute, for the expertise of qualified healthcare professionals. The content on AVADE® Behavioral Health, sourced from reliable information, does not constitute medical or professional healthcare advice, diagnosis, or treatment. It is crucial to consult healthcare providers for specific guidelines related to medical or behavioral health conditions. This material does not guarantee that any technique or strategy is safe or effective for any specific needs. Personal Safety Training, Inc., does not dictate policies or procedures for behavioral health violence prevention, self-defense tactics, or any physical interventions. Agencies are responsible for developing their own policies and evaluating the recommendations based on their circumstances.

The author and publisher do not guarantee the completeness or accuracy of the information and assume no risk for its use. Any implied warranty are expressly disavowed.

References for Module 9

https://988lifeline.org/

https://www.apa.org/

https://www.cdc.gov/

https://mhanational.org/

https://www.nami.org/

https://www.nimh.nih.gov/

https://www.psychiatry.org/

https://www.samhsa.gov/

Video: What is OCD?
youtube.com/watch?v=1MJVG8kWBbc&t=2s

Video: What is OCD?
youtube.com/watch?v=ivyLkTcvanQ&t=2s

Video: What is OCD?
youtube.com/watch?v=2wW88fzYZaA&t=7s

American Psychiatric Association. *Diagnostic and Statistical Manual of Mental Disorders Fifth Edition DSM-5®*. American Psychiatric Association Publishing. Washington, DC 2013

Boland, Robert, MD, Marcia L. Verduin, MD, Pedro Ruiz, MD. *Kaplan & Saddock's Synopsis of Psychiatry 12th Edition*. Philadelphia, PA. Wolters Kluwer, 2022

Brown, Catana, PhD., Virginia C. Stoffel PhD, and Jaime Muñoz PhD. *Occupational Therapy in Mental Health, A Vision for Participation*. Philadelphia, PA. F.A Davis Company, 2015.

Buser, Steven, MD. *DSM-5® Insanely Simplified, Unlocking the Spectrums within DSM_5 and ICD-10*. Asheville, NC. Chiron Publications, 2014

Duckworth, Ken, MD. *You Are Not Alone, The NAMI Guide to Navigating Mental Health*. New York, NY. Zando, 2022

Glick, Rachel Lipson, MD, Scott L. Zeller, MD, Jon S. Berlin, MD. *Emergency Psychiatry Principles and Practice. 2nd Edition*. Philadelphia, PA. Wolters Kluwer, 2021

Mental Health America. *Where to Start, A Survival Guide To Anxiety, Depression, and Other Mental Health Challenges*. New York, NY. Penguin Random House LLC, 2023

Morrissey, Jean and Patrick Callaghan. *Communication Skills for Mental Health Nurses*. Berkshire, England. McGraw-Hill Education, Maiden, 2011

Morrison, James. *DSM-5® Made Easy, The Clinicians Guide to Diagnosis*. New York, NY. The Guilford Press, 2014

Townsend, Mary C. *Psychiatric Mental Health Nursing, Concepts of Care in Evidenced Based Practice 8th Edition*. Philadelphia, PA. F.A Davis Company, 2015.

MODULE 10

Post-Traumatic Stress Disorder (PTSD)

Stress-related symptoms due to experiencing or witnessing a traumatic event

Module 10:
Post-Traumatic Stress Disorder (PTSD)

Post-Traumatic Stress Disorder (PTSD) Defined

> Post-traumatic stress disorder (PTSD) is a mental health condition that can occur in people who have experienced or witnessed a traumatic event, series of events, or set of circumstances. An individual may experience this as emotionally or physically harmful or life-threatening and may affect mental, physical, social, and/or spiritual well-being.

Examples include natural disasters, serious accidents, terrorist acts, war/combat, rape/sexual assault, historical trauma, intimate partner violence and bullying.

PTSD has been known by many names in the past, such as "shell shock" during the years of World War I and "combat fatigue" after World War II, but PTSD does not just happen to combat veterans. PTSD can occur in all people of any ethnicity, nationality or culture, and at any age.[1]

Studies have found that most people recover and do not develop PTSD after exposure to a major traumatic event. However, some people find themselves feeling worse as time passes and experience the symptoms of PTSD. Several factors before and after a traumatic event seem to increase the likelihood of PTSD. For example, the risk is greater when the traumatic event is more severe, violent, occurs over a longer period of time, or involves harm to oneself or the loss of a loved one. Being around reminders of the traumatic event can also increase the risk. In general, women are more likely than men and younger people are more likely than older to develop PTSD. People who had adverse childhood experiences, especially exposure to traumatic events, are more susceptible, as are people with chronic medical or psychiatric illness.

PTSD Facts and Statistics

- Most people will experience at least one traumatic event in their lifetime that has the potential to cause PTSD.[2]
- PTSD affects approximately 3.5 percent of U.S. adults every year.

---

1 https://www.psychiatry.org/patients-families/ptsd

2 https://www.forbes.com/health/mind/ptsd-statistics/

- The lifetime prevalence of PTSD in adolescents ages 13-18 is 8 percent.
- An estimated one in 11 people will be diagnosed with PTSD in their lifetime.
- Women are twice as likely as men to have PTSD.
- Three ethnic minorities—U.S. Latinos, African Americans, and Native Americans/Alaska Natives—are disproportionately affected and have higher rates of PTSD than non-Latino whites.
- About one in three people who experience severe trauma will develop PTSD.
- Of people diagnosed with PTSD, almost 1/3 fall into the category of having severe symptoms.
- People who have served in the military are more likely to develop PTSD than the general population of civilians.
- People who experience sexual assault have a higher likelihood of developing PTSD than those who experience other types of trauma.
- Almost one-third of all rape victims will develop PTSD at some point in their lives.
- The Substance Abuse and Mental Health Services Administration estimates that one in three first responders develop PTSD.
- Almost 80% of people with PTSD also have another mental health condition.

Signs and Symptoms of PTSD

Symptoms of PTSD may last months to years. PTSD symptoms may include:

- Flashbacks, or feeling like the event is happening again
- Trouble sleeping or nightmares
- Feeling alone or detached from others
- Losing interest in activities
- Having angry outbursts or other extreme reactions
- Feeling worried, guilty, or sad
- Frightening thoughts
- Having trouble concentrating
- Having physical pain like headaches or stomachaches
- Avoidance of memories, thoughts, or feelings about what is closely associated with traumatic events
- Problems remembering
- Negative beliefs about themselves or others
- Irritability
- Feeling very vigilant
- Startling easily

Symptoms of anxiety, depression, and substance use also are seen with people who have PTSD.

PTSD Causes

PTSD can occur at any age and is directly associated with exposure to trauma. Adults and children who have PTSD represent a relatively small portion of those who have been exposed to trauma. This difference is not yet well understood but we do know that there are risk factors that can increase a person's likelihood to develop PTSD. Risk factors can include prior experiences of trauma and factors that may promote resilience, such as social support. This is also an ongoing area of research.

We do know that for some, our "fight-or-flight" biological instincts, which can be life-saving during a crisis, can leave us with ongoing symptoms. Because the body is busy increasing its heart rate, pumping blood to muscles, preparing the body to fight or flee, all our physical resources and energy are focused on getting out of harm's way. Therefore, there has been discussion that the posttraumatic stress response may not a disorder per se, but rather a variant of a human response to trauma.

Whether you think of these symptoms as a stress response variant or PTSD, consider them a consequence of our body's inability to effectively return to "normal" in the months after its extraordinary response to a traumatic event.

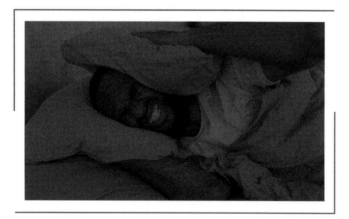

Risk Factors for PTSD

- Anyone who was a victim, witnessed, or has been exposed to a life-threatening situation.
- Survivors of violent acts, such as domestic violence, rape, sexual, physical and/or verbal abuse or physical attacks.
- Survivors of unexpected dangerous events, such as a car accident, natural disaster, or terrorist attack.
- Combat veterans or civilians exposed to war.
- People who have learned of or experienced an unexpected and sudden death of a friend or relative.
- Emergency responders who help victims during traumatic events.
- Children who are neglected and/or abused (physically, sexually, or verbally).

Why do some people develop PTSD while other people do not?

Not everyone who lives through a dangerous event develops PTSD—many factors play a part. Some of these factors are present before the trauma; others play a role during and after a traumatic event.

Additional risk factors that may increase the likelihood of developing PTSD include:

- Exposure to previous traumatic experiences, particularly during childhood
- Getting hurt or seeing people hurt or killed
- Feeling horror, helplessness, or extreme fear
- Having little or no social support after the event
- Dealing with stressors after the event, such as the loss of a loved one, pain, injury, or loss of job or home
- Having a personal history or family history of mental illness or substance use

Resilience factors that may reduce the likelihood of developing PTSD include:

- Seeking out and receiving support from friends, family, or support groups
- Learning to feel okay with one's actions in response to a traumatic event
- Having a coping strategy for getting through and learning from a traumatic event
- Being prepared and able to respond to upsetting events as they occur, despite feeling fear

Types of PTSD

The types of PTSD can be classified based on the duration, onset, and severity of symptoms:

- **Acute PTSD**: Symptoms last less than three months.
- **Chronic PTSD**: Symptoms last three months or longer.
- **Delayed-Onset PTSD**: Symptoms appear at least six months after the traumatic event.
- **Complex PTSD**: Results from prolonged or repeated trauma, often involving emotional and relational difficulties.

PTSD Crisis

> A PTSD crisis is a severe episode where symptoms of post-traumatic stress disorder become overwhelming and unmanageable, leading to significant distress and impairment in functioning, with a heightened risk of self-harm or suicidal behavior, requiring immediate intervention and support.

These crisis symptoms can include:

- **Re-experiencing symptoms of PTSD** including flashbacks, nightmares, and intrusive thoughts related to the traumatic event.
- **Avoidance symptoms of PTSD** include avoiding reminders of the traumatic event and emotional numbing, such as feeling detached from others and losing interest in previously enjoyed activities.
- **Arousal and reactivity symptoms of PTSD** include hypervigilance, sudden bursts of anger or irritability, difficulty sleeping, and concentration problems.
- **Cognitive and mood symptoms of PTSD** include persistent negative thoughts and feelings, a sense of hopelessness, and severe emotional distress such as anxiety and depression.
- **Physical symptoms of PTSD** include sweating, shaking, or heart palpitations when reminded of the trauma.
- **Self-harm, substance abuse, aggression, withdrawal, and suicidal thoughts or actions.**
- **Panic attacks with intense fear** and physical symptoms, and dissociation, which involves feeling disconnected from oneself or reality.

If someone with PTSD is exhibiting these crisis symptoms, it's crucial to seek immediate help from mental health professionals, crisis intervention services, or emergency services to ensure their safety and provide appropriate care.

Crisis and De-Escalation Interventions for PTSD

- Use a trauma-informed approach.
- Use positive interpersonal communication skills.
- Use the daily habits of de-escalation.
- **Guidelines for PTSD crisis and de-escalation strategies:**
  - **Contact crisis intervention teams.** Contact mental health crisis intervention teams if the situation escalates and professional intervention is needed.
  - **Contact the Suicide and Crisis Lifeline.** If you or someone you know is struggling or having thoughts of suicide, call or text the 988 Suicide & Crisis Lifeline at 988 or chat at 988lifeline.org. In life-threatening situations, call 911.
  - **Ensure safety.** Assess the environment to remove any potentially harmful objects and maintain physical distance to avoid escalating the situation.

- **Use active listening and empathy** by giving full attention to the person without judgment, showing empathy and understanding, and validating their emotions by acknowledging their difficulties.
- **Practice clear and simple communication** by using straightforward language, avoiding complexity, and being prepared to repeat information calmly if necessary to understand.
- **Provide reassurance and support** by letting the person know they are safe and not alone, using supportive statements, and being patient to allow them to process and respond at their own pace.
- **Use grounding techniques** to help the person stay connected to the present moment, such as focusing on their surroundings or guiding them through deep breathing exercises to reduce anxiety.
- **Use distraction techniques** that involve less stressful activities to divert attention from distressing thoughts, such as listening to music, drawing, taking a walk, watching a favorite TV show, or doing a puzzle to promote calmness and relaxation.
- **Encourage positive coping mechanisms** by suggesting healthy strategies like talking to a friend, writing in a journal, or engaging in a hobby while gently discouraging negative coping methods such as substance abuse or self-harm.
- **Set clear boundaries and limits** by communicating them respectfully to avoid engaging in harmful behaviors during the crisis, and ensure consistency in applying these limits to prevent confusion and frustration.
- **Encourage small steps** by assisting them in setting manageable goals and celebrating small victories along the way. Promote self-care by encouraging activities such as exercise, healthy eating, and adequate sleep to help improve their mood.

- **Guidelines to avoid PTSD crisis escalation:**
  - **Avoid overstimulation** to prevent overwhelming the person's senses and escalating anxiety by minimizing exposure to loud noises, bright lights, or crowded spaces.
  - **Avoid minimizing their experience** by refraining from downplaying or dismissing their feelings, experiences, or trauma, as invalidating their emotions can lead to increased feelings of isolation and distress.
  - **Respect personal boundaries** and avoid forcing physical contact as it may be perceived as intrusive or triggering, maintaining a respectful distance to honor their comfort and autonomy.
  - **Avoid confrontation** by refraining from arguing, debating, or challenging their beliefs or experiences, as this can lead to defensiveness and increased distress in the individual.
  - **Avoid rushing the individual** by giving them the necessary time to process their emotions and thoughts, refraining from pressuring them to talk or make decisions before they feel ready.
  - **Avoid using judgmental or stigmatizing language**, as it can worsen their self-esteem and amplify feelings of shame or guilt.
  - **Respect their coping mechanisms**, even if they seem unusual, and avoid criticizing or belittling their strategies for managing stress or trauma.
  - **Avoid making assumptions** about what they need or how they feel; instead, ask open-ended questions and actively listen to understand their perspective.
  - **Avoid introducing sudden changes** as they can heighten anxiety and distress; instead, strive to maintain a predictable and stable environment to promote a sense of security and well-being.

- **Avoid overwhelming the person with information** by providing it in manageable doses; this approach prevents information overload, making it easier for them to process and understand.
- **Avoid triggering language** or discussing topics that may trigger traumatic memories or cause distress; instead, redirect the conversation to more neutral or calming subjects to ensure their comfort and well-being.

- Build a trusting relationship and work in an open, engaging, and non-judgmental manner.
- Be aware that stigma and discrimination can be associated with a diagnosis of Post-Traumatic Stress Disorder.
- Work as a multidisciplinary team and offer guidance and support (family, caregivers).
- Encourage them to meet their ADL's (Activities of Daily Living).
- Show environmental awareness (safely remove any objects that the person could use to harm themselves).
- Seek immediate suicide intervention when needed (see Module 16).

Effective de-escalation and crisis intervention for PTSD requires a combination of compassion, empathy, active listening, and practical actions to ensure immediate safety and long-term support. By creating a safe and supportive environment, engaging appropriate resources, and following up with continuous care, individuals experiencing a crisis can be guided toward stability and recovery.

Addressing the risks associated with a PTSD crisis requires a proactive and compassionate approach. By implementing training, support systems, and clear protocols and promoting a supportive workplace culture, organizations can effectively manage these risks and ensure the safety and well-being of all staff members. Mental health is a crucial aspect of overall health, and taking steps to support it benefits both individuals and the organization as a whole.

PTSD Treatments

> **Disclaimer: Personal Safety Training Inc. makes no claim as to what type of treatment is needed for any mental health disorder.**

Effective treatment for PTSD typically involves a combination of psychotherapy and medication, tailored to individual preferences and co-existing conditions. Psychotherapy approaches such as Cognitive Processing Therapy, EMDR, and Exposure Therapy help individuals confront trauma and develop coping strategies, while group therapy can reduce feelings of isolation and shame. Medications, primarily SSRIs, are often used alongside therapy, but their effectiveness varies and may come with side effects. Complementary health approaches, including aqua therapy, acupuncture, mindfulness practices, and service dogs, can also support PTSD treatment by managing daily stressors and preventing symptom exacerbation. Immediate support and compassion following a traumatic event are crucial, though individuals should not be forced to discuss the trauma until they are ready.

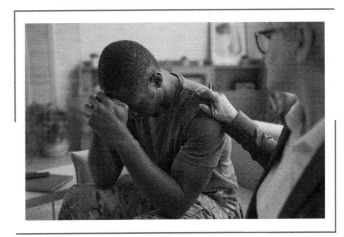

IF YOU OR SOMEONE YOU KNOW IS IN CRISIS AND CONSIDERING SELF-HARM OR SUICIDE:

- Call 911 for emergency services.
- Visit the nearest hospital emergency room.
- Call or text 988 to connect with the 988 Suicide and Crisis Lifeline, offering 24-hour, confidential support. *Para ayuda en español, llame al 988.*
- Support is also available via live chat at 988lifeline.org. AVADE® does not monitor this website for crisis messages, provide medical advice, or make referrals.

PSTI LEGAL DISCLAIMER

The information in this training book is a supplement, not a substitute, for the expertise of qualified healthcare professionals. The content on AVADE® Behavioral Health, sourced from reliable information, does not constitute medical or professional healthcare advice, diagnosis, or treatment. It is crucial to consult healthcare providers for specific guidelines related to medical or behavioral health conditions. This material does not guarantee that any technique or strategy is safe or effective for any specific needs. Personal Safety Training, Inc., does not dictate policies or procedures for behavioral health violence prevention, self-defense tactics, or any physical interventions. Agencies are responsible for developing their own policies and evaluating the recommendations based on their circumstances.

The author and publisher do not guarantee the completeness or accuracy of the information and assume no risk for its use. Any implied warranty are expressly disavowed.

References for Module 10

https://988lifeline.org/

https://www.apa.org/

https://www.cdc.gov/

https://mhanational.org/

https://www.nami.org/

https://www.nimh.nih.gov/

https://www.psychiatry.org/

https://www.samhsa.gov/

Video: What is PTSD?
youtube.com/watch?v=IojLqCgQb2Q&t=85s

Video: What is PTSD?
youtube.com/watch?v=uoJBvXAUvA8

Video: What is PTSD?
youtube.com/watch?v=YMC2jt_QVEE&t=4s

American Psychiatric Association. *Diagnostic and Statistical Manual of Mental Disorders Fifth Edition DSM-5®*. American Psychiatric Association Publishing. Washington, DC 2013

Boland, Robert, MD, Marcia L. Verduin, MD, Pedro Ruiz, MD. *Kaplan & Saddock's Synopsis of Psychiatry 12th Edition*. Philadelphia, PA. Wolters Kluwer, 2022

Brown, Catana, PhD., Virginia C. Stoffel PhD, and Jaime Muñoz PhD. *Occupational Therapy in Mental Health, A Vision for Participation*. Philadelphia, PA. F.A Davis Company, 2015.

Buser, Steven, MD. *DSM-5® Insanely Simplified, Unlocking the Spectrums within DSM_5 and ICD-10*. Asheville, NC. Chiron Publications, 2014

Duckworth, Ken, MD. *You Are Not Alone, The NAMI Guide to Navigating Mental Health*. New York, NY. Zando, 2022

Glick, Rachel Lipson, MD, Scott L. Zeller, MD, Jon S. Berlin, MD. *Emergency Psychiatry Principles and Practice. 2nd Edition*. Philadelphia, PA. Wolters Kluwer, 2021

Mental Health America. *Where to Start, A Survival Guide To Anxiety, Depression, and Other Mental Health Challenges*. New York, NY. Penguin Random House LLC, 2023

Morrissey, Jean and Patrick Callaghan. *Communication Skills for Mental Health Nurses*. Berkshire, England. McGraw-Hill Education, Maiden, 2011

Morrison, James. *DSM-5® Made Easy, The Clinicians Guide to Diagnosis*. New York, NY. The Guilford Press, 2014

Townsend, Mary C. *Psychiatric Mental Health Nursing, Concepts of Care in Evidenced Based Practice 8th Edition*. Philadelphia, PA. F.A Davis Company, 2015.

MODULE 11

Substance Use Disorder (SUD)

Harmful or hazardous use of substances leading to impairment or distress

Module 11:
Substance Use Disorder (SUD)

Substance Use Disorder (SUD) Defined

> Substance use disorder (SUD) is a complex condition in which there is uncontrolled use of a substance despite harmful consequences. People with SUD have an intense focus—sometimes called an addiction—on using a certain substance(s) such as alcohol, tobacco, or other psychoactive substances, to the point where their ability to function in day-to-day life becomes impaired. People keep using the substance even when they know it is causing or will cause problems.

Repeated substance use can cause changes in how the brain functions. These changes can last long after the immediate intoxication wears off. Intoxication is the intense pleasure, euphoria, and calm that is caused by the substance; these symptoms are different for each substance. With continued use of a substance, tolerance can develop, where someone may require larger amounts in order to feel these effects. Additionally, discontinuing use can lead to symptoms of withdrawal and intense cravings to return to use, often experienced as anxiety.

People with a substance use disorder may have distorted thinking and behaviors. Changes in the brain's structure and function are what cause people to have intense cravings, changes in personality, abnormal movements, and other behaviors. Brain imaging studies show changes in the areas of the brain that relate to judgment, decision-making, learning, memory, and behavioral control.[1]

> The coexistence of both a mental health and a substance use disorder is referred to as a co-occurring disorder (see Module 12).

The DSM-5 recognizes substance-related disorders resulting from the use of 10 separate classes of drugs: Alcohol, Caffeine, Cannabis, Hallucinogens, Inhalants, Opioids, Sedatives, Hypnotics/anxiolytics, Stimulants (including amphetamine-type substances, cocaine, and other stimulants), and Tobacco.

---

1 https://www.psychiatry.org/patients-families/addiction-substance-use-disorders/what-is-a-substance-use-disorder

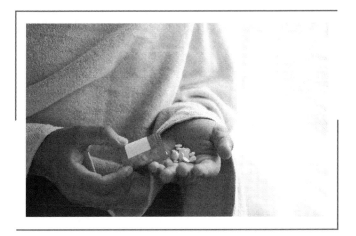

Substance Use Disorder Facts and Statistics[2]

- SUDs affect over 20 million Americans aged 12 and over.
- Over 70,000 drug overdose deaths occur in the US annually.
- The number of overdose deaths increases at an annual rate of 4.0%.
- Alcohol kills over 95,000 Americans every year.
- Almost three-quarters of law enforcement agencies in the western and midwestern areas of the U.S. view methamphetamine and fentanyl as the greatest threats to their populations.
- Over 20% of the U.S. population aged 12 and older have used illegal drugs or misused prescription drugs within the past year.
- Over 40% of Americans aged 12 and over drink alcohol.
- Substance use disorders are more likely to affect young males.
- Over 20% of males and 17% of females used illegal drugs or misused prescription drugs within the last year.
- 22% of males and 17% of females used illegal drugs or misused prescription drugs within the last year.
- Over half of Americans increased their alcohol consumption during the COVID-19 lockdowns.
- Fentanyl is a factor in more than half of all overdose deaths.

Signs and Symptoms of Substance Use Disorder

Symptoms of a substance use disorder include behavioral, physical, and social changes.

Behavioral signs/symptoms

- Mood swings and irritability
- Lying about how much or how often you drink or use drugs
- Withdrawing and isolating from friends and family
- Stopping activities, they once enjoyed
- Neglecting responsibilities like work, school, or household chores
- Declining performance or problems at work or school
- Financial or legal trouble
- Engaging in risky behaviors to get substances, or as a result of being intoxicated

Physical signs/symptoms

- Bloodshot eyes
- Pupils larger or smaller than usual
- Changes in appetite or sleep patterns
- Deterioration of physical appearance, personal grooming habits
- Runny nose or sniffling
- Sudden weight loss or weight gain
- Tremors, slurred speech, or impaired coordination

2 https://drugabusestatistics.org/

- Exhaustion
- Unexplained changes in physical appearance
- Unusual smells on breath, body, or clothing

Social signs/symptoms
- Failure to complete major tasks at work, school or home
- Social, work or leisure activities are given up or cut back because of substance use
- Skipping school or missing work
- Having frequent fights, accidents, or legal trouble
- Secretive or suspicious behavior
- Neglecting to eat
- Withdrawing from friends and family
- Giving up important social, occupational, or recreational activities because of substance use
- Substance use in risky settings
- Continuing to use, even when it puts you in danger

Substance Use Disorder Causes

There is no known cause of substance use disorder, but several risks have been identified. A person may be more likely to develop a substance use disorder if one of several factors are present.[3]

3 https://www.verywellhealth.com/substance-abuse-disorder-5105009

Substance Use Disorder Risk Factors

Biological factors
A person's genes, ethnicity, gender, and the presence of mental health disorders may all increase the risk of developing an addiction. In fact, it is estimated that nearly two-thirds of people in treatment programs for addiction are men. In addition, more than one in four adults living with serious mental health problems also has a substance use problem.

Environment and culture
A person's environment—such as experiencing abuse or neglect during childhood, peer pressure during adolescence, or intense stress levels at any age—can raise the risk of developing a substance use disorder.

Environmental risk factors for youth
- Favorable parental attitudes towards the behavior
- Poor parental monitoring
- Parental substance use
- Family rejection of sexual orientation or gender identity
- Association with delinquent or substance-using peers
- Lack of school connectedness
- Low academic achievement
- Childhood sexual abuse

Age
There are specific ages that make a person more likely to develop a substance use problem. Adolescence is a particularly risky time due to the developing, not-yet-mature brain. Drug use impacts the impulse control part of the brain. Thus, drug use causes changes in the brain that can result in a lack of self-control and poor decision-making and judgment. In addition, teenagers are at greater risk of becoming addicted compared to those who begin substance use as adults.

Types of Substance Use Disorder

Depending on the substance and symptoms, people can fall into different substance use categories:

- **Mild substance use disorder** is a term used to describe a less severe form of substance-related problems (meeting two to three of the criteria below).

- **Moderate substance use disorder** signifies a significant level of problematic substance use, falling between mild and severe cases (meeting four to five of the criteria below).

- **Severe substance use disorder** is a condition characterized by problematic patterns of substance use that significantly impair an individual's ability to function in day-to-day life (meeting six or more of the criteria below).

The diagnostic criteria for substance use disorder include a wide range of signs and symptoms resulting from substance use. The DSM-5 spells out specific criteria for a diagnosis of substance use disorder, including:

- **Amount:** Ingesting larger amounts of alcohol or drugs than intended

- **Control:** An unsuccessful desire to quit using or reduce the amount of use

- **Time:** Spending a lot of time obtaining the substance and/or planning to use or thinking about using

- **Cravings:** A strong desire and cravings to use the substance

- **Obligations:** A pattern of being unable to meet major responsibilities at work, at , or home

- **Social:** Recurring or ongoing social problems linked with substance use, but regardless of the problems, the substance use continues

- **Activities:** Losing interest in hobbies, foregoing important social engagements, and/or missing leisure activities because of substance use

- **Hazard:** Continued risky behavior (such as drinking and driving) regardless of hazardous consequences

- **Harm:** Using substances continually, regardless of knowing about recurrent physical or psychological problems caused by the substance use

- **Tolerance:** An adaptation of the body over time, characterized by the brain attempting to adjust to the abnormally high level of drugs or alcohol in the body. This results in the need to increase the amount of alcohol (or drug) ingested to get the desired effect. It may also result in experiencing a diminished effect when using the same amount of the substance. Overall, tolerance causes the need for more and more of a substance over time to get the same level of intoxication.

- **Withdrawal:** Experiencing negative symptoms, called withdrawal symptoms, when stopping the use of the substance, or using the substance to avoid having withdrawal symptoms. Withdrawal symptoms can include shakiness, sweating, increase in pulse, nausea and vomiting, insomnia, hallucinations, and seizures. Withdrawal symptoms differ depending on the type of substance a person used before detoxing.

Substance Use Disorder Crisis

> A substance use crisis is a severe phase of substance use disorder marked by significant harm, such as overdose, severe withdrawal, dangerous behaviors, or mental health crises, requiring immediate intervention and support.

- **Intense cravings:** An overwhelming desire or compulsion to use substances, which can result in increased consumption and potential overdose.
- **Physical health deterioration:** Noticeable decline in physical health due to substance abuse, such as rapid weight loss, chronic fatigue, or organ damage.
- **Mental health symptoms:** Severe mood swings, anxiety, paranoia, or hallucinations related to substance use.
- **Risk-taking behavior:** Engaging in dangerous activities while under the influence, such as driving under the influence (DUI) or risky sexual behavior.
- **Social and relationship problems:** Strained relationships with family, friends, or colleagues due to substance abuse-related issues.
- **Financial and legal issues:** Facing financial difficulties or legal consequences (like arrests or lawsuits) because of substance abuse.
- **Isolation:** Withdrawing from social interactions and neglecting responsibilities due to preoccupation with substance use.
- **Suicidal ideation:** Expressing thoughts of self-harm or suicide, especially during periods of intense substance use or withdrawal.

A SUD crisis requires immediate attention and intervention from healthcare professionals or addiction specialists to prevent further harm and promote recovery. If someone with Substance Use Disorder is exhibiting these crisis symptoms, it's crucial to seek help from health professionals, crisis intervention services, or emergency services to ensure their safety and provide appropriate care.

Crisis and De-Escalation Interventions for Substance Use Disorder

- Use a trauma-informed approach.
- Use positive interpersonal communication skills.
- Use the daily habits of de-escalation.
- **Guidelines for substance use crisis and de-escalation strategies:**
  - **Contact crisis intervention teams.** Contact mental health crisis intervention teams if the situation escalates and professional intervention is needed.
  - **Contact the Suicide and Crisis Lifeline.** If you or someone you know is struggling or having thoughts of suicide, call or text the 988 Suicide & Crisis Lifeline at 988 or chat at 988lifeline.org. In life-threatening situations, call 911.
  - **Ensure safety.** Assess the environment to remove any potentially harmful objects and maintain physical distance to avoid escalating the situation.

- **Seek to establish trust and rapport** by using empathetic language and actively listening to validate their feelings and experiences during a crisis.
- **Assess the crisis** by evaluating its severity, identifying potential risks, and pinpointing triggers or stressors contributing to the situation.
- **Provide psychoeducation** by educating individuals about the impact of substance use on their health, relationships, and well-being, including discussing the potential consequences of continued substance use during a crisis.
- **Encourage healthy coping strategies** such as deep breathing, mindfulness, and grounding techniques, assisting in identifying and utilizing positive coping skills to manage stress and cravings.
- **Develop a collaborative safety plan**, including crisis steps and contacts for emergency services, support networks, and treatment providers, along with relapse warning signs and prevention strategies. Connect individuals with substance abuse treatment programs, counseling, and support groups, offering assistance with appointments and healthcare navigation.
- **Connect individuals to medical professionals** to manage physical health and withdrawal symptoms, while addressing co-occurring mental health issues like anxiety, depression, or trauma as part of immediate care.
- **Engage individuals using motivational change** to explore readiness for change, identify personal goals, and discuss the benefits of treatment and positive lifestyle changes. Involve support systems like family and friends, providing education and guidance on how they can assist during a crisis.
- **Provide regular follow-up** to track progress, reinforce positive behaviors, and address setbacks. Offer continuous support, encouragement, and resources for sustained recovery and well-being.

■ **Guidelines to avoid substance use escalation:**

- **Avoid confronting or accusing the individual** about their substance use; instead, use non-judgmental language and refrain from blaming them for their addiction.
- **Do not enable or facilitate substance use** by refraining from providing access to alcohol or drugs, participating in substance use with them, or financially supporting their habits.
- **Avoid overreacting** by maintaining composure and staying calm, refraining from reacting with anger, frustration, or panic, which can escalate tensions in challenging situations.
- **Avoid minimizing or ignoring the problem** by refraining from downplaying the severity of their substance use or dismissing their concerns, and by not ignoring warning signs of a crisis or potential overdose.
- **Avoid judging or stigmatizing** by refraining from using language or labels to describe their addiction and by avoiding making assumptions about their motives or character based on their substance use.
- **Avoid forcing treatment** by respecting their autonomy and readiness for change, refraining from pressuring them into treatment or making decisions about their recovery.
- **Avoid lecturing or preaching** about substance use dangers; prioritize providing support, empathy, and understanding instead.
- **Avoid neglecting co-occurring mental health issues** like depression or anxiety; prioritize comprehensive care addressing both substance use and mental health.

- **Avoid encouraging negative coping mechanisms** like avoidance or denial; instead, promote healthy coping strategies and provide support resources.
- **Avoid dismissing their feelings** or experiences about substance use; instead, validate their emotions and provide non-judgmental support.

- Build a trusting relationship and work in an open, engaging, and non-judgmental manner.
- Be aware that stigma and discrimination can be associated with a diagnosis of Substance Use Disorder.
- Work as a multidisciplinary team and offer guidance and support (family, caregivers).
- Encourage them to meet their ADL's (Activities of Daily Living).
- Show environmental awareness (safely remove any objects that the person could use to harm themselves).
- Seek immediate suicide intervention when needed (see Module 16).

Effective de-escalation and crisis intervention for substance use disorders requires a combination of compassion, empathy, active listening, and practical actions to ensure immediate safety and long-term support. By creating a safe and supportive environment, engaging appropriate resources, and following up with continuous care, individuals experiencing a crisis can be guided toward stability and recovery.

Addressing the risks associated with a substance use disorder crisis requires a proactive and compassionate approach. By implementing training, support systems, and clear protocols and promoting a supportive workplace culture, organizations can effectively manage these risks and ensure the safety and well-being of all staff members. Mental health is a crucial aspect of overall health, and taking steps to support it benefits both individuals and the organization as a whole.

Substance Use Disorder Treatments

Disclaimer: Personal Safety Training Inc. makes no claim as to what type of treatment is needed for any mental health disorder.

Treatment for substance use disorder varies in intensity based on individual needs and may include medications and different treatment programs:

Medications
- **Detoxification/withdrawal:** Medications are provided to manage withdrawal symptoms during detox, tailored to the specific substance used.
- **Post-detox medications:** Medications like methadone, naltrexone, and buprenorphine/naloxone for opioid addiction, and naltrexone, acamprosate, and disulfiram for alcohol use, help reduce cravings and stabilize brain function.

Inpatient treatment
- **Medically-managed intensive inpatient:** Detox centers with medical staff to assist during the initial withdrawal phase.
- **Residential/inpatient treatment:** Facilities where individuals live full-time, receiving therapy, support groups, and education in a safe environment.

Intensive outpatient treatment
An intensive program offering group and individual therapy, education, and other modalities, attended for specific hours and days per week.

Outpatient treatment
A less intensive program providing a long-term structure, serving as follow-up treatment with fewer hours and days per week for those who have completed more intensive programs.

IF YOU OR SOMEONE YOU KNOW IS IN CRISIS AND CONSIDERING SELF-HARM OR SUICIDE:

- Call 911 for emergency services.
- Visit the nearest hospital emergency room.
- Call or text 988 to connect with the 988 Suicide and Crisis Lifeline, offering 24-hour, confidential support. *Para ayuda en español, llame al 988.*
- Support is also available via live chat at 988lifeline.org. *AVADE® does not monitor this website for crisis messages, provide medical advice, or make referrals.*

PSTI LEGAL DISCLAIMER

The information in this training book is a supplement, not a substitute, for the expertise of qualified healthcare professionals. The content on AVADE® Behavioral Health, sourced from reliable information, does not constitute medical or professional healthcare advice, diagnosis, or treatment. It is crucial to consult healthcare providers for specific guidelines related to medical or behavioral health conditions. This material does not guarantee that any technique or strategy is safe or effective for any specific needs. Personal Safety Training, Inc., does not dictate policies or procedures for behavioral health violence prevention, self-defense tactics, or any physical interventions. Agencies are responsible for developing their own policies and evaluating the recommendations based on their circumstances.

The author and publisher do not guarantee the completeness or accuracy of the information and assume no risk for its use. Any implied warranty are expressly disavowed.

References for Module 11

https://988lifeline.org/

https://www.apa.org/

https://www.cdc.gov/

https://mhanational.org/

https://www.nami.org/

https://www.nimh.nih.gov/

https://www.psychiatry.org/

https://www.samhsa.gov/

Video: What is Addiction?
youtube.com/watch?v=Vrb99pSgW7I&t=74s

Video: Substance Use Disorder
youtube.com/watch?v=Hgn7MJjMfkk&t=39s

Video: Understanding Substance Misuse, Abuse, Dependence, and Addiction
youtube.com/watch?v=G9IuVQlCGZk

American Psychiatric Association. *Diagnostic and Statistical Manual of Mental Disorders Fifth Edition DSM-5®*. American Psychiatric Association Publishing. Washington, DC 2013

Boland, Robert, MD, Marcia L. Verduin, MD, Pedro Ruiz, MD. *Kaplan & Saddock's Synopsis of Psychiatry 12th Edition*. Philadelphia, PA. Wolters Kluwer, 2022

Brown, Catana, PhD., Virginia C. Stoffel PhD, and Jaime Muñoz PhD. *Occupational Therapy in Mental Health, A Vision for Participation*. Philadelphia, PA. F.A Davis Company, 2015.

Buser, Steven, MD. *DSM-5® Insanely Simplified, Unlocking the Spectrums within DSM_5 and ICD-10*. Asheville, NC. Chiron Publications, 2014

Duckworth, Ken, MD. *You Are Not Alone, The NAMI Guide to Navigating Mental Health*. New York, NY. Zando, 2022

Glick, Rachel Lipson, MD, Scott L. Zeller, MD, Jon S. Berlin, MD. *Emergency Psychiatry Principles and Practice. 2nd Edition*. Philadelphia, PA. Wolters Kluwer, 2021

Mental Health America. *Where to Start, A Survival Guide To Anxiety, Depression, and Other Mental Health Challenges*. New York, NY. Penguin Random House LLC, 2023

Morrissey, Jean and Patrick Callaghan. *Communication Skills for Mental Health Nurses*. Berkshire, England. McGraw-Hill Education, Maiden, 2011

Morrison, James. *DSM-5® Made Easy, The Clinicians Guide to Diagnosis*. New York, NY. The Guilford Press, 2014

Townsend, Mary C. *Psychiatric Mental Health Nursing, Concepts of Care in Evidenced Based Practice 8th Edition*. Philadelphia, PA. F.A Davis Company, 2015.

AVADE | Behavioral Health Advanced Student Guide | Co-Occurring Disorder | Page | 141

MODULE 12

Co-Occurring Disorder

The coexistence of a substance use and a mental health disorder

Module 12: Co-Occurring Disorder

Co-Occurring Disorder Defined

> Co-occurring disorder is a term that describes the coexistence of a substance use disorder and a mental health disorder. The term can also refer to other combinations of disorders, such as a mental disorder and an intellectual disability. Co-occurring disorders may interact with each other and affect the course, prognosis, and treatment of both conditions. Co-occurring disorders are common among people with substance use problems.

The presence of two or more disorders can complicate diagnosis and treatment. Integrating both screening and treatment for mental and substance use disorders leads to a better quality of care and health outcomes for those living with co-occurring disorders by treating the whole person.

People with co-occurring disorders are more likely to be hospitalized than people with a mental or substance use disorder alone.

Co-Occurring Disorder Facts and Statistics

- Over half of individuals with co-occurring disorders received neither mental health services nor substance use treatment.

- Less than 10% of individuals with co-occurring disorders receive both mental health services and substance use treatment.[1]

- Most of us know someone personally who struggles with a dual diagnosis, or the presence of a substance use disorder and coexisting mental health disorder.

- Battling a dual diagnosis is more challenging because of the complexity of each specific case, needing to factor in the various mental health conditions and substance use disorders that can co-occur.

- More than 9 million Americans struggle with co-occurring disorders, according to the Substance Abuse and Mental Health Services Administration.

- Statistics indicate that roughly half of the almost 20 million adults with a substance use disorder also have a coexisting mental health condition.

---

1 https://nida.nih.gov/research-topics/comorbidity/comorbidity-substance-use-other-mental-disorders-infographic

- Compared with people with mental disorders or SUDs alone, people with co-occurring disorders are more likely to be hospitalized.
- Comorbidity is important because it is the rule rather than the exception with mental health disorders.[2]

Signs and Symptoms of Co-Occurring Disorder

The symptoms of co-occurring disorders include those associated with the particular substance use problem and mental health condition affecting an individual.

People with co-occurring disorders are at high risk for additional problems such as symptomatic relapses, hospitalizations, financial challenges, social isolation, family problems, homelessness, sexual and physical victimization, incarceration, and serious medical illnesses.

There are certain signs and symptoms that are often present with co-occurring disorders, such as:

- Unpredictable mood swings
- Irritability or anger issues
- Inability to keep a job
- Inability to maintain healthy relationships
- Financial difficulties
- Impaired social functioning
- Emotional instability
- Ignoring obligations and responsibilities
- Withdrawing from friends and family
- Erratic or unpredictable behavior
- Legal problems
- Increasing consumption of alcohol or drugs
- Heightened suicide risk
- Exhibits withdrawal symptoms when not using the substance

Co-Occurring Disorder Causes

With co-occurring disorders, either condition – substance use or mental health disorder – can develop first. Oftentimes, people struggling with a mental illness will use drugs or alcohol to try and cope with their symptoms (this is called self-medication). In other cases, people have used drugs or alcohol for some time, which then triggered or aggravated psychological problems. Studies show that certain drugs or long-term substance use can exacerbate the symptoms of mental illness.

Co-occurring disorders are caused by a combination of genetic predispositions, environmental exposures, psychological issues, social influences, brain chemistry imbalances, and early developmental factors.

Causes may include:

- **Genetic factors:** A family history of mental health disorders or substance use disorders can increase the risk of developing both.

---

2 https://store.samhsa.gov/sites/default/files/pep20-02-01-004.pdf

- **Environmental factors:** Exposure to trauma, abuse, or high-stress environments can contribute to the development of both mental health and substance use disorders.
- **Psychological factors:** Mental health disorders like depression, anxiety, or PTSD can lead individuals to use substances as a coping mechanism, which can then develop into a substance use disorder.
- **Social factors:** Peer pressure, social isolation, and lack of support can contribute to substance use and exacerbate mental health conditions.
- **Brain chemistry:** Imbalances in brain chemistry can predispose individuals to both mental health disorders and substance use disorders.
- **Developmental factors:** Early exposure to substance use or mental health issues during critical developmental periods can increase the risk of developing co-occurring disorders.

Co-Occurring Risk Factors

The following risk factors increase a person's vulnerability to developing a co-occurring disorder:

- Any mental illness
- Recurrent substance abuse
- Lack of appropriate treatment for either of the above
- A history of trauma or a traumatic life event
- Genetic or family history of mental health disorders and/or addiction

How common are co-occurring disorders?

People with mental health disorders are more likely to have a substance use disorder than those who do not. Roughly half of individuals who have either a mental illness or a substance use disorder will have the other at some point in their lives, according to the National Institute on Drug Abuse.

Types of Co-Occurring Disorder

While some instances of co-occurring disorders may be more frequent than others (see common ones here), any combination of addiction and mental illness is considered to be a "co-occurring disorder."

Examples of common co-occurring disorders include:

- Alcohol addiction and depression
- Schizophrenia and substance use disorder
- Anxiety disorder and drug addiction
- Major depressive disorder and an alcohol use disorder
- Obsessive-compulsive disorder (OCD) and marijuana abuse
- Bipolar disorders
- Psychotic disorders and addiction (e.g., schizophrenia)
- PTSD and addiction
- OCD and addiction

Co-Occurring Disorder Crisis

> A co-occurring disorder crisis is a severe episode where both mental health and substance use disorders intensify, leading to extreme distress, dangerous behaviors, and the need for immediate professional intervention.

Mental health symptoms

- **Severe anxiety or panic attacks**: Intense fear, rapid heartbeat, sweating, trembling, or shortness of breath.
- **Severe depression**: Persistent sadness, hopelessness, withdrawal, fatigue, or suicidal thoughts.
- **Psychotic symptoms**: Hallucinations, delusions, or paranoia.
- **Manic episodes**: Elevated mood, increased energy, rapid speech, impulsive behavior, or grandiose ideas.
- **Self-harm or suicidal behavior**: Self-injury, suicidal thoughts, plans, or previous attempts.

Substance use symptoms

- **Intoxication**: Slurred speech, impaired coordination, euphoria, agitation, or aggression.
- **Withdrawal**: Shaking, sweating, nausea, vomiting, hallucinations, or seizures when not using the substance.
- **Overdose**: Unconsciousness, slow or irregular breathing, bluish skin, or unresponsiveness.
- **Compulsive drug-seeking behavior**: Inability to control use, neglecting responsibilities, or engaging in risky behaviors to obtain substances.

Combined symptoms

- **Agitation or aggression**: Irritability, hostility, physical altercations, or verbal outbursts.
- **Severe mood swings**: Rapid, unpredictable changes in mood from extreme highs to lows.
- **Cognitive impairment**: Confusion, disorientation, memory problems, or difficulty concentrating.
- **Isolation and withdrawal**: Avoiding social interactions, neglecting personal hygiene, or withdrawing from family and friends.
- **Medical emergencies**: Complications like dehydration, malnutrition, or physical injury related to substance use or mental health conditions.
- **Legal or financial problems**: Legal issues due to substance-related behavior, financial distress, or inability to manage finances.

If someone with Co-Occurring Disorder is exhibiting these crisis symptoms, it's crucial to seek immediate help from mental health professionals, crisis intervention services, or emergency services to ensure their safety and provide appropriate care.

Crisis and De-Escalation Interventions for Co-Occurring Disorder

- Use a trauma-informed approach.
- Use positive interpersonal communication skills.
- Use the daily habits of de-escalation.
- **Guidelines for co-occuring disorder crisis and de-escalation strategies:**
  - **Contact crisis intervention teams.** Contact mental health crisis intervention teams if the situation escalates and professional intervention is needed.
  - **Contact the Suicide and Crisis Lifeline.** If you or someone you know is struggling or having thoughts of suicide, call or text the 988 Suicide & Crisis Lifeline at 988 or chat at 988lifeline.org. In life-threatening situations, call 911.

- **Ensure safety.** Assess the environment to remove any potentially harmful objects and maintain physical distance to avoid escalating the situation.

- **Stay calm and composed**, using a soft, gentle tone of voice, maintaining a non-threatening body posture, and avoiding sudden movements that might startle the person.

- **Use active and attentive listening** by showing full engagement in the conversation through eye contact, nodding, and using verbal acknowledgments like "I understand" or "Go on." Additionally, reflect and paraphrase what the person has said in your own words to demonstrate understanding, such as "It sounds like you're feeling overwhelmed because..."

- **Use clear and concise language**, repeat important information when needed, and avoid using technical terms or complex language.

- **Show empathy and validation** by acknowledging their feelings without judgment, using phrases like "It's okay to feel this way" or "I can see why you'd feel this way." Additionally, express empathy by showing that you care and understand their pain through statements such as "I'm here for you" or "That sounds really tough."

- **Offer reassurance** by letting them know they are not alone, help is available, and you are there to support them.

- **Assess the crisis** by evaluating its severity, identifying potential risks, and pinpointing triggers or stressors contributing to the situation.

- **Encourage healthy coping strategies** such as deep breathing, mindfulness, and grounding techniques, assisting in identifying and utilizing positive coping skills to manage stress and cravings.

- **Develop a collaborative safety plan**, including crisis steps and contacts for emergency services, support networks, and treatment providers, along with relapse warning signs and prevention strategies. Connect individuals with substance abuse treatment programs, counseling, and support groups, offering assistance with appointments and healthcare navigation.

- **Engage individuals using motivational change** to explore readiness for change, identify personal goals, and discuss the benefits of treatment and positive lifestyle changes. Involve support systems like family and friends, providing education and guidance on how they can assist during a crisis.

- **Provide regular follow-up** to track progress, reinforce positive behaviors, and address setbacks. Offer continuous support, encouragement, and resources for sustained recovery and well-being.

■ **Guidelines to avoid co-occurring disorder escalation**

- **Avoid confrontational behavior** such as arguing, criticizing, or blaming, and steer clear of aggressive language or gestures that may escalate the situation.

- **Avoid disregarding triggers** that may exacerbate anxiety or distress, as ignoring or exposing them without consent can worsen the situation.

- **Avoid overreacting** to symptoms or behaviors by maintaining a calm and composed demeanor, as overreaction can heighten their emotional distress.

- **Avoid neglecting boundaries** by respecting personal space, especially during moments of crisis. Neglecting boundaries can worsen their distress.

- **Avoid pressuring them to change** or demanding immediate solutions, as well as forcing compliance with your expectations or treatment plans.

- **Avoid downplaying or minimizing their experiences**, feelings, or struggles, and refrain from making dismissive comments or invalidating their emotions.
- **Demonstrate empathy and understanding**, avoiding indifference or lack of concern, and refrain from making judgmental or insensitive remarks about their condition.
- **Avoid encouraging negative coping mechanisms** like avoidance or denial; instead, promote healthy coping strategies and provide support resources.
- **Avoid dismissing their feelings or experiences** about substance use; instead, validate their emotions and provide non-judgmental support.

- Build a trusting relationship and work in an open, engaging, and non-judgmental manner.
- Be aware that stigma and discrimination can be associated with a diagnosis of Co-Occurring Disorder.
- Work as a multidisciplinary team and offer guidance and support (family, caregivers).
- Encourage them to meet their ADL's (Activities of Daily Living).
- Show environmental awareness (safely remove any objects that the person could use to harm themselves).
- Seek immediate suicide intervention when needed (see Module 16).

Effective de-escalation and crisis intervention for co-occurring disorders requires a combination of compassion, empathy, active listening, and practical actions to ensure immediate safety and long-term support. By creating a safe and supportive environment, engaging appropriate resources, and following up with continuous care, individuals experiencing a crisis can be guided toward stability and recovery.

Addressing the risks associated with a co-occurring disorder crisis requires a proactive and compassionate approach. By implementing training, support systems, and clear protocols and promoting a supportive workplace culture, organizations can effectively manage these risks and ensure the safety and well-being of all staff members. Mental health is a crucial aspect of overall health, and taking steps to support it benefits both individuals and the organization as a whole.

Co-Occurring Disorder Treatments

> **Disclaimer: Personal Safety Training Inc. makes no claim as to what type of treatment is needed for any mental health disorder.**

The Substance Abuse and Mental Health Services Administration (SAMHSA) recommends an integrated treatment approach for co-occurring disorders, coordinating substance abuse and mental health interventions. This often includes behavioral treatments like cognitive-behavioral therapy or dialectical behavior therapy, combined with medication. Collaboration with clinicians and support organizations for housing, health, and work is also essential. Psychoeducational classes increase awareness of symptoms and the relationship between mental disorders and substance abuse, while relapse-prevention education helps clients recognize and manage substance abuse triggers. Dual-recovery groups provide supportive forums for discussing psychiatric symptoms, medication, substance-related impulses, and coping strategies.

IF YOU OR SOMEONE YOU KNOW IS IN CRISIS AND CONSIDERING SELF-HARM OR SUICIDE:

- Call 911 for emergency services.
- Visit the nearest hospital emergency room.
- Call or text 988 to connect with the 988 Suicide and Crisis Lifeline, offering 24-hour, confidential support. *Para ayuda en español, llame al 988.*
- Support is also available via live chat at 988lifeline.org. *AVADE® does not monitor this website for crisis messages, provide medical advice, or make referrals.*

PSTI LEGAL DISCLAIMER

The information in this training book is a supplement, not a substitute, for the expertise of qualified healthcare professionals. The content on AVADE® Behavioral Health, sourced from reliable information, does not constitute medical or professional healthcare advice, diagnosis, or treatment. It is crucial to consult healthcare providers for specific guidelines related to medical or behavioral health conditions. This material does not guarantee that any technique or strategy is safe or effective for any specific needs. Personal Safety Training, Inc., does not dictate policies or procedures for behavioral health violence prevention, self-defense tactics, or any physical interventions. Agencies are responsible for developing their own policies and evaluating the recommendations based on their circumstances.

The author and publisher do not guarantee the completeness or accuracy of the information and assume no risk for its use. Any implied warranty are expressly disavowed.

References for Module 12

https://988lifeline.org/

https://www.apa.org/

https://www.cdc.gov/

https://mhanational.org/

https://www.nami.org/

https://www.nimh.nih.gov/

https://www.psychiatry.org/

https://www.samhsa.gov/

Video: How Do You Deal with Dual Diagnosis?
youtube.com/watch?v=N9QqzsIiANY

Video: Comorbidity Explained
youtube.com/watch?v=sqV70WCYp_g

Video: What is Dual Diagnosis Treatment for Co-occurring Disorders?
youtube.com/watch?v=0mxjPlyP26A

American Psychiatric Association. *Diagnostic and Statistical Manual of Mental Disorders Fifth Edition DSM-5®*. American Psychiatric Association Publishing. Washington, DC 2013

Boland, Robert, MD, Marcia L. Verduin, MD, Pedro Ruiz, MD. *Kaplan & Saddock's Synopsis of Psychiatry 12th Edition*. Philadelphia, PA. Wolters Kluwer, 2022

Brown, Catana, PhD., Virginia C. Stoffel PhD, and Jaime Muñoz PhD. *Occupational Therapy in Mental Health, A Vision for Participation*. Philadelphia, PA. F.A Davis Company, 2015.

Buser, Steven, MD. *DSM-5® Insanely Simplified, Unlocking the Spectrums within DSM_5 and ICD-10*. Asheville, NC. Chiron Publications, 2014

Duckworth, Ken, MD. *You Are Not Alone, The NAMI Guide to Navigating Mental Health*. New York, NY. Zando, 2022

Glick, Rachel Lipson, MD, Scott L. Zeller, MD, Jon S. Berlin, MD. *Emergency Psychiatry Principles and Practice. 2nd Edition*. Philadelphia, PA. Wolters Kluwer, 2021

Mental Health America. *Where to Start, A Survival Guide To Anxiety, Depression, and Other Mental Health Challenges*. New York, NY. Penguin Random House LLC, 2023

Morrissey, Jean and Patrick Callaghan. *Communication Skills for Mental Health Nurses*. Berkshire, England. McGraw-Hill Education, Maiden, 2011

Morrison, James. *DSM-5® Made Easy, The Clinicians Guide to Diagnosis*. New York, NY. The Guilford Press, 2014

Townsend, Mary C. *Psychiatric Mental Health Nursing, Concepts of Care in Evidenced Based Practice 8th Edition*. Philadelphia, PA. F.A Davis Company, 2015.

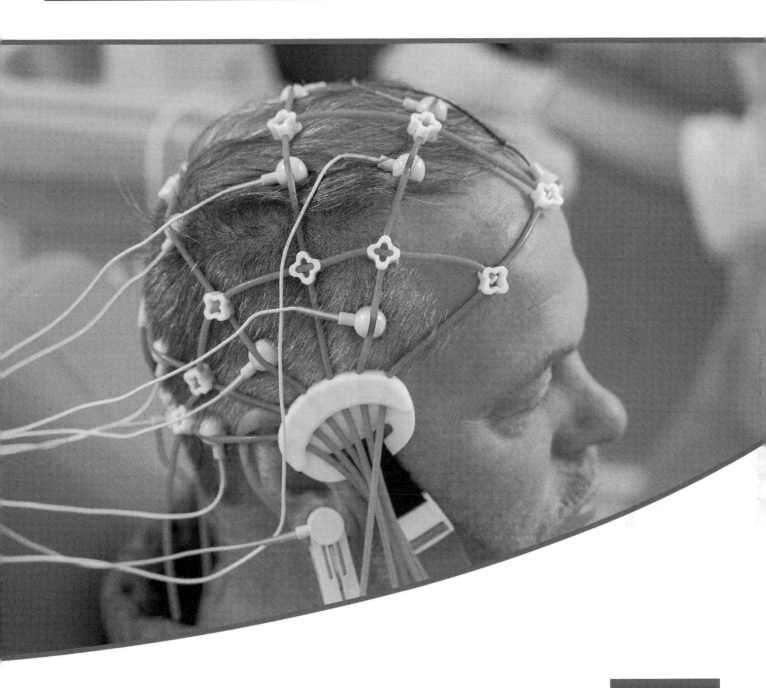

MODULE 13

Neurocognitive Disorders

A decline in cognitive function due to brain injury or disease

Module 13: Neurocognitive Disorders

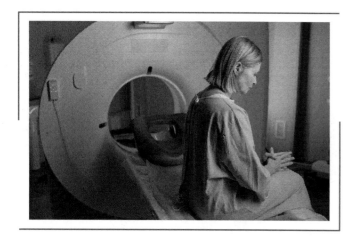

Neurocognitive Disorders Defined

> Neurocognitive disorders are a category of conditions characterized by a decline in cognitive function due to damage or disease affecting the brain. These disorders can impact memory, attention, learning, language, perception, and executive functions. These disorders can vary in severity and progression, and they often require comprehensive medical management.

Neurocognitive disorders, mild and major, include a group of conditions that were once all grouped under the umbrella term "dementia." The conditions involve similar cognitive impairments and decline and most often affect the elderly. The primary symptoms across the conditions involve declines in cognitive performance in areas including attention, executive function, learning and memory, language, motor skills, or social cognition. Since cognition is so critical to daily human functioning, these disorders can be extremely debilitating and lead to severe reductions in individuals' quality of life.

The term "dementia" is still used, but usually to refer to degenerative dementias that are more likely to affect older adults. It is now less likely to be used for conditions resulting from, say, trauma or substance abuse, that may emerge in younger patients.

The DSM-5 has introduced a substantial shift in the diagnostic schema regarding Dementia. The term Dementia has been replaced with Neurocognitive Disorder (NCD). The spectrum distinguishes mild NCDs from major NCDs.[1]

The NCDs include a long list of subtypes that are distinguished from one another by the specific cause of the disorder. Subtypes include:

- Alzheimer's Disease
- Vascular Dementia
- Traumatic Brain Injury (TBI).
- HIV-Associated Neurocognitive Disorders (HAND)
- Parkinson's Disease
- Lewy Body Disease
- Huntington's Disease
- Prion Disease
- Frontotemporal Dementia
- Chronic Substance Use

[1] https://www.psychologytoday.com/us/conditions/neurocognitive-disorders-mild-and-major

Neurocognitive Disorders Facts and Statistics

- Neurocognitive disorders are estimated to affect 1 to 2 percent of people by age 65 and as much as 30 percent of the population by age 85.

- Alzheimer's disease accounts for the majority of cases of neurocognitive disorders (NCDs).

- Experts think between 60% to 80% of people with dementia have Alzheimer's disease. More than 5 million Americans have been diagnosed with Alzheimer's.

- Although dementia mainly affects older people, it is not a normal part of aging.[2]

- The estimated proportion of the general population aged 60 and over with dementia at a given time is between 5-8%.

- Worldwide, around 50 million people have dementia, and there are nearly 10 million new cases every year.[3]

- Dementia has a physical, psychological, social, and economic impact, not only on people with dementia but also on their caregivers, families, and society.

- Alzheimer's disease is currently ranked as the sixth leading cause of death in the United States.

- Dementia patients can occupy up to 25% of beds in hospitals.

- 21% of hospital stays are followed by a readmission within 30 days.

- Dementia patients have an average of 23 inpatient days.

Signs and Symptoms of Neurocognitive Disorders

Neurocognitive disorders (NCDs) can affect many parts of the brain and can cause a variety of symptoms, including:

- **Thinking**: Difficulty remembering (memory loss), difficulty focusing, difficulty finding words, paranoid beliefs, delusions, problem-solving, and hallucinations

- **Mood**: Anxiety, depression, and apathy

- **Behavior**: Changes in normal behavior, aggression, yelling, wandering, manipulating objects, and inappropriate sexual conduct

- **Movement**: Trouble walking, keeping balance, or performing fine motor skills

- **Communication**: Difficulty seeing, understanding others, or following a conversation

- **Daily activities**: Trouble performing daily activities, like driving, planning, organizing, and managing money

- **Other symptoms**: Confusion, disorientation, agitation, vision problems, increased anxiety, forgetfulness, difficulty performing tasks, and loss of independence

---

2 https://www.psychiatry.org/patients-families/alzheimers/what-is-alzheimers-disease

3 https://www.who.int/news-room/fact-sheets/detail/dementia

Causes of Neurocognitive Disorders/ Dementia

Neurocognitive disorders can be caused by neurodegenerative diseases, vascular issues, brain injuries, infections, substance abuse, nutritional deficiencies, genetic factors, chronic conditions, severe mental illnesses, and aging.

Neurocognitive disorders are not developmental; they are acquired conditions representing underlying brain pathology resulting in a decline in cognitive faculties. They are caused by brain damage in areas that affect learning and memory, planning and decision making, the ability to correctly use and understand language, hand-eye coordination, and/or the ability to act within social norms, such as dressing appropriately for the weather or occasion, showing empathy, and performing routine tasks.

Dementia is caused by damage to or loss of nerve cells and their connections in the brain. Depending on the area of the brain affected by the damage, dementia can affect people differently and cause different symptoms.

Dementia are often grouped by what they have in common, such as the protein or proteins deposited in the brain or the part of the brain that's affected. Some diseases look like dementias, such as those caused by a reaction to medications or vitamin deficiencies, and they might improve with treatment.

Diagnosing dementia and its type can be challenging. To diagnose the cause of dementia, a physician must recognize the pattern of the loss of skills and function and determine what the individual is still able to do. The physician will also review the individual's medical history and symptoms and conduct a physical examination. He or she will likely ask someone close to the patient about their symptoms as well.

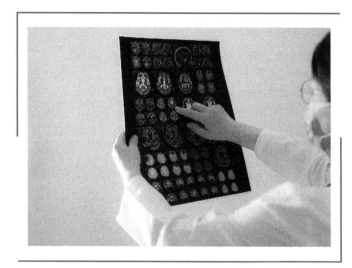

Risk Factors for Neurocognitive Disorders

- **Age**: Advanced age is a significant risk factor for developing neurocognitive disorders.
- **Genetics**: Family history of neurocognitive disorders or genetic mutations.
- **Cardiovascular health**: Conditions like hypertension, heart disease, and stroke.
- **Lifestyle factors**: Poor diet, lack of exercise, and smoking.
- **Chronic diseases**: Diabetes, obesity, and other chronic illnesses.
- **Traumatic Brain Injury**: Past head injuries or repeated concussions.
- **Mental health disorders**: Severe mental illnesses such as depression and schizophrenia.
- **Substance abuse**: Long-term use or abuse of drugs and alcohol.
- **Environmental factors**: Exposure to toxins or pollutants.
- **Educational level**: Lower levels of education and cognitive engagement.

Types of Neurocognitive Disorders

- **Alzheimer's Disease**: an irreversible, progressive brain disorder that slowly destroys memory and thinking skills and, eventually, the ability to carry out the simplest tasks.

- **Vascular Dementia**: the result of injuries to vessels that supply blood to the brain, often after a stroke or a series of strokes.

- **Traumatic Brain Injury (TBI)**: a serious medical issue that affects how your brain works. You can get a TBI from a hard bump or jolt to your head or if you're hit with something that penetrates your skull.

- **HIV-Associated Neurocognitive Disorders (HAND)**: neurological disorders associated with HIV infection and AIDS. It is a syndrome of progressive deterioration of memory, cognition, behavior, and motor function in HIV-infected individuals during the late stages of the disease when immunodeficiency is severe.

- **Parkinson's Disease**: a progressive disorder that affects the nervous system and causes movement problems, such as tremors, stiffness, and slowed movement.

- **Lewy Body Disease**: a disease associated with abnormal deposits of a protein in the brain, which affects chemicals in the brain that can lead to problems with thinking, movement, behavior, and mood.

- **Huntington's Disease**: a very rare disease that causes nerve cells in the brain to decay over time. It affects a person's movements, thinking ability, and mental health. It's often passed down through a changed gene from a parent.

- **Prion Disease**: such as Creutzfeldt-Jakob disease or Bovine Spongiform Encephalopathy ("mad cow disease") are a group of very rare neurodegenerative diseases that can affect humans and animals. Prion disease happens when normal proteins in your brain turn into abnormal proteins known as prions (pronounced "PREE-Ons").

- **Frontotemporal Dementia**: an umbrella term for a group of uncommon brain disorders that primarily affect the frontal and temporal lobes of the brain, which are generally associated with personality, behavior, and language.

- **Chronic substance use**: Chronic use of different substances is associated with neural dysfunctions and related cognitive deficits. Neurocognitive disorders encompass reward, negative affect, and control deficits underlying core addiction symptoms, and broader cognitive sequela affecting everyday functioning.

Understanding the Progression of Neurocognitive Disorders

Dementia typically progresses through seven stages, though this can vary depending on the affected brain area:

1. **No impairment**: No visible symptoms, but tests may detect issues.
2. **Very mild decline**: Slight behavioral changes, but the individual remains independent.
3. **Mild decline**: Noticeable thinking and reasoning changes, difficulty with planning, frequent repetition, and trouble remembering recent events.
4. **Moderate decline**: Increased difficulty with planning, remembering recent events, traveling, and handling money.
5. **Moderately severe decline**: Difficulty remembering phone numbers or names, confusion about the time or day, needing assistance with daily functions like choosing clothes.

6. **Severe decline**: Forgetting spouse's name, needing help with restroom use and eating, personality and emotional changes, potential sleep disturbances, outbursts, paranoia, delusions, and hallucinations.
7. **Very severe decline**: Inability to speak thoughts, inability to walk, spending most of the time in bed.

Neurocognitive Disorders Crisis

> A neurocognitive disorder crisis involves a severe worsening of symptoms like confusion, agitation, aggression, or significant cognitive decline, posing immediate safety risks and requiring urgent healthcare intervention.

Crisis symptoms in individuals with neurocognitive disorders include:

- **Severe confusion or delirium**: Sudden mental status changes, characterized by increased disorientation, confusion, and possible hallucinations or delusions.
- **Agitation and aggression**: Increased irritability, restlessness, or aggression, often leading to physical or verbal outbursts.
- **Wandering and getting lost**: A tendency to wander away from safe environments and an inability to recognize familiar places or people.
- **Severe anxiety or depression**: Intense episodes of anxiety or depression, often accompanied by increased emotional distress or crying spells.
- **Inability to perform daily activities**: Significant decline in performing basic self-care tasks, including incontinence or refusal to eat and drink.
- **Paranoia and suspicion**: Increased paranoia or suspicion towards caregivers or family members, often involving accusations of theft or harm.

If someone with a Neurocognitive Disorder is exhibiting these crisis symptoms, it's crucial to seek immediate help from mental health professionals, crisis intervention services, or emergency services to ensure their safety and provide appropriate care.

Crisis and De-Escalation Interventions for Neurocognitive Disorders

- Use a trauma-informed approach.
- Use positive interpersonal communication skills.
- Use the daily habits of de-escalation.
- **Guidelines for neurocognitive disorders crisis and de-escalation strategies:**
  - **Contact crisis intervention teams.** Contact mental health crisis intervention teams if the situation escalates and professional intervention is needed.
  - **Contact the Suicide and Crisis Lifeline.** If you or someone you know is struggling or having thoughts of suicide, call or text the 988 Suicide & Crisis Lifeline at 988 or chat at 988lifeline.org. In life-threatening situations, call 911.

- **Ensure safety.** Assess the environment to remove any potentially harmful objects and maintain physical distance to avoid escalating the situation.
- **Stay calm and reassuring.** Approach the individual with a calm and reassuring demeanor, using a gentle tone of voice and non-threatening body language to convey safety and support and prevent escalating anxiety.
- **Validate their feelings and experiences.** Acknowledge their emotions and experiences without judgment or criticism. Validate their concerns and reassure them that their feelings are understood and accepted.
- **Maintain structure and routine.** Provide stability and security by adhering to familiar routines and environments. Avoid sudden changes or disruptions that may lead to increased confusion or distress.
- **Use simple and clear communication.** Convey information and instructions using simple and concise language. Break down tasks or information into smaller, manageable steps to enhance understanding and communication clarity.
- **Provide visual and written cues.** Utilize visual aids, written instructions, or picture schedules to support comprehension and memory. These cues can guide behavior and reduce confusion by offering visual prompts.
- **Engage in calming activities.** Encourage participation in calming activities like deep breathing, listening to gentle music, or sensory stimulation. Provide distractions or hobbies they enjoy to redirect focus and reduce agitation effectively.
- **Ensure safety and remove hazards.** Assess the environment for potential safety risks and eliminate any hazards or dangerous objects. Create a safe and supportive space to prevent accidents or injuries during moments of crisis effectively.
- **Involve supportive caregivers and professionals.** Collaborate with healthcare professionals, caregivers, and support networks to develop a coordinated crisis intervention plan for individuals with neurocognitive disorders. Seek guidance and assistance from specialists experienced in managing such disorders during crisis situations for optimal support and care.
- **Practice self-care.** Prioritize your well-being and manage stress to remain calm and effective in providing support to individuals in crisis. Seek support from fellow caregivers or professionals to prevent burnout and ensure consistent and quality care delivery.

- **Guidelines to avoid neurocognitive disorders escalation:**
    - **Avoid aggressive or confrontational approaches.** Aggressive or confrontational behavior can escalate agitation and anxiety in individuals with neurocognitive disorders. It's crucial to refrain from raising your voice, using threatening gestures, or getting into arguments, as these actions may worsen the situation.
    - **Avoid overstimulation.** Reduce exposure to loud noises, bright lights, or chaotic surroundings that can overwhelm and increase distress in individuals with neurocognitive disorders. Establishing a calm and quiet environment can aid in grounding and reducing feelings of being overwhelmed.
    - **Avoid rushing or pressuring.** Give the person with neurocognitive disorders additional time to process information and make decisions during a crisis. Avoid pressuring or rushing them into tasks or responses, recognizing that cognitive processing may be slower in such situations.

- **Avoid ignoring their feelings or experiences.** Dismissing or disregarding their emotions, fears, or concerns can worsen their distress and feelings of invalidation. Show empathy, validate their experiences, and offer understanding without judgment to prevent escalation of distress.

- **Avoid inflexibility.** Stay flexible and adapt your approach to accommodate their unique needs, preferences, and capabilities. Avoid imposing rigid rules or expectations that could lead to frustration or resistance.

- **Avoid making assumptions.** Refrain from assuming their abilities, intentions, or experiences based on their diagnosis. Instead, take the time to comprehend their unique strengths, challenges, and communication style.

- **Avoid overloading with information:** Prevent cognitive overload by presenting information clearly, simply, and concisely. During a crisis, refrain from overwhelming them with excessive or complex explanations.

- **Avoid criticism or blame.** Criticizing or blaming the person for their behavior or symptoms can worsen feelings of shame, guilt, or defensiveness. It's more helpful to focus on offering support, understanding, and constructive feedback.

- **Avoid isolation or abandonment.** During a crisis, it's crucial to avoid isolating or abandoning the person, as this can exacerbate their distress. Maintain a supportive presence, offer reassurance, and involve their support network or healthcare providers as necessary to provide comprehensive care.

- **Avoid unnecessary physical restraints.** Reserve physical restraints for extreme situations where there's immediate danger to themselves or others. Prioritize seeking guidance from healthcare professionals or trained experts before resorting to physical interventions.

- Build a trusting relationship and work in an open, engaging, and non-judgmental manner.

- Be aware that stigma and discrimination can be associated with Neurocognitive Disorder.

- Work as a multidisciplinary team and offer guidance and support (family, caregivers).

- Encourage them to meet their ADL's (Activities of Daily Living).

- Show environmental awareness (safely remove any objects that the person could use to harm themselves).

- Seek immediate suicide intervention when needed (see Module 16).

Effective de-escalation and crisis intervention for neurocognitive disorders requires a combination of compassion, empathy, active listening, and practical actions to ensure immediate safety and long-term support. By creating a safe and supportive environment, engaging appropriate resources, and following up with continuous care, individuals experiencing a crisis can be guided toward stability and recovery.

Addressing the risks associated with a neurocognitive disorders crisis requires a proactive and compassionate approach. By implementing training, support systems, and clear protocols and promoting a supportive workplace culture, organizations can effectively manage these risks and ensure the safety and well-being of all staff members. Mental health is a crucial aspect of overall health, and taking steps to support it benefits both individuals and the organization as a whole.

Neurocognitive Disorders Treatments

> Disclaimer: Personal Safety Training Inc. makes no claim as to what type of treatment is needed for any mental health disorder.

Neurocognitive disorders are treated and managed in several ways:

- **Psychotherapy**, such as cognitive behavioral therapy and family-focused therapy.
- **Medications**, such as mood stabilizers, antipsychotic medications and, to a lesser extent, antidepressants.
- **Self-management strategies**, like education and recognition of an episode's early symptoms.
- **Complementary health approaches**, such as aerobic exercise meditation, faith and prayer can support, but not replace, treatment.

For individuals with bipolar disorder, collaborating closely with mental health professionals to develop a personalized treatment plan that addresses their specific needs and preferences is essential. Combination approaches often yield the best results in managing bipolar symptoms effectively.

While there is no cure for most neurocognitive disorders, certain treatments can temporarily alleviate symptoms. Doctors may prescribe medications such as antidepressants, cholinesterase inhibitors, and memantine to manage memory loss, depression, and other symptoms. Ongoing psychotherapy and psychosocial support are essential for understanding and managing the disorder, establishing caregiving regimens, and maintaining quality of life. Non-drug therapies, such as occupational therapy, modifying the environment, and simplifying tasks, are also important in managing symptoms and ensuring safety. Spouses, partners, and family members often participate in therapy sessions to provide the necessary support.

Several dementia symptoms and behavior problems might be treated initially using non-drug therapies, such as:

- **Occupational therapy**. A therapist can facilitate making the home safer and teach coping behaviors. The purpose is to prevent accidents, such as falls; manage behavior, and prepare the individual for the dementia progression.
- **Modifying the environment**. Reducing clutter and noise can make it easier for someone with dementia to focus and function. Hiding objects that can threaten safety, such as knives and car keys. Monitoring systems can alert you if the person with dementia wanders.
- **Simplifying tasks**. Breaking tasks into easier steps and focusing on success, not failure. Structure and routine also help reduce confusion in people with dementia.

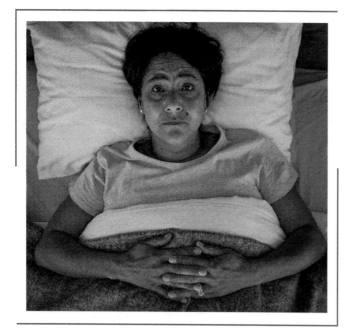

Sundowning

Sundowning is increased confusion that people living with Alzheimer's and dementia may experience from dusk through night. Also called "sundowner's syndrome," it is not a disease but a set of symptoms or dementia-related behaviors that may include difficulty sleeping, anxiety, agitation, hallucinations, pacing, and disorientation. Although the exact cause is unknown, sundowning may occur due to disease progression and changes in the brain.

Around 20% of people diagnosed with Alzheimer's disease experience sundowning at some point.

From late afternoon into the night, people living with Alzheimer's or dementia may experience:

- Increased confusion
- Anxiety or agitation
- Difficulty sleeping
- Pacing and wandering
- Disorientation

Risk factors that may contribute to trouble sleeping and sundowning:

- Mental and physical exhaustion from a full day of activities.
- Navigating a new or confusing environment.
- A mixed-up "internal body clock." The person living with Alzheimer's may feel tired during the day and awake at night.
- Low lighting can increase shadows, which may cause the person to become confused by what they see. They may experience hallucinations and become more agitated.
- Noticing stress or frustration in those around them may cause the person living with dementia to become stressed as well.
- Dreaming while sleeping can cause disorientation, including confusion about what's a dream and what's real.
- Less need for sleep, which is common among older adults.

Strategies to help manage sleep issues and sundowning:

- Encourage the person living with dementia to get plenty of rest.
- Schedule activities such as doctor appointments, trips and bathing in the morning or early afternoon hours when the person living with dementia is more alert.
- Encourage a regular routine of waking up, eating meals and going to bed.
- When possible, spend time outside in the sunlight during the day.
- Make notes about what happens before sundowning events and try to identify triggers.

- Reduce stimulation during the evening hours. For example, avoid watching TV, doing chores or listening to loud music. These distractions may add to the person's confusion.

- Offer a larger meal at lunch and keep the evening meal lighter.

- Keep the home well lit in the evening to help reduce the person's confusion.

- Try to identify activities that are soothing to the person, such as listening to calming music, looking at photographs or watching a favorite movie.

- Take a walk with the person to help reduce their restlessness.

- Talk to the person's doctor about the best times of day for taking medication.

- Try to limit daytime naps if the person has trouble sleeping at night.

- Reduce or avoid alcohol, caffeine and nicotine, which can all affect the ability to sleep.

IF YOU OR SOMEONE YOU KNOW IS IN CRISIS AND CONSIDERING SELF-HARM OR SUICIDE:

- Call 911 for emergency services.
- Visit the nearest hospital emergency room.
- Call or text 988 to connect with the 988 Suicide and Crisis Lifeline, offering 24-hour, confidential support. *Para ayuda en español, llame al 988.*
- Support is also available via live chat at 988lifeline.org. *AVADE® does not monitor this website for crisis messages, provide medical advice, or make referrals.*

PSTI LEGAL DISCLAIMER

The information in this training book is a supplement, not a substitute, for the expertise of qualified healthcare professionals. The content on AVADE® Behavioral Health, sourced from reliable information, does not constitute medical or professional healthcare advice, diagnosis, or treatment. It is crucial to consult healthcare providers for specific guidelines related to medical or behavioral health conditions. This material does not guarantee that any technique or strategy is safe or effective for any specific needs. Personal Safety Training, Inc., does not dictate policies or procedures for behavioral health violence prevention, self-defense tactics, or any physical interventions. Agencies are responsible for developing their own policies and evaluating the recommendations based on their circumstances.

The author and publisher do not guarantee the completeness or accuracy of the information and assume no risk for its use. Any implied warranty are expressly disavowed.

References for Module 13

https://988lifeline.org/

https://www.apa.org/

https://www.cdc.gov/

https://mhanational.org/

https://www.nami.org/

https://www.nimh.nih.gov/

https://www.psychiatry.org/

https://www.samhsa.gov/

Video: Dementia—Causes, Symptoms, and Treatment Options
youtube.com/watch?v=nLdLfmFzLSo

Video: What is dementia?
youtube.com/watch?v=fmaEql66gB0

Video: What is Alzheimer's disease?
youtube.com/watch?v=wfLP8fFrOp0

American Psychiatric Association. *Diagnostic and Statistical Manual of Mental Disorders Fifth Edition DSM-5®*. American Psychiatric Association Publishing. Washington, DC 2013

Boland, Robert, MD, Marcia L. Verduin, MD, Pedro Ruiz, MD. *Kaplan & Saddock's Synopsis of Psychiatry 12th Edition*. Philadelphia, PA. Wolters Kluwer, 2022

Brown, Catana, PhD., Virginia C. Stoffel PhD, and Jaime Muñoz PhD. *Occupational Therapy in Mental Health, A Vision for Participation*. Philadelphia, PA. F.A Davis Company, 2015.

Buser, Steven, MD. *DSM-5® Insanely Simplified, Unlocking the Spectrums within DSM_5 and ICD-10*. Asheville, NC. Chiron Publications, 2014

Duckworth, Ken, MD. *You Are Not Alone, The NAMI Guide to Navigating Mental Health*. New York, NY. Zando, 2022

Ford-Martin, Paula and Stephanie Booth. "Types of Dementia: What You Should Know." May 16, 2024. https://www.webmd.com/alzheimers/guide/alzheimers-dementia.

Glick, Rachel Lipson, MD, Scott L. Zeller, MD, Jon S. Berlin, MD. *Emergency Psychiatry Principles and Practice. 2nd Edition*. Philadelphia, PA. Wolters Kluwer, 2021

Mayo Clinic. "Dementia." Accessed June 19, 2024. https://www.mayoclinic.org/diseases-conditions/dementia/symptoms-causes/syc-20352013.

Mental Health America. *Where to Start, A Survival Guide To Anxiety, Depression, and Other Mental Health Challenges*. New York, NY. Penguin Random House LLC, 2023

Morrissey, Jean and Patrick Callaghan. *Communication Skills for Mental Health Nurses*. Berkshire, England. McGraw-Hill Education, Maiden, 2011

Morrison, James. *DSM-5® Made Easy, The Clinicians Guide to Diagnosis*. New York, NY. The Guilford Press, 2014

Phillippi, Renee. *Dementia for Caregivers, Strategies for behavioral issues and practical tips for caring for your loved one at home*. Independently published, 2022

Seniorguidance.org. "How to Deal with Dementia Behavior Problems." Accessed June 19, 2024. https://www.seniorguidance.org/senior-living/how-to-deal-with-dementia-behavior-problems/.

Snow, Teepa. *Dementia Caregiver Guide*. Efland, NC. Positive Approach, LLC, 2017

Townsend, Mary C. *Psychiatric Mental Health Nursing, Concepts of Care in Evidenced Based Practice 8th Edition*. Philadelphia, PA. F.A Davis Company, 2015.

MODULE 14

Borderline Personality Disorder

Pervasive instability in moods, self-image, behavior, and relationships

Module 13: Borderline Personality Disorder

Borderline Personality Disorder (BPD) Defined

> Borderline personality disorders is a severe mental health condition characterized by frequent mood swings, an unstable self-image, and intense, often unstable relationships. The disorder significantly impairs an individual's ability to regulate emotions, leading to impulsive behaviors, distorted self-perception, and strained interpersonal relationships.

While the disorder's basic description and diagnostic process seem straightforward enough, the lived experience of the disorder is far more complex.[1] Borderline personality disorder is a mental illness that severely impacts a person's ability to manage their emotions. This loss of emotional control can increase impulsivity, affect how a person feels about themselves, and negatively impact their relationships with others.[2]

For a diagnosis of BPD, individuals must meet at least five out of the nine criteria according to the DSM-V:

- Perceived or real fears of abandonment
- Intense mood swings or brief periods of severe depression or anxiety
- Impulsivity
- Unstable or changing relationships
- Self-injury, suicidal ideation, or suicidal behavior
- Chronic feelings of emptiness
- Inappropriate, intense anger and rage
- Unstable self-image
- Stress-related paranoia or severe dissociative symptoms

Borderline Personality Disorder Facts and Statistics

- BPD is one of the most commonly misdiagnosed mental health conditions.
- 5.9% of the population will display BPD characteristics at some point in their life.[3]

---

1 https://www.nami.org/borderline-personality-disorder/how-to-describe-borderline-personality-disorder-to-those-who-dont-understand/

2 https://www.nimh.nih.gov/health/topics/borderline-personality-disorder

3 https://www.mhanational.org/conditions/borderline-personality-disorder

- BPD accounts for 20% of the psychiatric inpatient population.
- Over four million people have BPD in America alone.
- While BPD is not as well-known as other disorders, it is actually more common than illnesses such as schizophrenia.
- Women are far more likely to be diagnosed with BPD than men.
- 75% of people diagnosed with BPD are women
- 70% of people with BPD will make at least one suicide attempt in their lifetimes.[4]
- 8-10% of people with BPD will complete suicide.
- This rate is more than 50 times the rate of suicide in the general population.
- Misdiagnosis: 1.6% is the recorded percentage of people with BPD, the actual prevalence may be even higher.
- Over 40% of people with BPD had been previously misdiagnosed with other disorders like bipolar disorder or major depressive disorder.

Signs and Symptoms of Borderline Personality Disorder

Many symptoms of borderline personality disorder are similar to those found in other disorders, such as anxiety disorder, schizophrenia, and other personality disorders.[5] Some of the most common signs or symptoms of BPD include:

- Intense mood swings, quick changes in values or interests, and impulsivity or recklessness
- A distorted self-image or sense of self, making it difficult to find a clear sense of purpose and direction
- Excessive self-criticism, including struggling to remember their own positive qualities
- A pattern of intense and unstable relationships with family, friends, and loved ones
- Impulsive and often dangerous behaviors, such as spending large amounts of money, unsafe sex practices, substance abuse, reckless driving, and binge eating
- Self-harming behaviors, such as cutting, burning, skin-picking, scratching, punching or hitting, biting, pinching, or bone-breaking
- Feelings of emptiness, intense sadness, or loneliness
- Frequent, prolonged, or intense anger that can contribute to feelings of shame, regret, or self-loathing
- Feelings of dissociation, such as feeling disconnected from oneself, observing oneself from outside one's body, or feelings of unreality

It is important to recognize that not everyone with borderline personality disorder may experience all of these symptoms. The frequency, duration and type of symptoms can depend on the person and their condition.

---

4 https://www.verywellmind.com/borderline-personality-disorder-statistics-425481

5 https://www.mhanational.org/conditions/borderline-personality-disorder

The symptoms of borderline personality disorder can be summarized as instability in mood, thinking, behavior, personal relationships, and self-image.

Borderline Personality Causes and Risk Factors

Researchers aren't sure what causes borderline personality disorder, but studies suggest that genetic, environmental, and social factors may increase the risk of developing it. These factors may include:

- **Family history**: People who have a close family member (such as a parent or sibling) with the illness may be at a higher risk of developing borderline personality disorder.

- **Brain structure and function**: Research shows that people with borderline personality disorder may have structural and functional changes in the brain, especially in the areas that control impulses and emotion regulation. However, the studies do not demonstrate whether these changes were risk factors for the illness or if such changes were caused by the disorder.

- **Environmental, cultural, and social factors**: Many people with borderline personality disorder report experiencing traumatic life events, such as abuse, abandonment, or hardship during childhood. Others may have been exposed to unstable, invalidating relationships or conflicts.

Although these factors may increase a person's risk, it doesn't mean it is certain that they'll develop borderline personality disorder. Likewise, people without these risk factors may develop the disorder in their lifetime.

Risk factors for BPD include:

- Abandonment in childhood or adolescence
- Disrupted family life
- Poor communication in the family
- Sexual, physical, or emotional abuse

Types of Borderline Personality Disorder

Theodore Millon, a prominent psychologist, proposed the following four subtypes of BPD, each with distinct characteristics:[6]

1. **Discouraged Borderline**: Exhibits a mixture of avoidant, depressive, and dependent personality traits. They may appear clingy and dependent on others for validation.

2. **Impulsive Borderline**: Characterized by histrionic and antisocial traits. These individuals are often energetic, flirtatious, and thrill-seeking, but may also engage in reckless behavior.

3. **Petulant Borderline**: Shows negativistic (passive-aggressive) and depressive features. They tend to be irritable, impatient, and stubborn, with

---

6 https://americanaddictioncenters.org/co-occurring-disorders/bpd

a tendency to alternate between feeling unworthy and displaying anger.

4. **Self-Destructive Borderline**: Combines depressive and masochistic (self-defeating) traits. These individuals are often prone to self-harm, substance abuse, and other self-destructive behaviors.

Borderline Personality Disorder Crisis

> A borderline personality disorder (BPD) crisis is an intense emotional episode marked by overwhelming distress, impulsivity, self-destructive behaviors, and severe mood swings, requiring immediate intervention and support.

Indicators of a BPD crisis may include:

- **Emotional intensity**: Individuals may experience extreme emotional pain, anger, or sadness that can rapidly escalate.
- **Impulsivity**: There can be impulsive behaviors such as self-harm, substance abuse, or suicidal threats and actions.
- **Interpersonal conflicts**: Intense and unstable relationships may become more volatile during a crisis.
- **Distorted thinking**: Paranoid thoughts, dissociation, and extreme black-and-white thinking may intensify.
- **Increased impulsivity**: Engaging in risky behaviors without considering the consequences.
- **Threats or acts of self-harm**: This can include cutting, burning, or other forms of self-injury.
- **Suicidal ideation or attempts**: Expressing a desire to die or making plans to commit suicide.
- **Severe mood swings**: Rapid changes in mood, from intense anger to deep sadness.
- **Intense fear of abandonment**: Real or perceived threats of abandonment can trigger a crisis.

If someone with Borderline Personality Disorder is exhibiting these crisis symptoms, it's crucial to seek immediate help from mental health professionals, crisis intervention services, or emergency services to ensure their safety and provide appropriate care.

Crisis and De-Escalation Interventions for Borderline Personality Disorder

- Use a trauma-informed approach.
- Use positive interpersonal communication skills.
- Use the daily habits of de-escalation.
- **Guidelines for borderline personality disorder crisis and de-escalation strategies:**
  - **Contact crisis intervention teams.** Contact mental health crisis intervention teams if the situation escalates and professional intervention is needed.
  - **Contact the Suicide and Crisis Lifeline.** If you or someone you know is struggling or having thoughts of suicide, call or text the 988 Suicide & Crisis Lifeline at 988 or chat at 988lifeline.org. In life-threatening situations, call 911.

- **Ensure safety.** Assess the environment to remove any potentially harmful objects and maintain physical distance to avoid escalating the situation.
- **Stay calm and composed.** Maintain a calm demeanor and manage your own emotions to help soothe the person. Speak in a soft, gentle tone.
- **Use active listening.** Show that you are fully engaged and listening to their concerns. Use verbal and non-verbal cues to indicate you are paying attention.
- **Validate their feelings.** Acknowledge their emotions without judgment. Say things like, "I understand that you're feeling very upset right now."
- **Use simple and clearlLanguage.** Avoid complex explanations or instructions. Keep your communication straightforward and to the point.
- **Offer reassurance.** Provide comfort and assurance that you are there to support them and help them through the situation.
- **Avoid confrontation.** Do not argue or confront them about their feelings or behaviors. Stay non-confrontational to reduce their defensive reactions.
- **Set boundaries respectfully.** Clearly and respectfully communicate any necessary boundaries. Ensure these are consistent and predictable.
- **Use grounding techniques.** Help them focus on the present moment with grounding exercises, such as describing their surroundings or engaging in deep breathing.
- **Engage in distraction.** Offer distractions that can help shift their focus away from distressing thoughts, such as engaging in a favorite activity or a simple task.
- **Seek professional help when necessary.** Recognize when the situation requires professional intervention and facilitate access to mental health services.

■ Guidelines to avoid borderline personality disorder crisis escalation:

- **Avoid judgment and criticism** to prevent increased defensiveness and emotional distress.
- **Avoid confrontational or argumentative interactions** to prevent escalating emotions and leading to a heightened crisis state.
- **Avoid invalidating their emotions** to ensure they feel heard and validated, reducing their distress.
- **Avoid inconsistent boundaries** by ensuring rules and expectations are clear and consistent to prevent confusion and frustration.
- **Avoid overloading with information** to prevent overwhelming them; keep communication simple and to the point.
- **Avoid escalating the situation** by not matching their emotional intensity or showing frustration, and instead stay calm and composed.
- **Avoid neglecting safety measures** by ensuring a safe environment, removing potentially harmful objects, and maintaining a calm space.
- **Avoid ignoring their triggers** by being mindful of known triggers and not exposing them to these without proper preparation and support.

■ Build a trusting relationship and work in an open, engaging, and non-judgmental manner.

■ Be aware that stigma and discrimination can be associated with Neurocognitive Disorder.

■ Work as a multidisciplinary team and offer guidance and support (family, caregivers).

■ Encourage them to meet their ADL's (Activities of Daily Living).

- Show environmental awareness (safely remove any objects that the person could use to harm themselves).
- Seek immediate suicide intervention when needed (see Module 16).

Effective de-escalation and crisis intervention for borderline personality disorder requires a combination of compassion, empathy, active listening, and practical actions to ensure immediate safety and long-term support. By creating a safe and supportive environment, engaging appropriate resources, and following up with continuous care, individuals experiencing a crisis can be guided toward stability and recovery.

Addressing the risks associated with a borderline personality disorder crisis requires a proactive and compassionate approach. By implementing training, support systems, and clear protocols and promoting a supportive workplace culture, organizations can effectively manage these risks and ensure the safety and well-being of all staff members. Mental health is a crucial aspect of overall health, and taking steps to support it benefits both individuals and the organization as a whole.

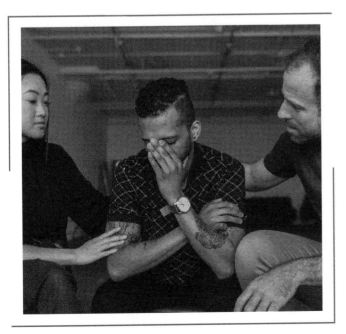

Borderline Personality Disorder Treatments

> **Disclaimer:** Personal Safety Training Inc. makes no claim as to what type of treatment is needed for any mental health disorder.

Borderline personality disorder (BPD) has historically been seen as difficult to treat, but evidence-based treatments have shown that many individuals with BPD can experience significant improvements in symptoms, functioning, and quality of life. It is crucial that treatment is provided by a licensed mental health professional, as untrained providers may offer ineffective or harmful interventions.

Psychotherapy is the primary treatment for BPD, typically involving one-on-one or group sessions with a trained therapist. Key therapies include:

- **Dialectical Behavior Therapy (DBT):** Specifically designed for BPD, DBT incorporates mindfulness and teaches skills to manage emotions, reduce self-destructive behaviors, and improve relationships.
- **Cognitive Behavioral Therapy (CBT):** Helps individuals identify and alter distorted beliefs and behaviors, reducing mood swings, anxiety, and self-harming behaviors.

Medications are not usually the primary treatment for BPD but may be prescribed to address specific symptoms or co-occurring disorders. Medication management often involves coordinated care from multiple medical professionals due to potential side effects and the need for careful monitoring.

Overall, while the treatment journey can be lengthy and requires patience and support, sticking with appropriate therapy significantly improves outcomes for individuals with BPD.

IF YOU OR SOMEONE YOU KNOW IS IN CRISIS AND CONSIDERING SELF-HARM OR SUICIDE:

- Call 911 for emergency services.
- Visit the nearest hospital emergency room.
- Call or text 988 to connect with the 988 Suicide and Crisis Lifeline, offering 24-hour, confidential support. *Para ayuda en español, llame al 988.*
- Support is also available via live chat at 988lifeline.org. *AVADE® does not monitor this website for crisis messages, provide medical advice, or make referrals.*

PSTI LEGAL DISCLAIMER

The information in this training book is a supplement, not a substitute, for the expertise of qualified healthcare professionals. The content on AVADE® Behavioral Health, sourced from reliable information, does not constitute medical or professional healthcare advice, diagnosis, or treatment. It is crucial to consult healthcare providers for specific guidelines related to medical or behavioral health conditions. This material does not guarantee that any technique or strategy is safe or effective for any specific needs. Personal Safety Training, Inc., does not dictate policies or procedures for behavioral health violence prevention, self-defense tactics, or any physical interventions. Agencies are responsible for developing their own policies and evaluating the recommendations based on their circumstances.

The author and publisher do not guarantee the completeness or accuracy of the information and assume no risk for its use. Any implied warranty are expressly disavowed.

References for Module 14

https://988lifeline.org/

https://www.apa.org/

https://www.cdc.gov/

https://mhanational.org/

https://www.nami.org/

https://www.nimh.nih.gov/

https://www.psychiatry.org/

https://www.samhsa.gov/

Video: What is Borderline Personality Disorder?
youtube.com/watch?v=EaMUhG1KWZA

Video: What is Borderline Personality Disorder?
youtube.com/watch?v=OCBHv_MMYB8

Video: What is Borderline Personality Disorder?
youtube.com/watch?v=KSPhc2NJA2Q

American Psychiatric Association. *Diagnostic and Statistical Manual of Mental Disorders Fifth Edition DSM-5®*. American Psychiatric Association Publishing. Washington, DC 2013

Boland, Robert, MD, Marcia L. Verduin, MD, Pedro Ruiz, MD. *Kaplan & Saddock's Synopsis of Psychiatry 12th Edition*. Philadelphia, PA. Wolters Kluwer, 2022

Brown, Catana, PhD., Virginia C. Stoffel PhD, and Jaime Muñoz PhD. *Occupational Therapy in Mental Health, A Vision for Participation*. Philadelphia, PA. F.A Davis Company, 2015.

Buser, Steven, MD. *DSM-5® Insanely Simplified, Unlocking the Spectrums within DSM_5 and ICD-10*. Asheville, NC. Chiron Publications, 2014

Duckworth, Ken, MD. *You Are Not Alone, The NAMI Guide to Navigating Mental Health*. New York, NY. Zando, 2022

Glick, Rachel Lipson, MD, Scott L. Zeller, MD, Jon S. Berlin, MD. *Emergency Psychiatry Principles and Practice. 2nd Edition*. Philadelphia, PA. Wolters Kluwer, 2021

Mental Health America. *Where to Start, A Survival Guide To Anxiety, Depression, and Other Mental Health Challenges*. New York, NY. Penguin Random House LLC, 2023

Morrissey, Jean and Patrick Callaghan. *Communication Skills for Mental Health Nurses*. Berkshire, England. McGraw-Hill Education, Maiden, 2011

Morrison, James. *DSM-5® Made Easy, The Clinicians Guide to Diagnosis*. New York, NY. The Guilford Press, 2014

Townsend, Mary C. *Psychiatric Mental Health Nursing, Concepts of Care in Evidenced Based Practice 8th Edition*. Philadelphia, PA. F.A Davis Company, 2015.

Autism Spectrum Disorder (ASD)

Neurological and development disorder affecting interactions with others

Module 15: Autism Spectrum Disorder (ASD)

Autism Spectrum Disorder Defined

> Autism spectrum disorder (ASD) is a neurological and developmental disorder that affects how people interact with others, communicate, learn, and behave. Although autism can be diagnosed at any age, it is described as a "developmental disorder" because symptoms generally appear in the first two years of life.

According to the Diagnostic and Statistical Manual of Mental Disorders (DSM-5), people with ASD often have:

- Difficulty with communication and interaction with other people
- Restricted interests and repetitive behaviors
- Symptoms that affect their ability to function in school, work, and other areas of life

Autism is known as a "spectrum" disorder because there is wide variation in the type and severity of symptoms people experience.

People of all genders, races, ethnicities, and economic backgrounds can be diagnosed with ASD. Although ASD can be a lifelong disorder, treatments, and services can improve a person's symptoms and daily functioning. The American Academy of Pediatrics recommends that all children receive screening for autism. Caregivers should talk to their child's healthcare provider about ASD screening or evaluation.

The American Psychiatric Association changed the term autism to autism spectrum disorder in 2013. ASD is now an umbrella term that covers the different levels of autism.[1] The autism spectrum includes conditions that providers used to consider separate, including:

- Autism
- Asperger Syndrome
- Pervasive developmental disorder—not otherwise specified (PDD-NOS).

1 https://my.clevelandclinic.org/health/diseases/8855-autism

Autism Spectrum Disorder Facts and Statistics

- Approximately 1 in 36 children has been identified with autism spectrum disorder (ASD), according to the CDC.[2]
- ASD is reported to occur in all racial, ethnic, and socioeconomic groups.
- ASD is nearly 4 times more common among boys than among girls.
- Autism spectrum disorder is one of the fastest-growing developmental disorders in the United States.
- ASD is more common than childhood cancer, diabetes, and AIDS combined.[3]
- ASD is a developmental disability that often presents with challenges before the age of 3 and lasts throughout a person's lifetime.
- Individuals with ASD may be very creative and find a passion and talent for music, theater, art, dance, and singing quite easily.
- Children with autism are 160 times more likely to drown than typical children. Therefore, it is very important to teach them to swim and to keep an eye on children around water.
- 35% of adults with ASD have not had a job or received postgraduate education after leaving high school. Many services required by law end abruptly after high school, leaving young ASD adults under-supported.
- About 10% of people with autism spectrum disorder also have another genetic, neurological, or metabolic disorder.

Signs and Symptoms of Autism Spectrum Disorder

The list below gives some examples of common types of behaviors in people diagnosed with ASD. Not all people with ASD will have all behaviors, but most will have several of the behaviors listed below.[4]

Social communication/interaction behaviors may include:

- Making little or inconsistent eye contact
- Appearing not to look at or listen to people who are talking
- Infrequently sharing interest, emotion, or enjoyment of objects or activities (including infrequent pointing at or showing things to others)
- Not responding or being slow to respond to one's name or to other verbal bids for attention
- Having difficulties with the back and forth of conversation
- Often talking at length about a favorite subject without noticing that others are not interested or without giving others a chance to respond
- Displaying facial expressions, movements, and gestures that do not match what is being said
- Having an unusual tone of voice that may sound sing-song or flat and robot-like
- Having trouble understanding another person's point of view or being unable to predict or understand other people's actions
- Difficulties adjusting behaviors to social situations
- Difficulties sharing in imaginative play or in making friends

---

2 https://www.cdc.gov/autism/data-research/index.html

3 https://www.massgeneral.org/children/autism/lurie-center/30-facts-to-know-about-autism-spectrum-disorder

4 https://www.nimh.nih.gov/health/topics/autism-spectrum-disorders-asd

Restrictive/repetitive behaviors may include:

- Repeating certain behaviors or having unusual behaviors, such as repeating words or phrases (a behavior called echolalia)
- Having a lasting intense interest in specific topics, such as numbers, details, or facts
- Showing overly focused interests, such as with moving objects or parts of objects
- Becoming upset by slight changes in a routine and having difficulty with transitions
- Being more sensitive or less sensitive than other people to sensory input, such as light, sound, clothing, or temperature

People with ASD may also experience sleep problems and irritability.

People on the autism spectrum also may have many strengths, including:

- Being able to learn things in detail and remember information for long periods of time
- Being strong visual and auditory learners
- Excelling in math, science, music, or art

Autism Spectrum Disorder Causes

Scientists have not discovered a single cause of autism. They believe several factors may contribute to this developmental disorder.

- **Genetics.** If one child in a family has ASD, another sibling is more likely to develop it, too. Likewise, identical twins are highly likely to both develop autism if it is present. Relatives of children with autism show minor signs of communication difficulties. Scans reveal that people on the autism spectrum have certain abnormalities of the brain's structure and chemical function.

- **Environment.** Scientists are currently researching many environmental factors that are thought to play a role in contributing to ASD. Many prenatal factors may contribute to a child's development, such as a mother's health. Other postnatal factors may affect development as well. Despite many claims that have been highlighted by the media, strong evidence has been shown that vaccines do not cause autism.

Types of Autism Spectrum Disorder

Autism spectrum disorder (ASD) is a group of related neurological conditions that affect brain development. It's characterized by difficulties with social interactions, communication, and behavioral issues, such as repetitive actions and narrow interests.[5]

- **Asperger's Syndrome.** This is on the milder end of the autism spectrum. A person with Asperger's may be very intelligent and able to handle their daily life. They may be really focused on topics that interest them and discuss them nonstop. But they have a much harder time socially.

5 https://www.webmd.com/brain/autism/autism-spectrum-disorders

- **Pervasive developmental disorder, not otherwise specified (PDD-NOS).** This diagnosis included most children whose autism was more severe than Asperger's syndrome but not as severe as autistic disorder.

- **Autistic Disorder.** This older term is further along the autism spectrum than Asperger's and PDD-NOS. It includes the same types of symptoms but at a more intense level.

- **Childhood Disintegrative Disorder.** This was the rarest and most severe part of the spectrum. It describes children who develop normally and then quickly lose many social, language, and mental skills, usually between ages 2 and 4. Often, these children also develop a seizure disorder.

- **Psychotic Depression.** Psychotic depression occurs when psychotic features such as hallucinations and delusions are accompanied by a major depressive episode, though psychotic symptoms generally have a depressive theme such as guilt, worthlessness, and death.

Autism Spectrum Disorder Crisis

> An ASD crisis refers to an intense, overwhelming reaction to a situation that triggers extreme distress or anxiety in an individual with autism. This may manifest as a meltdown or shutdown, characterized by behaviors such as screaming, crying, self-harm, aggression, or complete withdrawal. This may require immediate medical intervention.

A person with Autism Spectrum Disorder (ASD) in crisis may exhibit a range of behaviors, including:

- **Meltdowns:** Sudden, intense emotional outbursts that can include shouting, screaming, crying, kicking, lashing out, or biting. Meltdowns can be distressing for the person experiencing them and their supporters and can pose a risk of harm.

- **Withdrawal:** Withdrawing from a situation, isolating themselves, or finding a quiet space when they feel overwhelmed.

- **Communication challenges:** Difficulty expressing needs or emotions verbally or increased repetitive or self-stimulatory behaviors, such as rocking, finger-tapping, or saying the same phrase over and over. This is known as "stimming" and can help create sensory balance or self-soothe.

- **Sensory overload:** Being overwhelmed by sensory stimuli, such as loud sounds, bright lights, textures, or smells.

- **Acute agitation:** Momentary behaviors of oppositional or disturbing activities, such as echolalia (repeating of words) and repetitive beating, or more severe behaviors, such as dangerous self-injuries or aggressions.

If someone with Autism Spectrum Disorder is exhibiting these crisis symptoms, it's crucial to seek immediate help from mental health professionals, crisis intervention services, or emergency services to ensure their safety and provide appropriate care.

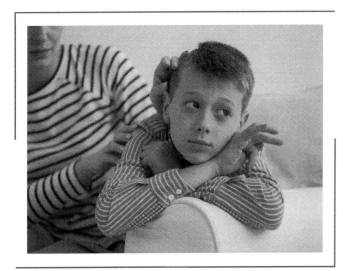

Crisis and De-Escalation Interventions for Autism Spectrum Disorder

- Use a trauma-informed approach.
- Use positive interpersonal communication skills.
- Use the daily habits of de-escalation.
- **Guidelines for ASD crisis and de-escalation strategies:**
  - **Contact crisis intervention teams.** Contact mental health crisis intervention teams if the situation escalates and professional intervention is needed.
  - **Contact the Suicide and Crisis Lifeline.** If you or someone you know is struggling or having thoughts of suicide, call or text the 988 Suicide & Crisis Lifeline at 988 or chat at 988lifeline.org. In life-threatening situations, call 911.
  - **Ensure safety.** Assess the environment to remove any potentially harmful objects and maintain physical distance to avoid escalating the situation.
  - **Maintain a calm demeanor,** control your emotions, use clear, simple language, and employ visual aids to communicate effectively.
  - **Minimize sensory overload** by reducing noise and bright lights, and provide sensory tools like fidget toys, weighted blankets, or noise-canceling headphones.
  - **Actively listen and validate their feelings** to show engagement, provide reassurance, and offer supportive statements like "I'm here for you" or "We'll work through this together."
  - **Use distraction techniques** by redirecting focus to calming activities such as listening to music, drawing, or playing with a preferred toy.
  - **Set clear, respectful boundaries** about acceptable behaviors and apply limits consistently to avoid confusion and frustration.
  - **Involve trusted family members or friends** for additional support and reassurance, and contact mental health crisis intervention teams if professional intervention is needed.
  - **Be patient,** stay non-confrontational, and avoid power struggles by agreeing to disagree when necessary.
  - **Use positive reinforcement** by acknowledging their efforts, encouraging positive behaviors, offering relaxation, and celebrating successes in managing intense emotions.
- **Guidelines to avoid ASD crisis escalation:**
  - **Avoid distress by understanding triggers:** identify specific triggers like certain noises, lights, or social situations, and continuously monitor the environment to minimize potential triggers.
  - **Avoid sensory overload** by minimizing sudden loud noises, bright or flashing lights, and strong or unpleasant smells.

- **Avoid unexpected changes** by maintaining routines and providing warnings before transitions to reduce anxiety and agitation.
- **Avoid complex or unclear communication** by providing clear, concrete instructions and speaking at a moderate pace to facilitate understanding.
- **Avoid physical discomfort** by ensuring their clothing is not itchy or tight and maintaining a comfortable environment that is neither too hot nor too cold to reduce stress levels.
- **Avoid invading personal space** by not standing too close or touching without consent and ensuring that individuals are not crowded, as these situations can escalate anxiety.
- **Avoid negative social interactions** by refraining from criticism, judgment, bullying, or teasing, as these can significantly escalate stress and anxiety.
- **Avoid unpredictable events**, such as sudden interruptions or surprises, as they can be unsettling and overwhelming.
- **Avoid demanding tasks** by not placing high demands or unrealistic expectations and by providing clear instructions for complex tasks to prevent frustration and anxiety.
- **Avoid emotional overload** by managing intense emotions and ensuring adequate emotional support during stressful times to prevent escalating distress.
- **Avoid physical discomfort** by addressing pain or illness promptly and ensuring basic needs like hunger and thirst are met to prevent escalation and irritability.

- Build a trusting relationship and work in an open, engaging, and non-judgmental manner.
- Be aware that stigma and discrimination can be associated with a diagnosis of ASD.
- Work as a multidisciplinary team and offer guidance and support (family, caregivers).
- Encourage them to meet their ADL's (Activities of Daily Living).
- Show environmental awareness (safely remove any objects that the person could use to harm themselves).
- Seek immediate suicide intervention when needed (see Module 16).

Effective de-escalation and crisis intervention for autism spectrum disorder requires a combination of compassion, empathy, active listening, and practical actions to ensure immediate safety and long-term support. By creating a safe and supportive environment, engaging appropriate resources, and following up with continuous care, individuals experiencing a crisis can be guided toward stability and recovery.

Addressing the risks associated with a autism spectrum disorder crisis requires a proactive and compassionate approach. By implementing training, support systems, and clear protocols and promoting a supportive workplace culture, organizations can effectively manage these risks and ensure the safety and well-being of all staff members. Mental health is a crucial aspect of overall health, and taking steps to support it benefits both individuals and the organization as a whole.

Autism Spectrum Disorder Treatments

> **Disclaimer: Personal Safety Training Inc. makes no claim as to what type of treatment is needed for any mental health disorder.**

Given that ASD is a developmental condition that begins early in life, having a cascading effect on developmental milestones, there is no known cure. But there is effective treatment available.

Treatment options include:

- **Education and development**, including specialized classes and skills training, time with therapists (such as speech, language, and occupational Therapists) and other specialists
- **Behavioral treatments**, such as applied behavior analysis (ABA)
- **Medication for co-occurring symptoms**, combined with therapy
- **Complementary and alternative medicine (CAM)**, such as supplements and changes in diet

People with ASD may face a wide range of issues, which means that there is no single best treatment for ASD. Working closely with a healthcare provider is important in finding the right combination of treatment and services.

IF YOU OR SOMEONE YOU KNOW IS IN CRISIS AND CONSIDERING SELF-HARM OR SUICIDE:

- Call 911 for emergency services.
- Visit the nearest hospital emergency room.
- Call or text 988 to connect with the 988 Suicide and Crisis Lifeline, offering 24-hour, confidential support. *Para ayuda en español, llame al 988.*
- Support is also available via live chat at 988lifeline.org. *AVADE® does not monitor this website for crisis messages, provide medical advice, or make referrals.*

PSTI LEGAL DISCLAIMER

The information in this training book is a supplement, not a substitute, for the expertise of qualified healthcare professionals. The content on AVADE® Behavioral Health, sourced from reliable information, does not constitute medical or professional healthcare advice, diagnosis, or treatment. It is crucial to consult healthcare providers for specific guidelines related to medical or behavioral health conditions. This material does not guarantee that any technique or strategy is safe or effective for any specific needs. Personal Safety Training, Inc., does not dictate policies or procedures for behavioral health violence prevention, self-defense tactics, or any physical interventions. Agencies are responsible for developing their own policies and evaluating the recommendations based on their circumstances.

The author and publisher do not guarantee the completeness or accuracy of the information and assume no risk for its use. Any implied warranty are expressly disavowed.

References for Module 15

https://988lifeline.org/

https://www.apa.org/

https://www.cdc.gov/

https://mhanational.org/

https://www.nami.org/

https://www.nimh.nih.gov/

https://www.psychiatry.org/

https://www.samhsa.gov/

Video: What is Autism Spectrum Disorder? youtube.com/watch?v=MTW7H5UQ8Ts&t=9s

Video: What is Autism Spectrum Disorder? youtube.com/watch?v=Bgyq5cTiHto

Video: What is Autism? youtube.com/watch?v=tEBsTX2OVgI

American Psychiatric Association. *Diagnostic and Statistical Manual of Mental Disorders Fifth Edition DSM-5®*. American Psychiatric Association Publishing. Washington, DC 2013

Boland, Robert, MD, Marcia L. Verduin, MD, Pedro Ruiz, MD. *Kaplan & Saddock's Synopsis of Psychiatry 12th Edition*. Philadelphia, PA. Wolters Kluwer, 2022

Brown, Catana, PhD., Virginia C. Stoffel PhD, and Jaime Muñoz PhD. *Occupational Therapy in Mental Health, A Vision for Participation*. Philadelphia, PA. F.A Davis Company, 2015.

Buser, Steven, MD. *DSM-5® Insanely Simplified, Unlocking the Spectrums within DSM_5 and ICD-10*. Asheville, NC. Chiron Publications, 2014

Duckworth, Ken, MD. *You Are Not Alone, The NAMI Guide to Navigating Mental Health*. New York, NY. Zando, 2022

Glick, Rachel Lipson, MD, Scott L. Zeller, MD, Jon S. Berlin, MD. *Emergency Psychiatry Principles and Practice. 2nd Edition*. Philadelphia, PA. Wolters Kluwer, 2021

Mental Health America. *Where to Start, A Survival Guide To Anxiety, Depression, and Other Mental Health Challenges*. New York, NY. Penguin Random House LLC, 2023

Morrissey, Jean and Patrick Callaghan. *Communication Skills for Mental Health Nurses*. Berkshire, England. McGraw-Hill Education, Maiden, 2011

Morrison, James. *DSM-5® Made Easy, The Clinicians Guide to Diagnosis*. New York, NY. The Guilford Press, 2014

Townsend, Mary C. *Psychiatric Mental Health Nursing, Concepts of Care in Evidenced Based Practice 8th Edition*. Philadelphia, PA. F.A Davis Company, 2015.

MODULE 16

Suicide Prevention

Provide support, education, and resources aimed at reducing suicide risk

Module 16:
Suicide Prevention

Suicide Prevention Defined

> Suicide prevention involves recognizing warning signs, providing timely intervention, and offering continuous support to individuals at risk. Strategies include understanding and identifying behaviors indicating suicidal thoughts, such as drastic mood changes, social withdrawal, and expressions of hopelessness. Prompt intervention involves engaging the individual in conversation, expressing concern, and ensuring they are not left alone.

Continuous support is essential through a network of family, friends, and mental health professionals. Encouraging ongoing therapy, support groups, and regular check-ins helps monitor well-being and address ongoing concerns. Additionally, education and training for all involved parties in recognizing distress signs and offering initial support is crucial. Creating a supportive environment where individuals feel safe to express their feelings without judgment ensures they receive the care and support they need.

Suicide touches whole communities. Each person who dies by suicide leaves behind people who knew that person, along with the impact of suicide and the bereavement that follows.

Everyone has a role to play in preventing suicide. For instance, faith communities can work to prevent suicide simply by helping people navigate the struggles of life to find a sustainable sense of hope, meaning, and purpose in addition to encouraging individuals to engage in behavioral health care.

> A person dies by suicide **every 11 minutes** in the United States.

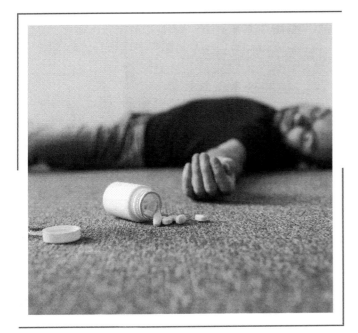

Suicide Facts and Statistics[1]

- When it comes to suicide and suicide attempts, there are rate differences depending on demographic characteristics such as age, gender, ethnicity, and race. Nonetheless, suicide occurs in all demographic groups.
- Suicide is a leading cause of death in the U.S.
- A person dies by suicide every 11 minutes in the United States.[2]
- On average, there are 132 suicides per day.
- More people die from suicide than from homicide.
- Suicide is a serious public health problem.
- Suicide has a far-reaching impact and affects people of all ages.
- Almost fifty thousand people died by suicide in 2022.[3]
- There were over 1.5 million suicide attempts in 2022.

- Men are three to four times more likely to commit suicide than women.
- Firearms account for over half of all suicide deaths.
- Over 90% of individuals in the U.S. believe suicide can be prevented.
- For every suicide there are three hospitalizations for self-harm.[4]
- Worldwide more than 700,000 people die due to suicide every year.
- For every suicide there are many more people who attempt suicide.
- A prior suicide attempt is an important risk factor for suicide in the general population.
- Veterans are at a 57% higher risk of suicide than their non-veteran peers.

Warning Signs and Symptoms of Suicide for Adults

The risk is greater if a behavior is new or has increased, and if it seems related to a painful event, loss, or change.

- Talking about or making plans for suicide.
- Acting anxious or agitated, behaving recklessly.
- Talking about being a burden to others.
- Talking about feeling trapped or in unbearable pain.
- Increasing the use of alcohol or drugs.
- Talking about feeling hopeless or having no reason to live.
- Sleeping too little or too much.
- Withdrawing or feeling isolated.
- Showing rage or talking about seeking revenge.
- Displaying extreme mood swings.

---

1 https://www.nimh.nih.gov/health/statistics/suicide#

2 https://www.withhopefoundation.org/suicide-facts

3 https://afsp.org/suicide-statistics/

4 https://www.cdc.gov/suicide/facts/index.html

Warning Signs and Symptoms of Suicide for Youth

It's time to take action if you notice these signs in family or friends:

- Talking about or making plans for suicide.
- Expressing hopelessness about the future.
- Displaying severe/overwhelming emotional pain or distress.
- Showing worrisome changes in behavior, particularly in combination with the warning signs above, including significant:
  - Withdrawal from or changing social connections/situations
  - Changes in sleep (increased or decreased)
  - Anger or hostility that seems out of character or out of context
  - Recent increased agitation or irritability

Suicidal Ideation and Planning

Suicidal Ideation

Suicidal ideation involves a persistent preoccupation with thoughts of suicide. This may include frequently contemplating methods of committing suicide, imagining what life would be like without you, or mentally rehearsing the act of suicide.

Suicidal Planning

When a person has a plan for suicide, it means they have moved beyond just thinking about ending their life (suicidal ideation) to actually formulating a specific strategy or method for doing so. This is a significant warning sign and indicates a higher level of risk.

Here's what it typically involves:

- **Method**: The individual has decided on a specific method they would use to end their life (e.g., firearms, medication overdose, hanging).
- **Timeframe**: They have thought about or chosen a specific time or date to carry out their plan.
- **Location**: They have identified a specific place where they intend to commit suicide.
- **Preparation**: They may have gathered the necessary means to carry out their plan, such as purchasing a weapon, collecting pills, or writing a note.

Having a plan often indicates a deeper level of distress and a higher immediacy of risk. It is a crucial indicator for mental health professionals, caregivers, and emergency responders to take immediate action to ensure the safety of the individual. Intervention strategies might include crisis counseling, hospitalization, and removing access to means of self-harm.

Understanding and identifying these elements can help in assessing the severity of the risk and determining the appropriate level of intervention to prevent suicide.

Suicide Risk Factors

Risk factors are characteristics that make it more likely that someone will consider, attempt, or die by suicide. They can't cause or predict a suicide attempt, but they're important to be aware of.

- Mental disorders, particularly mood disorders, schizophrenia, anxiety disorders, and certain personality disorders
- Substance use disorders
- Hopelessness
- Impulsive and/or aggressive tendencies
- History of trauma or abuse
- Major physical illnesses
- Previous suicide attempt(s)
- Family history of suicide
- Job or financial loss
- Loss of relationship(s)
- Easy access to lethal means
- Local clusters of suicide
- Lack of social support and sense of isolation
- Stigma associated with asking for help
- Lack of healthcare, especially mental health and substance abuse treatment
- Cultural and religious beliefs, such as the belief that suicide is a noble resolution of a personal dilemma
- Exposure to others who have died by suicide (in real life or via the media and Internet)

Suicide Methods

Understanding these methods can help inform targeted suicide prevention strategies, such as firearm regulations, safe medication disposal programs, mental health interventions, and public safety measures. It's crucial to always present this information responsibly and ensure it is used to promote safety and well-being.

- **Firearms**: the most common method of death by suicide, accounting for a little more than half of all suicide deaths
- **Hanging/strangulation**: the next most common method is suffocation/hangings
- **Poisoning/overdose**: the third most common method is drug overdose
- **Jumping from heights**: involves bridges, buildings, or other tall structures
- **Suffocation**: methods such as plastic bags or other means to cut off air supply
- **Drowning**: involves bodies of water like rivers, lakes, or oceans
- **Cutting or self-inflicted injury**: often involves sharp objects
- **Vehicle exhaust**: involves carbon monoxide poisoning
- **Electrocution**: less common but still reported in some regions
- **Intentional traffic collisions**: involves using a vehicle to cause fatal injuries

Crisis Warning Signs for Suicide

> Crisis warning signs for suicide are critical indicators that an individual may be at immediate risk of attempting suicide. These signs require urgent attention and intervention.

Key warning signs include:

- **Talking about wanting to die or kill oneself**: explicit statements about wanting to end their life.
- **Looking for a way to kill oneself**: seeking access to means such as firearms, pills, or other methods.
- **Talking about feeling hopeless or having no reason to live**: expressing a lack of purpose or hope for the future.
- **Talking about feeling trapped or in unbearable pain**: describing emotional or physical pain that seems intolerable.
- **Talking about being a burden to others**: believing that their existence is a problem for friends and family.
- **Increasing the use of alcohol or drugs**: escalating substance use as a way to cope with distress.
- **Acting anxious or agitated; behaving recklessly**: displaying heightened anxiety, restlessness, or risky behaviors.
- **Sleeping too little or too much**: significant changes in sleep patterns, such as insomnia or hypersomnia.
- **Withdrawing or feeling isolated**: pulling away from friends, family, and social activities.
- **Showing rage or talking about seeking revenge**: exhibiting anger or discussing plans for revenge.
- **Displaying extreme mood swings**: shifts from extreme sadness to sudden calm or happiness, which can indicate a decision to follow through with suicide.

These signs can appear suddenly or over time and might vary depending on the individual. Immediate intervention, such as contacting mental health professionals, crisis hotlines, or emergency services, is crucial when these warning signs are observed. **Early recognition and response can save lives.**

Crisis and De-Escalation Interventions for Suicide

- Use a trauma-informed approach.
- Use positive interpersonal communication skills.
- Use the daily habits of de-escalation.
- **Guidelines for suicide crisis and de-escalation strategies:**
  - **Contact the Suicide and Crisis Lifeline.** If you or someone you know is struggling or having thoughts of suicide, call or text the 988 Suicide & Crisis Lifeline at 988 or chat at 988lifeline.org. In life-threatening situations, call 911.
  - **Implement immediate safety measures** by removing access to any potential means of suicide (weapons, etc.), and ensuring constant supervision until professional assistance can be obtained.

- **Contact crisis intervention teams.** Contact mental health crisis intervention teams if the situation escalates and professional intervention is needed.
- **Ensure safety.** Assess the environment to remove any potentially harmful objects and maintain physical distance to avoid escalating the situation.
- **Use active listening and empathy** by allowing the person to freely express their thoughts and emotions without interruption or judgment, while also validating their feelings through understanding and compassion.
- **Address suicidal thoughts directly** by asking pointed questions about their intentions and plans without reacting negatively, maintaining a calm and supportive demeanor throughout the conversation.
- **Develop a safety plan** by identifying triggers and warning signs for suicidal thoughts, listing coping strategies to manage distress, and providing emergency contacts for support during crises.
- **Encourage professional help** by assisting in connecting with mental health professionals like therapists or counselors and offering to accompany them to appointments whenever possible.
- **Mobilize support networks** by encouraging them to seek support from trusted individuals like friends or family and connecting them with community resources such as support groups or crisis centers.
- **Offer crisis helpline numbers**, such as the National Suicide Prevention Lifeline (1-800-273-8255) or text (988), and emphasize the importance of reaching out to emergency services like 911 if there's an immediate threat.
- **Promote social interaction to reduce isolation** by encouraging engagement in supportive activities and scheduling regular check-ins to offer ongoing support and monitor well-being.
- **Encourage healthy habits** by recommending regular physical activity, emphasizing its mood-improving and stress-reducing benefits. Additionally, promote balanced nutrition and regular sleep for overall well-being.
- **Provide education on mental health**, emphasizing the significance of treatment and self-care practices. Acknowledge and celebrate any progress made to foster hope and resilience in coping with mental health challenges.

■ Guidelines to avoid suicide crisis escalation:

- **Avoid being judgmental** by refraining from criticizing or blaming the person for their feelings or situation, as this can escalate feelings of guilt and shame, worsening their crisis.
- **Avoid minimizing their feelings** by dismissing or downplaying their suicidal thoughts or emotions, as this can make them feel unheard or invalidated, leading to increased feelings of hopelessness.
- **Avoid using confrontational approaches** such as aggression, argumentation, or being confrontational, as these can escalate their emotional state and deter them from seeking help.
- **Avoid pressuring for immediate solutions** by demanding that they "snap out of it" or "get over it," as this can be overwhelming and counterproductive, given that recovery typically requires time and support.
- **Avoid overreacting with fear or panic** when faced with their suicidal ideation, as it can intensify their distress and anxiety, leading to further difficulties.
- **Avoid neglecting safety measures**, such as leaving them alone or not restricting access to means of suicide, as this can heighten the risk of harm.

- **Do not make false promises/offer reassurances that cannot be fulfilled**, as this can lead to a loss of trust and credibility, exacerbating feelings of isolation and distress.
- **Do not ignore warning signs** of suicidal behavior, such as discussions about death or possessions being given away, as doing so may result in missed opportunities for timely intervention and support.
- **Avoid being inflexible in interventions**, as this can create resistance and barriers to seeking help by not considering the individual's unique needs and preferences.
- **Do show empathy, understanding, and active listening** to avoid making the person feel disconnected and unheard, which can worsen their distress.

- Be aware that stigma and discrimination can be associated with suicide..
- Work as a multidisciplinary team and offer guidance and support (family, caregivers).
- Encourage them to meet their ADL's (Activities of Daily Living).
- Show environmental awareness (safely remove any objects that the person could use to harm themselves).
- Seek immediate suicide intervention when needed (see Module 16).

Effective de-escalation and crisis intervention for suicide prevention requires a combination of compassion, empathy, active listening, and practical actions to ensure immediate safety and long-term support. By creating a safe and supportive environment, engaging appropriate resources, and following up with continuous care, individuals experiencing a crisis can be guided toward stability and recovery.

Addressing the risks associated with suicide requires a proactive and compassionate approach. By implementing training, support systems, and clear protocols and promoting a supportive workplace culture, organizations can effectively manage these risks and ensure the safety and well-being of all staff members. Mental health is a crucial aspect of overall health, and taking steps to support it benefits both individuals and the organization as a whole.

LEVEL I · MODULE 16

 Behavioral Health Advanced Student Guide | Suicide Prevention   Page | 193

IF YOU OR SOMEONE YOU KNOW IS IN CRISIS AND CONSIDERING SELF-HARM OR SUICIDE:

- Call 911 for emergency services.
- Visit the nearest hospital emergency room.
- Call or text 988 to connect with the 988 Suicide and Crisis Lifeline, offering 24-hour, confidential support. *Para ayuda en español, llame al 988.*
- Support is also available via live chat at 988lifeline.org. AVADE® *does not monitor this website for crisis messages, provide medical advice, or make referrals.*

PSTI LEGAL DISCLAIMER

The information in this training book is a supplement, not a substitute, for the expertise of qualified healthcare professionals. The content on AVADE® Behavioral Health, sourced from reliable information, does not constitute medical or professional healthcare advice, diagnosis, or treatment. It is crucial to consult healthcare providers for specific guidelines related to medical or behavioral health conditions. This material does not guarantee that any technique or strategy is safe or effective for any specific needs. Personal Safety Training, Inc., does not dictate policies or procedures for behavioral health violence prevention, self-defense tactics, or any physical interventions. Agencies are responsible for developing their own policies and evaluating the recommendations based on their circumstances.

The author and publisher do not guarantee the completeness or accuracy of the information and assume no risk for its use. Any implied warranty are expressly disavowed.

References for Module 16

https://988lifeline.org/

https://www.apa.org/

https://www.cdc.gov/

https://mhanational.org/

https://www.nami.org/

https://www.nimh.nih.gov/

https://www.psychiatry.org/

https://www.samhsa.gov/

Video: Understanding Suicide and Self-Harm
youtube.com/watch?v=Qq-xrQKx1Pg&t=8s

Video: Why Do People Self-Harm?
youtube.com/watch?v=u-c0WqpAp_4

Video: Suicide Prevention Treatment
youtube.com/watch?v=fTlrHMuwHcQ&rco=1

Video: Youth Suicide Prevention
youtube.com/watch?v=TokWrCfq_Cc

American Psychiatric Association. *Diagnostic and Statistical Manual of Mental Disorders Fifth Edition DSM-5®*. American Psychiatric Association Publishing. Washington, DC 2013

Boland, Robert, MD, Marcia L. Verduin, MD, Pedro Ruiz, MD. *Kaplan & Saddock's Synopsis of Psychiatry 12th Edition*. Philadelphia, PA. Wolters Kluwer, 2022

Brown, Catana, PhD., Virginia C. Stoffel PhD, and Jaime Muñoz PhD. *Occupational Therapy in Mental Health, A Vision for Participation*. Philadelphia, PA. F.A Davis Company, 2015.

Buser, Steven, MD. *DSM-5® Insanely Simplified, Unlocking the Spectrums within DSM_5 and ICD-10*. Asheville, NC. Chiron Publications, 2014

Duckworth, Ken, MD. *You Are Not Alone, The NAMI Guide to Navigating Mental Health*. New York, NY. Zando, 2022

Glick, Rachel Lipson, MD, Scott L. Zeller, MD, Jon S. Berlin, MD. *Emergency Psychiatry Principles and Practice. 2nd Edition*. Philadelphia, PA. Wolters Kluwer, 2021

Mental Health America. *Where to Start, A Survival Guide To Anxiety, Depression, and Other Mental Health Challenges*. New York, NY. Penguin Random House LLC, 2023

Morrissey, Jean and Patrick Callaghan. *Communication Skills for Mental Health Nurses*. Berkshire, England. McGraw-Hill Education, Maiden, 2011

Morrison, James. *DSM-5® Made Easy, The Clinicians Guide to Diagnosis*. New York, NY. The Guilford Press, 2014

Townsend, Mary C. *Psychiatric Mental Health Nursing, Concepts of Care in Evidenced Based Practice 8th Edition*. Philadelphia, PA. F.A Davis Company, 2015.

MODULE 17

Post-Incident Response, Debriefing, and Documentation

Guidelines to follow after encountering a crisis incident

Module 17: Post-Incident Response, Debriefing, and Documentation

Post-Incident Response

Post-incident response, debriefing, and documentation are essential steps in managing workplace violence incidents. The post-incident response involves immediate actions to ensure safety, provide medical and psychological support, and communicate with staff. Debriefing allows affected employees to discuss the incident, gather information, identify gaps in procedures, and develop improvement strategies. Comprehensive documentation is crucial for legal compliance, providing evidence for investigations, aiding learning and improvement, and maintaining accountability. These processes help organizations manage the aftermath of incidents, support employees, and enhance future prevention and response strategies.

Post-incident responses include:

Triage (medical/hazmat)
Triage is the process of determining the priority of patients' or victims' treatments based on the severity of their condition. Initial first-aid treatment and protocols for hazardous materials and clean-up should be handled immediately.

Report the incident
Report the incident to police, security, risk management, human resources, etc. Follow standard operating procedures in reporting incidents.

Consider all involved
Staff, guests, visitors, patients, or anyone who was witness to the incident should be treated accordingly for medical and stress debriefing.

Provide for incident debriefing
Debriefing allows those involved with the incident to process the event and reflect on its impact. Depending on the situation, a thorough debriefing may need to take place. Even those not specifically involved in an incident may suffer emotional and psychological trauma.

Critical Incident Stress Debriefing (CISD)
CISD is a specific technique designed to assist others in dealing with physical or psychological symptoms that are generally associated with critical incident trauma exposure.

Research on the effectiveness of critical incident debriefing techniques has demonstrated that individuals who are provided critical stress debriefing within a 24- to 72-hour window after experiencing the critical incident have lower levels of short- and long-term crisis reactions and psychological trauma.

Employee Assistance Programs (EAP)

EAPs are intended to help employees deal with work or personal problems that might adversely impact their work performance, health, and well-being. EAPs generally include assessment, short-term counseling, and referral services for employees and their household members. Employee benefit programs offered by many employers, typically in conjunction with health insurance plans, provide for payment for EAPs.

Document incident to include any follow-up investigations

Post-incident documentation is absolutely critical for reducing liability risk, preventing recurrences, and assisting in follow-up investigations.

Initiate corrective actions to prevent recurrences

Preventing similar future incidents involves taking proactive corrective actions. Agency management, supervision, security, risk management, employee safety committees, the environment of care committee, etc., should initiate, track, and follow up on corrective actions.

Post-Incident Debriefing

Post-incident stress debriefing involves methods designed to help manage stress after a traumatic event. These techniques focus on providing emotional support, promoting mental well-being, and fostering a sense of safety and stability among affected individuals. Debriefing sessions typically include discussing the incident, expressing feelings, and receiving professional guidance to process the experience. These methods aim to alleviate stress, prevent long-term psychological effects, and support the overall recovery process.

> **The goal of debriefing is to reduce the chance of Post-Traumatic Stress symptoms and Post-Traumatic Stress Disorder (PTSD).**

Post-incident debriefing includes:

- **Always debrief.** Staff should debrief after every workplace violence incident, regardless of the severity. Oftentimes a brief discussion of the events and outcome is enough. Other times, a more intensive debriefing is needed.

- **Talk to co-workers.** Almost all workers have experienced or witnessed some type of workplace violence incident. Your co-workers can be a great resource to vent your concerns about your feelings after an incident.

- **Acknowledge humanness.** As humans, we are susceptible to the frailties of human nature. This acknowledgement creates an awareness that it is okay to seek and ask for help.

- **Be aware of post-event feelings.** Having the knowledge and awareness that you may experience strong feelings from an event can give you the confidence to seek help and discuss feelings with others.

- **Take advantage of your Employee Assistance Program (EAP).** Agencies realize that feelings may persist for longer than you might expect after an incident. Employee Assistance Programs can benefit employees and help them deal with post-incident stress or other work/personal problems. EAPs are intended to help employees deal with problems or issues that might adversely affect their work performance, health, and well-being. EAPs generally include assessment, short-term counseling, and referral services for employees and their household members.

- **Know the signs and symptoms of Post-Traumatic Stress Disorder (PTSD).** PTSD is a psychological reaction occurring after experiencing a highly stressful event (such as wartime combat, physical violence, or a natural disaster). It's usually characterized by depression, anxiety, flashbacks, recurrent nightmares, and avoidance of reminders of the event.

- **Take the time to follow up with other staff.** As human beings, we often focus on the needs of others and not ourselves. Take the time to discuss workplace incidents, your feelings about the incidents, and how incidents in the workplace could improve.

- **Critical Incident Stress Debriefing (CISD).** Individuals who are exposed to an assault situation (as a witness or a victim) should consider some level of critical incident debriefing or counseling. The final extent of any traumatic situation may never be known or realistically estimated in terms of trauma, loss, and grief. In the aftermath of any critical incident, psychological reactions are quite common and are fairly predictable. CISD can be a valuable tool following a traumatic event.

Conducting an Incident Debrief

Staff should debrief after every workplace violence incident, regardless of the severity. Oftentimes a brief discussion of the events and outcome is enough. Other times, a more intensive debriefing is needed. **Debriefs are always positive!** After action, corrections should be done at a later date.

There are four primary steps for conducting an Incident Debrief:

1. **Wellness check**: The facilitator conducting the debrief asks each person involved and gets a verbal acknowledgement of their mental and physical wellness.

2. **What happened**: The facilitator conducting the debrief asks each person to briefly describe what they saw, heard, and experienced during the incident.

3. **What we did well**: The facilitator conducting the debrief will ask each person to briefly describe what the team did well in responding and dealing with the incident.

4. **How we can improve**: The facilitator conducting the debrief will ask each person to briefly describe what they believe the team (we) can improve upon in future incidents. Be positive!

BEHAVIORAL HEALTH
INCIDENT DEBRIEF PROCESS FORM

▸ Conducting an Incident Debrief

- ☑ After a workplace violence incident, it is important that **all personnel involved in the incident meet immediately following the incident to debrief.**
- ☑ The debrief should be **led and documented by the supervisor and/or person in charge on duty** at the time of the incident, in coordination with security personnel.

FOUR PRIMARY STEPS TO CONDUCTING AN INCIDENT DEBRIEF:

1. **Wellness Check:** The facilitator conducting the debrief *asks each person* involved and gets a *verbal acknowledgement* of their **mental** and **physical wellness**.
   - The debrief leader will **assist in determining if anyone requires immediate or follow up medical treatment** as a result of *injury sustained* as a *result of the incident*.
   - If any personnel are identified as *sustaining injury* or *experiencing extensive stress* as a result of the incident, the agency will need to **follow up and provide further support and resources**, in line with the facilities policy & procedures.

2. **What Happened:** The facilitator conducting the debrief *ask each person* to briefly **describe what they saw, heard and experienced** during the incident.
   - It is important to assist in creating an environment within the debrief that allows **ALL individuals involved** to appropriately decompress and gain their composure prior to returning to regular job duties.

3. **What Did We Do Well:** The facilitator conducting the debrief will *ask each person* to briefly **describe what the team (we) did well** in responding and dealing with the incident?
   - Often, individuals *immediately following an event* will still be experiencing a **high level of adrenaline**. This is especially true for those who may have not experienced a violent event very often.

4. **What Can we Improve Upon:** The facilitator conducting the debrief will ask each person to briefly describe what they believe the team (we) can improve upon in future incidents? Positive!!
   - An individual still experiencing an *adrenaline rush*, may not be aware of their need to decompress or how the incident may have impacted them emotionally and/or mentally. Because of this, as a **TEAM**, ensure that you encourage each other to take a moment and *assess your ability to return to your regular job duties*.

Staff should debrief after every workplace violence incident, *regardless of the severity*. Often times a brief discussion of the events and outcome is enough. Other times, a more intensive debriefing is needed. Debriefs are **always POSITIVE!** After action corrections should be *done at a later date*.

Remember: The goal of debriefing is to **reduce the chances of Post-Traumatic Stress Disorder** (PTSD) and **Post-Traumatic Stress Symptoms**.

A) **Wellness Check:** _____

B) **What Happened:** _____

C) **What Did We Do Well:** _____

D) **What Can We Improve Upon:** _____

Behavioral Health Crisis & De-Escalation Intervention Training
© Personal Safety Training Inc. | AVADE® Training

Post-Incident Documentation

Who–What–Where–When–Why–How?
The first rule in post-incident documentation is the "who, what, where, when, why, and how" rule of reporting. After writing an incident narrative, double-check to see if you have included the first rule of reporting.

Witnesses: Who was there?
Make sure to include anyone who was a witness to the incident. Staff, visitors, guests, and support services (police, fire, EMS, etc.) can be valuable witnesses should an incident be litigated.

Narrative characteristics
A proper narrative should describe in detail the characteristics of the violent offender/predator.

Before, during, and after
A thorough incident report will describe what happened before, during, and after the incident. Details matter!

First person vs. third person
The account of an incident can be described in the first person or the third person. This can be specific to your agency protocols or the preference of the person documenting the incident.

Post-follow-up (track and trend)
Most agencies use electronic documentation, which allows for easy retrieval, tracking, and trending. Using technology assists agencies in following up and initiating proactive corrections.

Follow standard operating procedures
Whether handwriting incident reports or using electronic documentation and charting, staff should consistently and thoroughly document all incidents relating to violence in the workplace.

Elements of Reporting Self-Defense Force

After any situation involving the defense of yourself or another person, proper documentation and reporting are crucial. The events of the assault or attempted assault should be reported to police/security. Police/security will document the incident and start an investigation. You should also document the account for your personal records. This can protect you in a possible legal situation that could arise out of using force to defend yourself. As you document your account of the incident, make sure to report to police/security any details you missed during your initial report to them.

What type of force/self-defense/technique was used during the incident?
Be specific in your documentation regarding the type of control, defense, and force used during the incident.

How long did the incident and resistance last?
Important to note the length of the resistance, as this is a factor relative to exhaustion and increasing the level of force.

Was any de-escalation used?
Verbal and non-verbal de-escalation techniques should be noted.

Were you in fear of injury (bodily harm) to yourself, others, or the subject?

Fear is a distressing emotion aroused by a perceived threat, impending danger, evil, or pain.

If so, why?

Fear is a basic survival mechanism occurring in response to a specific stimulus, such as pain or the threat of danger.

Explain thoroughly, and make sure to document completely.

The importance of documentation cannot be over-emphasized. Documentation ensures proper training standards are met, policies and procedures are understood, certification standards are met, liability and risk management are mitigated, and departmental and organizational requirements are maintained.

Every person must take into consideration their moral, legal, and ethical beliefs and rights, and understandings when using any type of force to defend themselves or others. Personal Safety Training Inc. makes no legal declaration, representation, or claim as to what force should be used or not used during a self-defense/assault incident or situation. Each individual must take into consideration their ability, agency policies and procedures, and laws in their state and/or country.

IF YOU OR SOMEONE YOU KNOW IS IN CRISIS AND CONSIDERING SELF-HARM OR SUICIDE:

- Call 911 for emergency services.
- Visit the nearest hospital emergency room.
- Call or text 988 to connect with the 988 Suicide and Crisis Lifeline, offering 24-hour, confidential support. *Para ayuda en español, llame al 988.*
- Support is also available via live chat at 988lifeline.org. *AVADE® does not monitor this website for crisis messages, provide medical advice, or make referrals.*

PSTI LEGAL DISCLAIMER

The information in this training book is a supplement, not a substitute, for the expertise of qualified healthcare professionals. The content on AVADE® Behavioral Health, sourced from reliable information, does not constitute medical or professional healthcare advice, diagnosis, or treatment. It is crucial to consult healthcare providers for specific guidelines related to medical or behavioral health conditions. This material does not guarantee that any technique or strategy is safe or effective for any specific needs. Personal Safety Training, Inc., does not dictate policies or procedures for behavioral health violence prevention, self-defense tactics, or any physical interventions. Agencies are responsible for developing their own policies and evaluating the recommendations based on their circumstances.

The author and publisher do not guarantee the completeness or accuracy of the information and assume no risk for its use. Any implied warranty are expressly disavowed.

AVADE® Level I
Behavioral Health Review

- TRAUMA-INFORMED CARE
- INTERPERSONAL COMMUNICATION
- THE ASSAULT CYCLE
- DE-ESCALATION TACTICS & TECHNIQUES
- ANXIETY DISORDER
- DEPRESSION DISORDER
- BIPOLAR DISORDER
- SCHIZOPHRENIA DISORDER
- OBSESSIVE-COMPULSIVE DISORDER
- POST-TRAUMATIC STRESS DISORDER (PTSD)
- SUBSTANCE USE DISORDER (SUD)
- CO-OCCURRING DISORDER
- NEUROCOGNITIVE DISORDERS
- BORDERLINE PERSONALITY DISORDER
- AUTISM SPECTRUM DISORDER (ASD)
- SUICIDE PREVENTION
- POST-INCIDENT RESPONSE, DEBRIEFING, AND DOCUMENTATION

Workplace violence is, unfortunately, on the rise. By learning and studying the AVADE® strategies, integrating them, teaching them, and modeling them to your co-workers, you can lessen your chances of being a victim of workplace violence. Integrate the AVADE® safety principles into your workplace/life-place for defusing tense situations. Learn to identify the signs and symptoms of potential violence. Above all, learn to trust your instincts and listen to your intuition.

Remember: your best tools for keeping yourself safe are your own mind and personal safety habits.

AVADE® Behavioral Health

LEVEL II

Self-Defense Tactics and Techniques

The Goal of Self-Defense

The goal of this section is to teach self-defense intervention tactics and techniques. Most incidents can be prevented using your awareness, vigilance, and avoidance. However, there may be times when you need to physically intervene to protect yourself or another person. **After any self-defense intervention, always escape and report immediately.** Before conducting any physical training, be sure to cover the following safety rules with your class. Safety is the most important rule in physical training.

In today's society, corporations, healthcare, schools, gaming, law enforcement, security, corrections, the military, and protective services agencies realize that self-defense tactics and techniques are essential for protecting themselves and the public they serve. These agencies also understand that mitigating liability begins with proper training and education in self-defense tactics and techniques.

The AVADE® training program is designed for agencies to reduce the potential for injury and liability risk when employees are lawfully defending themselves or controlling an aggressive individual. The tactics and techniques in this training curriculum are for incidents where the aggressor is physically combative, resistive, and unarmed.

This training manual provides training and education that is designed to empower individuals and to increase awareness, knowledge, skills, and actions with regard to the use of force, control and restraint, self-defense, and defending others with self-defense tactics and techniques.

This course stresses the importance of knowing your agency's policies and procedures in regard to using force and defending yourself or another person. The AVADE® training is intended to give the trainee the basic understanding of self-defense, use of force, control and restraint, reasonable force, and basic legal definitions of force. Personal Safety Training Inc. makes no legal declaration, representation, or claim as to what force should be used or not used during self-defense, use of force incident, or assault incident or situation. Each trainee must take into consideration their ability, agency policies and procedures, and laws in the state and country in which they reside.

Most individuals can learn and develop proficiency in the techniques taught in this training course. Basic self-defense fundamentals are followed by defensive blocking techniques, personal defensive techniques, vulnerable areas of the body, specific responses to holds, assaults, and post-incident response and documentation procedures.

AVADE® Training Safety Rules

1. Safety and waiver agreement
Each individual trained *must* complete the **Student Registration and Recertification Form**. The instructor will advise the student how to fill it out and answer any questions pertaining to it.

2. Weapons-free environment
NO WEAPONS are allowed anywhere in the training area. Instructor will advise participants in proper procedures in securing weapons and ammunition. Follow agency policy and procedures.

3. Remove jewelry, etc.
The following should not be worn during a class which involves hands-on training: all jewelry with sharp edges, pins or raised surfaces, or jewelry that encircles the neck.

4. No horseplay
Any participant who displays a disregard for safety to anyone in class will be asked to leave the class. Please practice only the technique currently being taught. **Do not practice unauthorized techniques.**

5. Pat out rule (used for partner techniques)
Upon hearing/feeling/seeing the "PAT," your partner applying the technique will immediately release the pressure of the technique to reduce discomfort/pain. The technique will be immediately and totally released on instructions from the instructor or when a safety monitor says "RELEASE," "STOP," or words similar to them.

6. Be a good "defender" and good "aggressor"
Essentially this means working together with your partner when practicing the techniques. Without cooperation while practicing self-defense or defensive control tactics techniques, time is wasted and injury potential is increased.

7. Practice techniques slowly at first
Gain balance and correctness slowly before practicing for speed. Proceed at the pace directed by your trainer.

8. Check equipment for added safety
The instructor will check *all* equipment used during the training to ensure proper function, working order and safety.

9. Advise instructor of any pre-existing injuries
Any injury or condition that could be further injured or aggravated should be brought to the immediate attention of your instructor, and your partner, prior to participating in any hands-on training.

10. Advise instructor of any injury during class
Any injury, regardless of what it is, needs to be reported to the primary instructor.

11. Safety is everyone's responsibility!
Safety is everyone's responsibility and everyone is empowered to immediately report or *yell out* any safety violation.

12. Training hazards
Always keep any items or training equipment and batons off the floor/ground and out of the way when not in use.

13. Safety markings
Colored wrist bands or blue tape marking is a visual aid for pre-existing injury. **Use caution.**

14. Leaving training area
If you must leave the training area for any reason, please advise your instructor prior to doing so.

AVADE® Level II Self-Defense Tactics and Techniques Modules

SELF-DEFENSE FUNDAMENTALS

DEFENSIVE BLOCKING TECHNIQUES

SELF-DEFENSE TECHNIQUES

POST-INCIDENT RESPONSE, DEBRIEFING, AND DOCUMENTATION

Self-defense is the right to use reasonable force to protect oneself or members of one's staff/family from bodily harm from the attack of an aggressor if you have reason to believe that you or they are in danger. Self-defense must always be your last resort. When it is used, the force used must be considered "reasonable." For instance, striking someone who yells an obscenity at you is not considered "reasonable force."

Individuals do have the right to self-defense. The application of force must follow any agency policy and procedure as well as state and federal law. The best self-defense is to avoid the situation and getaway. If avoidance and escape are not possible, a reasonable defense would be lawful as a last resort.

The best self-defense is to avoid the situation and getaway. If avoidance and escape are not possible, a reasonable defense would be lawful as a last resort. You have the right to defend yourself; however, any use of self-defense must follow any agency policy and procedure, as well as state and federal law.

The following information will provide a general understanding of what self-defense and use of force are, how you can legally protect yourself against assault, as well as the risk of liability associated with any type of self-defense or force.

Personal Safety Training Inc. makes no legal declaration, representation or claim as to what force should be used or not used during a self-defense, use of force incident, or assault incident or situation. Each trainee must take into consideration their ability, agency policies and procedures and laws in the state and country in which they reside.

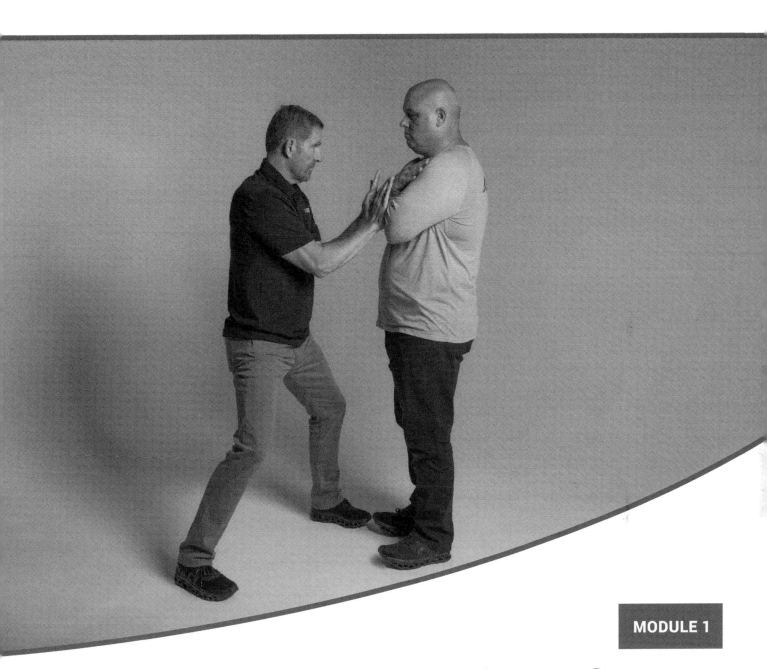

MODULE 1

Self-Defense Fundamentals

The foundation of the AVADE® hands-on tactics and techniques

Module 1: Self-Defense Fundamentals

Every tactic and technique requires the use of fundamental laws. If you don't understand the fundamental rules of self-defense, your ability to defend yourself is compromised. A basic understanding and use of these laws will give you an advantage in a situation where you might need to use force to defend yourself or another person.

> Fun·da·men·tal (from the Latin medieval: *fundāmentālis*: late Middle English)
> —synonyms 1. Indispensable, primary.
> —adjective 1. Serving as, or being an essential part of, a foundation or basis; basic; underlying: *fundamental principles; the fundamental structure.*

Self-Defense Fundamentals Overview

Stance | Balance | Stability

Defensive Movements

Core Energy Principle

Defensive Verbalization

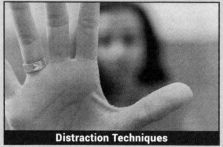
Distraction Techniques

Escape Strategies

Reactionary Gap

Hand Positions

On Target Training

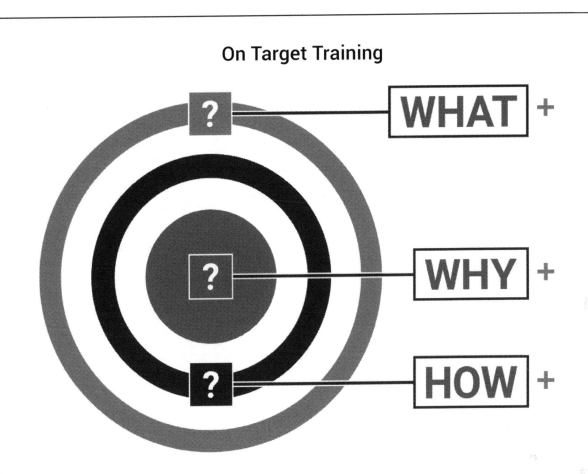

1. WHAT?
The WHAT describes a technique or tactic. The first step in teaching a hands-on technique is to explain what the technique is by the name of it. For example, we will be learning about defensive movement, and the first defensive movement technique is forward shuffle.

2. HOW?
The HOW is the manner or method, the technique or tactic is performed. The second step in teaching a hands-on technique is to explain and demonstrate how to do it. This step should be done a couple of times so that students can see it fully and completely.

3. WHY?
And most importantly is the WHY. It's the purpose, reason, intention, justification, or motive of a technique or tactic. The third step and most important step in teaching hands-on techniques are to explain why the technique is done a certain way and why you should have this technique in your arsenal of defenses. Without this understanding, the student is not bought into believing that the technique is needed or effective.

To really understand a technique or tactic, you must know the WHY (bullseye).

STANCE | BALANCE | STABILITY: BLADED STANCE

THE BLADED (DEFENSIVE) STANCE

All techniques are performed from the bladed stance/position.

Objective: Demonstrate how to correctly position your body to protect your vulnerable line and maintain stance, balance, and stability.

PERFORMANCE: BLADED STANCE

1. Face the clock (diagram on PowerPoint or imagine a clock in front of you) with your feet shoulder-width apart.
2. Step straight back with either left or right foot. Usually, individuals prefer to have their dominant foot to the rear.
3. If you stepped back with your right foot, turn your feet and body to the one o'clock position. If you stepped back with your left foot, turn your feet and body to the eleven o'clock position.
4. Keep your weight equal on both feet, and your knees slightly bent.

Caution: When back foot is behind front foot, you are positioned like being on a skateboard (common mistake - not stable).

PERFORMANCE: STABILITY TEST (BLADED STANCE)

Partner exercise (A and B)

1. Partner A places his/her feet together. Partner B gently pushes Partner A to the front, back, left side, and right side. Reverse roles.
2. Partner A stands with his/her feet shoulder-width apart. Partner B gently pushes partner A to the front, back, left side, and right side. Reverse roles.
3. Partner A now assumes the bladed stance. Partner B gently pushes Partner A to the front, back, left side, and right side. Reverse roles.

> **The Bladed Stance protects your "Vulnerable Line" away from the subject.**

DEFENSIVE MOVEMENTS: FORWARD SHUFFLE

Forward movement is used to engage a subject for control or defense.

FORWARD SHUFFLE

This defensive movement involves being able to move forward while maintaining balance and stability. All defensive tactics techniques are enhanced with defensive movement.

Objective: Demonstrate how to move forward correctly.

PERFORMANCE: FORWARD MOVEMENT

1. Assume the bladed stance.
2. Take a short step forward with your front foot (shuffle).
3. Follow up with a short step forward using your rear foot.
4. Continue forward, using forward shuffling movement.

Caution: If the feet come together, balance and stability are compromised (common mistake).

> The rule of defensive movement is:
> The foot that is closest to the direction you want to go always moves first.

DEFENSIVE MOVEMENTS: REAR SHUFFLE

Rear movement is used to disengage from an aggressor.

REAR SHUFFLE

This defensive movement involves being able to move to the rear (backward) while maintaining balance and stability. All defensive tactics techniques are enhanced with defensive movement.

Objective: Demonstrate how to correctly move to the rear.

PERFORMANCE: REAR MOVEMENT

1. Assume the bladed stance.
2. Take a short step back with the rear foot (shuffle).
3. Follow up with a short step back using your front foot.
4. Continue backward, using the rear shuffling movement.

Caution: If the feet come together, balance and stability are compromised (common mistake).

Caution: Backpedaling is another common mistake.

Caution: Beware of obstacles in your environment.

> The rule of defensive movement is:
> The foot that is closest to the direction you want to go always moves first.

DEFENSIVE MOVEMENTS: SIDE-TO-SIDE SHUFFLE

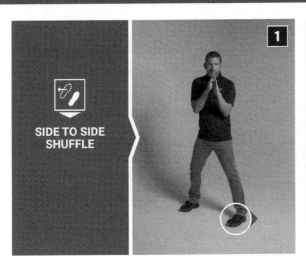

Side-to-side movement is used to avoid an attack from an aggressor.

SIDE-TO-SIDE SHUFFLE

This defensive movement involves being able to move side to side while maintaining balance and stability. All defensive tactics techniques are enhanced with defensive movement.

Objective: Demonstrate how to correctly move side to side.

PERFORMANCE: SIDE-TO-SIDE MOVEMENT

1. Assume the bladed stance.
2. Take a short step to the right using your right foot.
3. Follow up with a short step to the right using your left foot.
4. Take a short step to the left using your left foot.
5. Follow up with a short step to the left using your right foot.

Caution: If the feet come together, balance and stability are compromised (common mistake).

Caution: Crossing feet up is another common mistake.

Caution: Beware of obstacles in your environment.

> The rule of defensive movement is:
> The foot that is closest to the direction you want to go always moves first.

DEFENSIVE MOVEMENTS: FORWARD AND REAR PIVOTING

Pivoting is used to reposition or to enhance your energy when using personal defensive techniques or defensive control tactics.

FORWARD AND REAR PIVOTING

This defensive movement involves being able to pivot forward or back while maintaining balance and stability. All defensive tactics techniques are enhanced with defensive movement.

Objective: Demonstrate how to correctly pivot forward and backward.

PERFORMANCE: PIVOTING (FORWARD & BACK)

1. Assume the bladed stance.
2. Take an arcing step forward with your rear foot (forward pivot).
3. Take an arcing step backward with your front foot (rear pivot).
4. When pivoting forward or backward, always remain balanced and stable.
5. Pivots can be small movements or up to a 360-degree pivot.

Caution: If the feet come together, balance and stability are compromised (common mistake).

Caution: Crossing feet up is another common mistake.

Caution: Beware of obstacles in your environment.

ROBOT EXERCISE (THE BEST SELF-DEFENSE TECHNIQUE!)

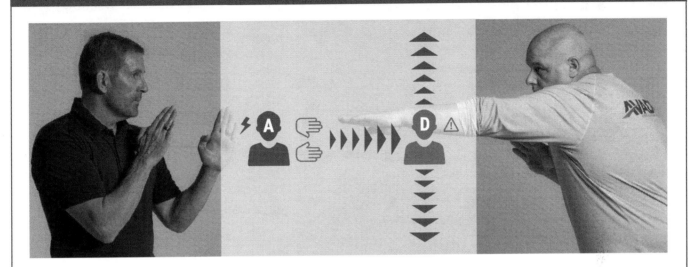

DEFENSIVE MOVEMENT "ROBOT EXERCISE"

The robot exercise involves being able to move in a lateral motion (side to side) to avoid an attack that is coming at you from a distance of 4' away or greater.

Objective: Demonstrate how to correctively avoid a forward attack by moving out of the way.

PERFORMANCE: "ROBOT EXERCISE"

1. The defender assumes a bladed defensive stance.
2. From 4–6' away, the attacker places hands out directly toward the defender.
3. Attacker moves forward toward the defender, attempting to gently touch either shoulder of the defender.
4. The defender waits for the last moment to move to either side, away from the attack.
5. Using sounds and/or movements will assist the defender in distracting the attacker.
6. Once out of the attack zone, defender can proceed to keep moving away from the attacker.

Caution: Do not move too late!

Caution: Do not move too soon, or the attacker will have time to adjust (reaction time) and follow/track you.

Caution: Crossing feet up is another common mistake.

Caution: Beware of obstacles in your environment.

CORE ENERGY PRINCIPLE

Energy and power are generated and developed from the core of the human body, even though a lot of emphasis is placed on the body's extremities.

The Core Energy Principle will:

- give you an advantage over aggressive subjects
- provide you power for counter blocks
- provide you power for defenses
- help you control and decentralize a physically resistive subject

CORE ENERGY

Our central and most essential part of our strength and power is our core energy. Without core energy, we rely on our extremities, which are not as strong as our central core. All defensive tactics techniques utilize this essential principle.

Objective: Demonstrate how to correctly use your core energy.

PERFORMANCE: CORE ENERGY

Partner exercise (A and B)

1. Partner A faces Partner B with his/her elbows away from their core.

2. Partner B moves forward toward Partner A. Partner A pushes Partner B back by pushing at their shoulders. How did it go? Reverse roles.

3. Partner A again faces Partner B with his/her elbows down towards their core. Partner B moves forward toward Partner A. Partner A pushes Partner B back by pushing at their shoulders. How did it go? Reverse roles.

Defensive Verbalization

During all defenses:
Use loud, repetitive defensive verbalizations.

NO!

STOP!

GET BACK!

LET ME GO!

LEAVE ME ALONE!

Why use defensive verbalization?

- Creates witnesses
- Establishes authority
- Keeps you breathing
- May be used as a distraction
- Alerts others of a confrontation
- Provides direction to the aggressor
- Mitigates liability risk for you and the agency

The Art of Distraction

> The Art of Distraction is a process by which we can buy valuable time to escape, defend, or control.

Distractions affect the senses, which take time for the mind to process the new information. Distractions have been used since ancient times. A valuable advantage!

- **Sounds:** Using a loud scream or yell can cause a momentary delay.
- **Movements:** Using your hands, eyes, and body can distract and cause a momentary delay.
- **Psychological:** Asking a question that is out of the ordinary can cause them a mental delay.
- **Lights:** Flashlights, the sun, emergency lights, etc., can cause a delay.

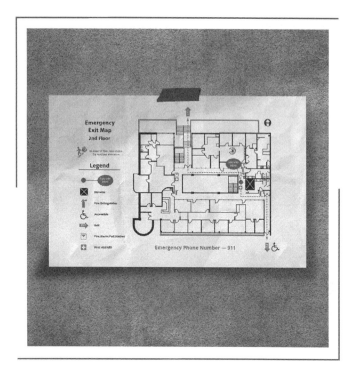

Escape Strategies

Escape is the act or instance of breaking free from danger or threat or from being trapped, restrained, confined, or isolated against your will.

Planning is the cognitive process of thinking about what you will do in the event of something happening.

REACTIONARY GAP EXERCISE

The "Reactionary Gap" is 4–6 feet: The distance between and you and an aggressor in which your ability to react/respond is impaired due to the close proximity of the aggressor.

When we are approaching individuals who are in the Assault Cycle (stressed, intoxicated, angry, escalated), we should approach them at a 45-degree angle versus approaching them head-on. We then proceed with our 5 Habits and maintain the appropriate distance from them.

- Action beats reaction within the Reactionary Gap.
- When we are too close to an individual, it can cause them anxiety and escalate them.
- When we lean in, we appear to be closer than we really are.
- A minimum distance of 4–6 feet is always recommended.
- Avoid using statements that can escalate a person.

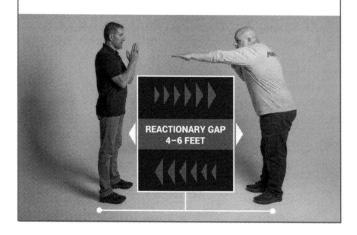

REACTIONARY GAP EXERCISE, PART ONE

"Reactionary Gap" is the distance between and individual and an aggressor in which the ability to react is impaired due to the close proximity of the aggressor.

1. Form two lines with participants facing each other at approximately 10' apart.
2. Have **Line A** approach **Line B** until they are arm's length away from them and able to touch their shoulder.
3. Have both **Line A** and **Line B** place their hands in the prayer position.
4. **Line A** will begin by quickly touching **Line B**'s shoulder with either hand. (Always coming back to the prayer position. The touching of the shoulder is simulating an unarmed attack)
5. **Line B** will try to defend against the shoulder attack by blocking with either hand or moving out of the way.
6. Reverse the roles of attacker and defender.
7. How did it go? Who didn't get hit?

> "Action beats reaction within the Reactionary Gap"

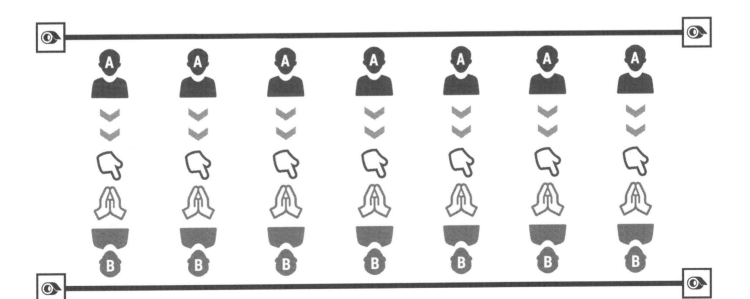

REACTIONARY GAP EXERCISE, PART TWO

"Reactionary Gap" is the distance between and individual and an aggressor in which the ability to react is impaired due to the close proximity of the aggressor.

1. Form two lines with participants facing each other at approximately 10' apart.
2. Now instruct Line B to stop Line A as they approach with 4–6' of distance away from them.
3. Line A will again attack Line B's shoulder from this new distance (4–6'). Notice that Line A must lunge in, in order to reach Line B's shoulder.
4. Line B, again will defend by blocking with either hand or moving out of the way.
5. How did it go, Line B?
6. Reverse the roles of attacker and defender.

> The minimum distance needed in order to react to an unarmed attack is 4–6' away from the attacker.

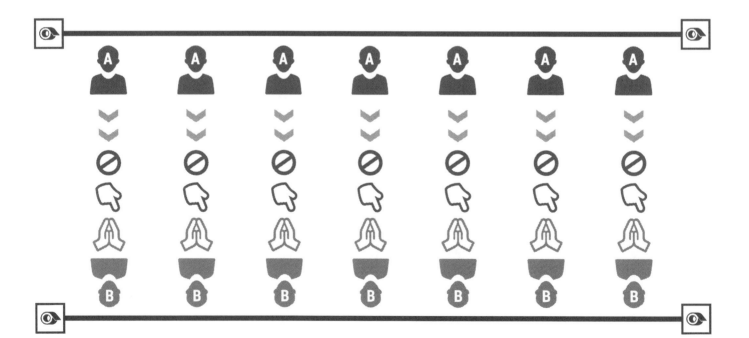

HAND POSITIONS

There are five basic hand positions.

Objective: Demonstrate how to correctly use your hands in the open, authority, stop, caution, and directive positions.

PERFORMANCE: OPEN OR AUTHORITY HAND POSITIONS

1. Assume the bladed stance.
2. Position your arms with your elbows down and your palms facing upward (Open).
3. Position your arms with your elbows down and your palms down (Authority).

PERFORMANCE: STOP OR CAUTION HAND POSITIONS

1. Assume the bladed stance.
2. Position your arms with your elbows down and your palms facing outward (Stop).
3. The non-verbal message says, "Don't come close to me," or a non-threatening message if you are moving forward (Caution).

PERFORMANCE: DIRECTIVE HAND POSITIONS

1. Assume the bladed stance.
2. Position your arms/hands, pointing with your open hand in the direction you want them to go (Directive).

Caution: Do not point when giving directions, as pointing is perceived as a derogatory gesture.
Caution: Closing your hands into a fist position may send a message of aggression.

MODULE 2

Defensive Blocking Techniques

Techniques to prevent and mitigate an imminent assault from an aggressor

Module 2:
Defensive Blocking Techniques

During all defenses use loud and repetitive defensive verbalizations (NO, STOP, GET BACK, STOP RESISTING, etc.) to direct the aggressor to stop attacking you, as well as using defensive movements—escape! After all defenses be sure to follow agency policies and procedures in regard to self-defense. Report and document immediately.

> Empower yourself and your staff by being able to correctly prevent and mitigate against an imminent assault from an aggressor.

Defensive Blocking Techniques Overview

Shoulder Block Defense

Elbow Block Defense

Turtle Block Defense

High Block Defense

Middle Block Defense

Outside Block Defense

Low Block Defense

SHOULDER BLOCK DEFENSE

SHOULDER BLOCK

SHOULDER BLOCK DEFENSE

This technique teaches individuals how to deflect an imminent assault.

Objective: Demonstrate how to properly use a defensive shoulder block against a physical assault to your head.

PERFORMANCE: SHOULDER BLOCK DEFENSE

1. Assume the bladed stance.
2. Bring your chin down.
3. Drop the arm that is in front of you while bringing your shoulder up to your chin.
4. You can slightly rotate your body towards your back side as the assault comes towards you, further deflecting the attack.

DURING ALL DEFENSES:

- Use loud, repetitive defensive verbalizations (No! Stop! Get back! Let me go! Leave me alone! etc.) to direct the aggressor to stop attacking you.
- Use defensive movements (Escape)!

AFTER ALL DEFENSES:

- Follow agency policies and procedures in regard to self-defense.
- Report and document immediately.

ELBOW BLOCK DEFENSE

This technique teaches individuals how to deflect an imminent assault.

Objective: Demonstrate how to properly use a defensive elbow block against a physical assault to your head.

PERFORMANCE: ELBOW BLOCK DEFENSE

1. Assume the bladed stance.
2. Bring your chin down.
3. Bring your front arm up to your face with your elbow directly in front, creating a shield in front of your face.
4. You can slightly rotate your body towards your backside as the assault comes towards you, further deflecting the attack.

DURING ALL DEFENSES:

- Use loud, repetitive defensive verbalizations (No! Stop! Get back! Let me go! Leave me alone! etc.) to direct the aggressor to stop attacking you.
- Use defensive movements (Escape)!

AFTER ALL DEFENSES:

- Follow agency policies and procedures in regard to self-defense.
- Report and document immediately.

TURTLE BLOCK DEFENSE

TURTLE BLOCK DEFENSE

This technique teaches individuals how to deflect an imminent assault.

Objective: Demonstrate how to properly use a defensive turtle block against a physical assault to your head and torso.

PERFORMANCE: TURTLE BLOCK DEFENSE

1. Assume the bladed stance.
2. Bring your chin down.
3. Bring both arms up in front of your face with your elbows directly in front, creating a shield in front of your body and face.
4. You can slightly rotate your body towards your backside as the assault comes towards you, further deflecting the attack.

Caution: Do not close your eyes or bend forward compromising your balance.

DURING ALL DEFENSES:

- Use loud, repetitive defensive verbalizations (No! Stop! Get back! Let me go! Leave me alone! etc.) to direct the aggressor to stop attacking you.
- Use defensive movements (Escape)!

AFTER ALL DEFENSES:

- Follow agency policies and procedures in regard to self-defense.
- Report and document immediately.

HIGH BLOCK DEFENSE

HIGH BLOCK DEFENSE

This technique teaches individuals how to deflect an imminent assault to their head.

Objective: Demonstrate how to properly use a high defensive block against a physical assault to your head.

PERFORMANCE: HIGH BLOCK DEFENSE

1. Assume the bladed stance.
2. Bring your chin down.
3. Bring your arm up in front of your face with your palm out, elbow close to your head, with your hand higher than your elbow.
4. Your hands can be open or closed.
5. You can use your support arm, strong-arm, or both arms to defend against an attack on your head.

DURING ALL DEFENSES:

- Use loud, repetitive defensive verbalizations (No! Stop! Get back! Let me go! Leave me alone! etc.) to direct the aggressor to stop attacking you.
- Use defensive movements (Escape)!

AFTER ALL DEFENSES:

- Follow agency policies and procedures in regard to self-defense.
- Report and document immediately.

MIDDLE BLOCK DEFENSE

MIDDLE BLOCK DEFENSE

This technique teaches individuals how to deflect an imminent rushing assault or grappling attack towards them.

Objective: Demonstrate how to properly use a defensive middle block against a physical assault coming at you.

PERFORMANCE: MIDDLE BLOCK DEFENSE

1. Assume the bladed stance.
2. Bring both arms up in front of you (palms out).
3. Push the aggressor away at the shoulders or torso area.
4. Use side-to-side movement after the middle block defense to get into a position of advantage or to continue to defend.

DURING ALL DEFENSES:

- Use loud, repetitive defensive verbalizations (No! Stop! Get back! Let me go! Leave me alone! etc.) to direct the aggressor to stop attacking you.
- Use defensive movements (Escape)!

AFTER ALL DEFENSES:

- Follow agency policies and procedures in regard to self-defense.
- Report and document immediately.

OUTSIDE BLOCK DEFENSE

OUTSIDE BLOCK DEFENSE

This technique teaches individuals how to deflect an imminent assault to either side of their head/body.

Objective: Demonstrate how to properly use a defensive outside block against a physical assault coming to either side of your head/body.

PERFORMANCE: OUTSIDE BLOCK DEFENSE

1. Assume the bladed stance.
2. Bring either your right or left (or both) arms up in front of your body and pivot towards the direction of the attack.
3. Your hands can be open or closed.
4. You can use your support arm, strong arm, or both arms to defend against an attack on either side of your body.

DURING ALL DEFENSES:

- Use loud, repetitive defensive verbalizations (No! Stop! Get back! Let me go! Leave me alone! etc.) to direct the aggressor to stop attacking you.
- Use defensive movements (Escape)!

AFTER ALL DEFENSES:

- Follow agency policies and procedures in regard to self-defense.
- Report and document immediately.

LOW BLOCK DEFENSE

LOW BLOCK

LOW BLOCK DEFENSE

This technique teaches individuals how to deflect an imminent attack to the lower area of the body.

Objective: Demonstrate how to properly use a low defensive block against a physical assault coming to the lower part of your body.

PERFORMANCE: LOW BLOCK DEFENSE

1. Assume the bladed stance.
2. Bring either your right or left (or both) arm down, sweeping in front of your body and moving the attack away.
3. Your hands can be open or closed.
4. You can use your support arm, strong-arm, or both arms to defend against an attack to the lower area of your body.

DURING ALL DEFENSES:
- Use loud, repetitive defensive verbalizations (No! Stop! Get back! Let me go! Leave me alone! etc.) to direct the aggressor to stop attacking you.
- Use defensive movements (Escape)!

AFTER ALL DEFENSES:
- Follow agency policies and procedures in regard to self-defense.
- Report and document immediately.

Self-Defense Techniques

MODULE 3

Defensive tactics for a physically violent aggressor

Module 3:
Self-Defense Techniques

Self-Defense Techniques Overview

Wrist Grab Defense

Two-Hand Wrist Grab Defense

Bite Defense

Hair Pull Defense

Front Strangle Defense

Rear Airway Choke Defense

Rear Carotid Choke Defense

Rear Bear Hold Defense

Self-Defense Techniques Caution

Personal Defensive Techniques are used for physical violence and deadly force situations.

> **Deadly force is force that is likely or intended to cause death or great bodily harm to you or another person.**

Any time force is used to defend yourself or others it must be a last resort and reasonable, and you must be able to articulate what you did, why you did it, and how you did it.

Any use of self-defense is based on your policies and procedures.

Vulnerable Areas of the Body

Knowledge of self-defense tactics is very important. Just as important is how and when you would utilize your self-defense tactics skills, if and when necessary. Without this knowledge and understanding, your interventions could be ineffective or expose you to unnecessary liability risk.

An individual *must always* consider their policies and procedures, as well as state and federal laws, when using force or self-defense interventions.

The "Vulnerable Areas" of the body diagram denote lower, medium, and high-risk target areas.

Low-Risk Target Areas

Low-Risk Target Areas are for situations where the subject is resisting or attacking you or another person with physical violence and aggression.

The subject's body would be considered low risk for the application of blocks and restraint techniques (excluding the head, neck, groin, and spine). The level of resultant trauma to these areas tends to be minimal or temporary, yet exceptions may occur.

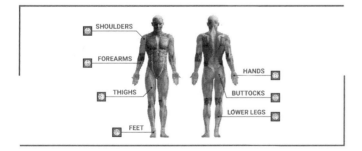

Medium-Risk Target Areas

Medium-Risk Target Areas are for situations where the subject is resisting or attacking you or another person with physical violence and aggression, or when the force applied to a Low-Risk Target Area fails to overcome the subject's resistance or attack.

Medium Risk Targets are areas of the human body that include joints and areas that are in close proximity to a High-Risk Target Area. The risk of potential injury is increased. The level of resultant trauma to these areas tends to be moderate to serious. Injury may last for longer periods of time or may be temporary.

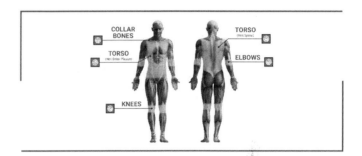

High-Risk Target Areas

High-Risk Target Areas are for situations where the subject is using deadly force that is likely to cause serious injury or death to you or another person.

Force directed to High-Risk Target Areas may cause a greater risk of injury to the subject. Staff must be justified and reasonable in using deadly force against a subject. The level of resultant trauma to these areas tends to be serious and/or long-lasting. Injury to the subject may include serious bodily injury, unconsciousness, shock, or death.

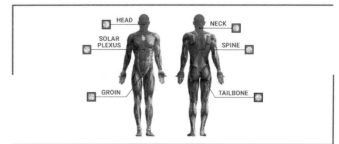

WRIST GRAB DEFENSE (PT. 1)

WRIST GRAB DEFENSE

It is a technique that teaches individuals how to defend themselves from a one-handed wrist grab assault.

Objective: Demonstrate how to defend against a one-handed wrist grab assault situation.

PERFORMANCE: WRIST GRAB DEFENSE

1. The defender stabilizes after being grabbed by the wrist.
2. The defender pulls elbow into their core (or moves forward to get their elbow into their core).
3. The defender turns palm upward, grabbing their hand with their free hand.
4. The defender then pulls their hand upward, using their core energy to break free of the assault.
5. The defender may need to use a distraction technique (by covering the eyes) or personal defensive technique to break free from the assault.

Special Note: If personal defense techniques are used in these defenses, it MUST be for physical violence or deadly force situations. Any time force is used to defend yourself or others, it must be a last resort, reasonable, and you must be able to articulate what you did, why you did it, and how you did it.

DURING ALL DEFENSES:
- Use loud, repetitive defensive verbalizations (No! Stop! Get back! Let me go! Leave me alone! etc.) to direct the aggressor to stop attacking you.
- Use defensive movements (Escape)!

AFTER ALL DEFENSES:
- Follow agency policies and procedures in regard to self-defense.
- Report and document immediately.

...continued, WRIST GRAB DEFENSE (PT. 2)

WRIST GRAB DEFENSE

WRIST GRAB DEFENSE

It is a technique that teaches individuals how to defend themselves from a one-handed wrist grab assault.

Objective: Demonstrate how to defend against a one-handed wrist grab assault situation.

PERFORMANCE: WRIST GRAB DEFENSE

1. The defender stabilizes after being grabbed by the wrist.
2. The defender pulls elbow into their core (or moves forward to get their elbow into their core).
3. The defender turns palm upward, grabbing their hand with their free hand.
4. The defender then pulls their hand upward, using their core energy to break free of the assault.
5. The defender may need to use a distraction technique (by covering the eyes) or personal defensive technique to break free from the assault.

Special Note: If personal defense techniques are used in these defenses, it MUST be for physical violence or deadly force situations. Any time force is used to defend yourself or others, it must be a last resort, reasonable, and you must be able to articulate what you did, why you did it, and how you did it.

DURING ALL DEFENSES:

- Use loud, repetitive defensive verbalizations (No! Stop! Get back! Let me go! Leave me alone! etc.) to direct the aggressor to stop attacking you.
- Use defensive movements (Escape)!

AFTER ALL DEFENSES:

- Follow agency policies and procedures in regard to self-defense.
- Report and document immediately.

TWO-HAND WRIST GRAB DEFENSE (PT. 1)

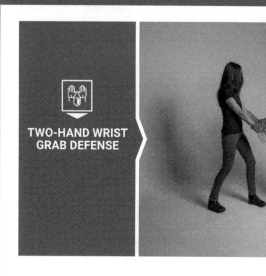

TWO-HAND WRIST GRAB DEFENSE

It is a technique that teaches individuals how to defend themselves from a two-handed wrist grab assault.

Objective: Demonstrate how to defend against a two-handed wrist grab assault situation.

PERFORMANCE: TWO-HAND WRIST GRAB DEFENSE

1. The defender stabilizes after being grabbed by the wrists.
2. The defender pulls both elbows into their core (or moves forward to get their elbows into core).
3. The defender turns palms upward while raising both hands upward in a circular outward motion to release the grab.
4. The defender may need to bring their palms back downward in a reverse circular motion to release the grab.
5. The defender may need to use a distraction technique or personal defensive technique to break free from assault.

Special Note: If personal defense techniques are used in these defenses, it MUST be for physical violence or deadly force situations. Any time force is used to defend yourself or others, it must be a last resort, reasonable, and you must be able to articulate what you did, why you did it, and how you did it.

DURING ALL DEFENSES:

- Use loud, repetitive defensive verbalizations (No! Stop! Get back! Let me go! Leave me alone! etc.) to direct the aggressor to stop attacking you.
- Use defensive movements (Escape)!

AFTER ALL DEFENSES:

- Follow agency policies and procedures in regard to self-defense.
- Report and document immediately.

...continued, TWO-HAND WRIST GRAB DEFENSE (PT. 2)

TWO-HAND WRIST GRAB DEFENSE

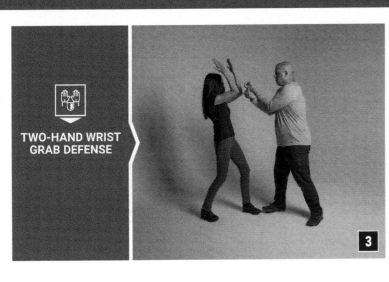

TWO-HAND WRIST GRAB DEFENSE

It is a technique that teaches individuals how to defend themselves from a two-handed wrist grab assault.

Objective: Demonstrate how to defend against a two-handed wrist grab assault situation.

PERFORMANCE: TWO-HAND WRIST GRAB DEFENSE

1. The defender stabilizes after being grabbed by the wrists.
2. The defender pulls both elbows into their core (or moves forward to get their elbows into core).
3. The defender turns palms upward while raising both hands upward in a circular outward motion to release the grab.
4. The defender may need to bring their palms back downward in a reverse circular motion to release the grab.
5. The defender may need to use a distraction technique or personal defensive technique to break free from assault.

Special Note: If personal defense techniques are used in these defenses, it MUST be for physical violence or deadly force situations. Any time force is used to defend yourself or others, it must be a last resort, reasonable, and you must be able to articulate what you did, why you did it, and how you did it.

DURING ALL DEFENSES:
- Use loud, repetitive defensive verbalizations (No! Stop! Get back! Let me go! Leave me alone! etc.) to direct the aggressor to stop attacking you.
- Use defensive movements (Escape)!

AFTER ALL DEFENSES:
- Follow agency policies and procedures in regard to self-defense.
- Report and document immediately.

BITE DEFENSE (PT. 1)

BITE DEFENSE

It is a technique that teaches individuals how to defend themselves from a bite assault.

Objective: Demonstrate how to defend against a bite assault situation.

Caution: The worst thing we can do when we are bitten is to pull away. A bite assault could be considered a deadly force situation.

PERFORMANCE: BITE DEFENSE

1. The defender stabilizes after being bitten on their arm or hand.
2. The defender distracts the aggressor by covering the aggressor's eyes with their free hand.
3. The defender *does not* pull away unless the aggressor opens their mouth.
4. The defender may need to grab the back of the aggressor's head and pull them in as they push the bitten limb/hand into the aggressor's mouth. Push-Pull! "Feed the Bite."
5. The defender may need to use a personal defensive technique to break free from the assault. If the aggressor falls back after being impacted by a personal defensive technique but does not open their mouth: **Move with them!**

Special Note: If personal defense techniques are used in these defenses, it MUST be for physical violence or deadly force situations. Any time force is used to defend yourself or others, it must be a last resort, reasonable, and you must be able to articulate what you did, why you did it, and how you did it.

DURING ALL DEFENSES:

- Use loud, repetitive defensive verbalizations (No! Stop! Get back! Let me go! Leave me alone! etc.) to direct the aggressor to stop attacking you.
- Use defensive movements (Escape)!

AFTER ALL DEFENSES:

- Follow agency policies and procedures in regard to self-defense.
- Report and document immediately.

LEVEL II · MODULE 3

...continued, BITE DEFENSE (PT. 2)

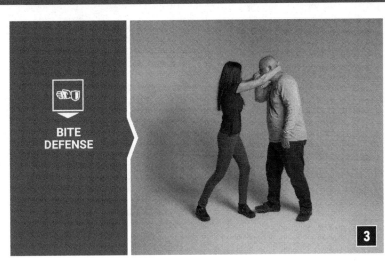

BITE DEFENSE

It is a technique that teaches individuals how to defend themselves from a bite assault.

Objective: Demonstrate how to defend against a bite assault situation.

Caution: The worst thing we can do when we are bitten is to pull away. A bite assault could be considered a deadly force situation.

PERFORMANCE: BITE DEFENSE

1. The defender stabilizes after being bitten on their arm or hand.
2. The defender distracts the aggressor by covering the aggressor's eyes with their free hand.
3. The defender *does not* pull away unless the aggressor opens their mouth.
4. The defender may need to grab the back of the aggressor's head and pull them in as they push the bitten limb/hand into the aggressor's mouth. Push-Pull! "Feed the Bite."
5. The defender may need to use a personal defensive technique to break free from the assault. If the aggressor falls back after being impacted by a personal defensive technique but does not open their mouth: **Move with them!**

Special Note: If personal defense techniques are used in these defenses, it MUST be for physical violence or deadly force situations. Any time force is used to defend yourself or others, it must be a last resort, reasonable, and you must be able to articulate what you did, why you did it, and how you did it.

DURING ALL DEFENSES:

- Use loud, repetitive defensive verbalizations (No! Stop! Get back! Let me go! Leave me alone! etc.) to direct the aggressor to stop attacking you.
- Use defensive movements (Escape)!

AFTER ALL DEFENSES:

- Follow agency policies and procedures in regard to self-defense.
- Report and document immediately.

REAR HAIR/COLLAR PULL DEFENSE

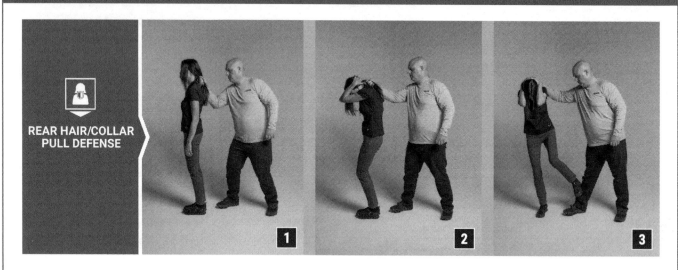

HAIR/COLLAR PULL DEFENSE

It is a technique that teaches individuals how to defend themselves from a hair/collar pull assault.

Objective: Demonstrate how to defend against a hair/collar pull.

Caution: The worst thing we can do when our hair is pulled is to pull away. Most hair pulls are done from behind the victim. A hair pull assault could be considered a deadly force situation, as the aggressor may pull the victim down from behind, causing a serious injury due to the fall/whiplash effect.

PERFORMANCE: HAIR/COLLAR PULL DEFENSE

1. The defender stabilizes after their hair has been pulled from behind.
2. The defender immediately interlaces their fingers together behind their head while bringing their chin down.
3. The defender does a slight quarter turn towards the aggressor.
4. The defender initiates a foot stomp onto the instep of the aggressor's foot.

Special Note: If personal defense techniques are used in these defenses, it MUST be for physical violence or deadly force situations. Any time force is used to defend yourself or others, it must be a last resort, reasonable, and you must be able to articulate what you did, why you did it, and how you did it.

DURING ALL DEFENSES:
- Use loud, repetitive defensive verbalizations (No! Stop! Get back! Let me go! Leave me alone! etc.) to direct the aggressor to stop attacking you.
- Use defensive movements (Escape)!

AFTER ALL DEFENSES:
- Follow agency policies and procedures in regard to self-defense.
- Report and document immediately.

FRONT HAIR/LAPEL PULL DEFENSE

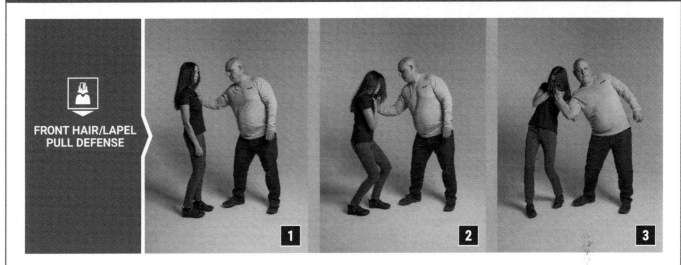

HAIR/LAPEL PULL DEFENSE

It is a technique that teaches individuals how to defend themselves from a hair/lapel pull assault.

Objective: Demonstrate how to defend against a hair/lapel pull.

Caution: The worst thing we can do when our hair is pulled is to pull away. Most hair pulls are done from behind the victim. A hair pull assault could be considered a deadly force situation, as the aggressor may pull the victim down from behind, causing a serious injury due to the fall/whiplash effect.

Special Note: If personal defense techniques are used in these defenses, it MUST be for physical violence or deadly force situations. Any time force is used to defend yourself or others, it must be a last resort, reasonable, and you must be able to articulate what you did, why you did it, and how you did it.

PERFORMANCE: HAIR/LAPEL PULL DEFENSE

1. The defender stabilizes after their hair/lapel has been pulled from the front.
2. The defender immediately interlaces their fingers together onto the hand of the aggressor while bringing their chin down.
3. The defender moves slightly forward toward the aggressor, getting their arm to bend.
4. Once the aggressor's arm is bent, the defender will place their elbow onto the same side of the aggressor's elbow and turn into the elbow until the release of hair/lapel.

DURING ALL DEFENSES:
- Use loud, repetitive defensive verbalizations (No! Stop! Get back! Let me go! Leave me alone! etc.) to direct the aggressor to stop attacking you.
- Use defensive movements (Escape)!

AFTER ALL DEFENSES:
- Follow agency policies and procedures in regard to self-defense.
- Report and document immediately.

FRONT STRANGLE DEFENSE

FRONT STRANGLE DEFENSE

It is a technique that teaches individuals how to defend themselves from a frontal strangle assault.

Objective: Demonstrate how to defend against a frontal strangle assault situation.

Note: A front strangle assault is more than likely done from close range unless a person has you up against a wall or pinned to the floor.

Special Note: If personal defense techniques are used in these defenses, it MUST be for physical violence or deadly force situations. Any time force is used to defend yourself or others, it must be a last resort, reasonable, and you must be able to articulate what you did, why you did it, and how you did it.

PERFORMANCE: FRONT STRANGLE DEFENSE

1. The defender stabilizes after being grabbed around the throat with both hands.
2. The defender can utilize a palm heel defense, knee defense, finger spears to the eyes, foot stomp, or any personal defense technique.
3. The defender may need to use repeated defensive moves to break free from this assault.
4. This assault is potentially life-threatening, and the defender will need to respond immediately to break free from the assault.

Special Note: If the front strangle assault is not a deadly force assault, the defender may use a distraction technique (by covering the eyes) and/or a middle block defense.

DURING ALL DEFENSES:

- Use loud, repetitive defensive verbalizations (No! Stop! Get back! Let me go! Leave me alone! etc.) to direct the aggressor to stop attacking you.
- Use defensive movements (Escape)!

AFTER ALL DEFENSES:

- Follow agency policies and procedures in regard to self-defense.
- Report and document immediately.

FRONT STRANGLE DEFENSE (SPECIAL SITUATION)

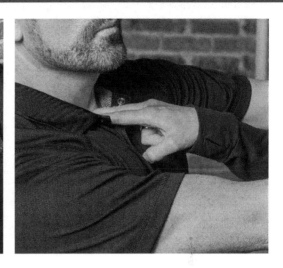

FRONT STRANGLE DEFENSE (SPECIAL SITUATION)

It is a technique that teaches individuals how to defend themselves from a frontal strangle assault.

Objective: Demonstrate how to defend against a frontal strangle assault situation.

Note: Typically, a front strangle assault is done from close range unless a person has you up against a wall or pinned to the floor.

Special Note: If personal defense techniques are used in these defenses, it MUST be for physical violence or deadly force situations. Any time force is used to defend yourself or others, it must be a last resort, reasonable, and you must be able to articulate what you did, why you did it, and how you did it.

PERFORMANCE: FRONT STRANGLE DEFENSE (SPECIAL SITUATION)

1. The defender stabilizes after being grabbed around the throat with both hands, arms extended.
2. The defender can utilize a finger spear technique to the bottom of the throat/top of the rib cage of the attacker.
3. Finger spear is done by placing two fingers together and pushing in and down.
4. The defender may need to turn their body sideways if the attacker's arms are long.
5. The defender may need to use other personal defense techniques.

DURING ALL DEFENSES:

- Use loud, repetitive defensive verbalizations (No! Stop! Get back! Let me go! Leave me alone! etc.) to direct the aggressor to stop attacking you.
- Use defensive movements (Escape)!

AFTER ALL DEFENSES:

- Follow agency policies and procedures in regard to self-defense.
- Report and document immediately.

REAR AIRWAY CHOKE DEFENSE

REAR AIRWAY CHOKE DEFENSE

It is a technique that teaches individuals how to defend themselves from a rear airway choke assault.

Objective: Demonstrate how to defend against a rear airway choke assault situation.

Note: A rear airway choke assault can compromise your ability to breathe and verbalize and render you unconscious. Individuals will need to respond *immediately* to this type of assault.

Special Note: If personal defense techniques are used in these defenses, it MUST be for physical violence or deadly force situations. Any time force is used to defend yourself or others, it must be a last resort, reasonable, and you must be able to articulate what you did, why you did it, and how you did it.

PERFORMANCE: REAR AIRWAY CHOKE DEFENSE

1. The defender stabilizes after being grabbed around the throat from behind.
2. The defender pulls the attacker's arm downward towards their core.
3. After the core is established, the defender will turn their head away from the attacker's elbow and place their palm under the attacker's elbow.
4. The defender will then pivot and push the attacker's elbow into the air to escape the assault.
5. The defender may need to use personal defense techniques to escape the assault.

DURING ALL DEFENSES:

- Use loud, repetitive defensive verbalizations (No! Stop! Get back! Let me go! Leave me alone! etc.) to direct the aggressor to stop attacking you.
- Use defensive movements (Escape)!

AFTER ALL DEFENSES:

- Follow agency policies and procedures in regard to self-defense.
- Report and document immediately.

REAR CAROTID CHOKE DEFENSE

REAR CAROTID CHOKE DEFENSE

It is a technique that teaches individuals how to defend themselves from a rear carotid choke assault.

Objective: Demonstrate how to defend against a rear carotid choke assault situation.

Note: A rear carotid choke assault can compromise your ability to breathe and verbalize and may render you unconscious. Individuals will need to respond *immediately* to this assault.

Special Note: If personal defense techniques are used in these defenses, it MUST be for physical violence or deadly force situations. Any time force is used to defend yourself or others, it must be a last resort, reasonable, and you must be able to articulate what you did, why you did it, and how you did it.

PERFORMANCE: REAR CAROTID CHOKE DEFENSE

1. The defender stabilizes and immediately place fingers into their carotid neck areas and pulls aggressor's arm downward to their core.
2. Once stabilized, the defender can bring their chin down and push up on the attackers elbow with the same side hand (shelf the elbow).
3. This position pushes the elbow onto the chin of the defender, allowing defender to breathe.
4. The defender can bite the arm of the attacker and use the hand, not at the elbow, for defense technique techniques. Defense techniques are used to escape.

DURING ALL DEFENSES:

- Use loud, repetitive defensive verbalizations (No! Stop! Get back! Let me go! Leave me alone! etc.) to direct the aggressor to stop attacking you.
- Use defensive movements (Escape)!

AFTER ALL DEFENSES:

- Follow agency policies and procedures in regard to self-defense.
- Report and document immediately.

REAR BEAR HOLD DEFENSE (PT. 1)

REAR BEAR HOLD DEFENSE

It is a technique that teaches individuals how to defend themselves from a rear bear-hold assault.

Objective: Demonstrate how to defend against a rear bear hold assault situation.

Note: A rear bear hold assault can compromise your ability to breathe as well as make you vulnerable to being picked up and thrown down or taken to another location.

Special Note: If personal defense techniques are used in these defenses, it MUST be for physical violence or deadly force situations. Any time force is used to defend yourself or others, it must be a last resort, reasonable, and you must be able to articulate what you did, why you did it, and how you did it.

PERFORMANCE: REAR BEAR HOLD DEFENSE

1. The defender stabilizes, immediately grabs attacker's hands, and bends forward using core.
2. Once bent forward, the defender launches their head back (head butt) into the face of the attacker.
3. The defender will head butt until arms are released.
4. Once arms are released, the defender may elbow or use other personal defense techniques to break free from the assault.
5. Defense techniques are used to escape.

Special Note: If the rear bear hold assault is not a deadly force assault, the defender may use a the finger pull technique. Pulling the aggressors finger that is exposed and pivoting away from them to defend.

DURING ALL DEFENSES:

- Use loud, repetitive defensive verbalizations (No! Stop! Get back! Let me go! Leave me alone! etc.) to direct the aggressor to stop attacking you.
- Use defensive movements (Escape)!

AFTER ALL DEFENSES:

- Follow agency policies and procedures in regard to self-defense.
- Report and document immediately.

...continued, REAR BEAR HOLD DEFENSE (PT. 2)

REAR BEAR HOLD DEFENSE

REAR BEAR HOLD DEFENSE

It is a technique that teaches individuals how to defend themselves from a rear bear-hold assault.

Objective: Demonstrate how to defend against a rear bear hold assault situation.

Note: A rear bear hold assault can compromise your ability to breathe as well as make you vulnerable to being picked up and thrown down or taken to another location.

Special Note: If personal defense techniques are used in these defenses, it MUST be for physical violence or deadly force situations. Any time force is used to defend yourself or others, it must be a last resort, reasonable, and you must be able to articulate what you did, why you did it, and how you did it.

PERFORMANCE: REAR BEAR HOLD DEFENSE

1. The defender stabilizes, immediately grabs attacker's hands, and bends forward using core.
2. Once bent forward, the defender launches their head back (head butt) into the face of the attacker.
3. The defender will head butt until arms are released.
4. Once arms are released, the defender may elbow or use other personal defense techniques to break free from the assault.
5. Defense techniques are used to escape.

Special Note: If the rear bear hold assault is not a deadly force assault, the defender may use a the finger pull technique. Pulling the aggressors finger that is exposed and pivoting away from them to defend.

DURING ALL DEFENSES:

- Use loud, repetitive defensive verbalizations (No! Stop! Get back! Let me go! Leave me alone! etc.) to direct the aggressor to stop attacking you.
- Use defensive movements (Escape)!

AFTER ALL DEFENSES:

- Follow agency policies and procedures in regard to self-defense.
- Report and document immediately.

MODULE 4

Post-Incident Response, Debriefing, and Documentation

Guidelines to follow after encountering a crisis incident

Module 4:
Post-Incident Response, Debriefing, and Documentation

Post-Incident Response

Post-incident response, debriefing, and documentation are essential steps in managing workplace violence incidents. The post-incident response involves immediate actions to ensure safety, provide medical and psychological support, and communicate with staff. Debriefing allows affected employees to discuss the incident, gather information, identify gaps in procedures, and develop improvement strategies. Comprehensive documentation is crucial for legal compliance, providing evidence for investigations, aiding learning and improvement, and maintaining accountability. These processes help organizations manage the aftermath of incidents, support employees, and enhance future prevention and response strategies.

Post-incident responses include:

Triage (medical/hazmat)
Triage is the process of determining the priority of patients' or victims' treatments based on the severity of their condition. Initial first-aid treatment and protocols for hazardous materials and clean-up should be handled immediately.

Report the incident
Report the incident to police, security, risk management, human resources, etc. Follow standard operating procedures in reporting incidents.

Consider all involved
Staff, guests, visitors, patients, or anyone who was witness to the incident should be treated accordingly for medical and stress debriefing.

Provide for incident debriefing
Debriefing allows those involved with the incident to process the event and reflect on its impact. Depending on the situation, a thorough debriefing may need to take place. Even those not specifically involved in an incident may suffer emotional and psychological trauma.

Critical Incident Stress Debriefing (CISD)
CISD is a specific technique designed to assist others in dealing with physical or psychological symptoms that are generally associated with critical incident trauma exposure.

Research on the effectiveness of critical incident debriefing techniques has demonstrated that individuals who are provided critical stress debriefing within a 24- to 72-hour window after experiencing the critical incident have lower levels of short- and long-term crisis reactions and psychological trauma.

Employee Assistance Programs (EAP)

EAPs are intended to help employees deal with work or personal problems that might adversely impact their work performance, health, and well-being. EAPs generally include assessment, short-term counseling, and referral services for employees and their household members. Employee benefit programs offered by many employers, typically in conjunction with health insurance plans, provide for payment for EAPs.

Document incident to include any follow-up investigations

Post-incident documentation is absolutely critical for reducing liability risk, preventing recurrences, and assisting in follow-up investigations.

Initiate corrective actions to prevent recurrences

Preventing similar future incidents involves taking proactive corrective actions. Agency management, supervision, security, risk management, employee safety committees, the environment of care committee, etc., should initiate, track, and follow up on corrective actions.

Post-Incident Debriefing

Post-incident stress debriefing involves methods designed to help manage stress after a traumatic event. These techniques focus on providing emotional support, promoting mental well-being, and fostering a sense of safety and stability among affected individuals. Debriefing sessions typically include discussing the incident, expressing feelings, and receiving professional guidance to process the experience. These methods aim to alleviate stress, prevent long-term psychological effects, and support the overall recovery process.

> The goal of debriefing is to reduce the chance of Post-Traumatic Stress symptoms and Post-Traumatic Stress Disorder (PTSD).

Post-incident debriefing includes:

- **Always debrief.** Staff should debrief after every workplace violence incident, regardless of the severity. Oftentimes a brief discussion of the events and outcome is enough. Other times, a more intensive debriefing is needed.

- **Talk to co-workers.** Almost all workers have experienced or witnessed some type of workplace violence incident. Your co-workers can be a great resource to vent your concerns about your feelings after an incident.

- **Acknowledge humanness.** As humans, we are susceptible to the frailties of human nature. This acknowledgement creates an awareness that it is okay to seek and ask for help.

- **Be aware of post-event feelings.** Having the knowledge and awareness that you may experience strong feelings from an event can give you the confidence to seek help and discuss feelings with others.

- **Take advantage of your Employee Assistance Program (EAP).** Agencies realize that feelings may persist for longer than you might expect after an incident. Employee Assistance Programs can benefit employees and help them deal with post-incident stress or other work/personal problems. EAPs are intended to help employees deal with problems or issues that might adversely affect their work performance, health, and well-being. EAPs generally include assessment, short-term counseling, and referral services for employees and their household members.

- **Know the signs and symptoms of Post-Traumatic Stress Disorder (PTSD).** PTSD is a psychological reaction occurring after experiencing a highly stressful event (such as wartime combat, physical violence, or a natural disaster). It's usually characterized by depression, anxiety, flashbacks, recurrent nightmares, and avoidance of reminders of the event.

- **Take the time to follow up with other staff.** As human beings, we often focus on the needs of others and not ourselves. Take the time to discuss workplace incidents, your feelings about the incidents, and how incidents in the workplace could improve.

- **Critical Incident Stress Debriefing (CISD).** Individuals who are exposed to an assault situation (as a witness or a victim) should consider some level of critical incident debriefing or counseling. The final extent of any traumatic situation may never be known or realistically estimated in terms of trauma, loss, and grief. In the aftermath of any critical incident, psychological reactions are quite common and are fairly predictable. CISD can be a valuable tool following a traumatic event.

Conducting an Incident Debrief

Staff should debrief after every workplace violence incident, regardless of the severity. Oftentimes a brief discussion of the events and outcome is enough. Other times, a more intensive debriefing is needed. **Debriefs are always positive!** After action, corrections should be done at a later date.

There are four primary steps for conducting an Incident Debrief:

1. **Wellness check**: The facilitator conducting the debrief asks each person involved and gets a verbal acknowledgement of their mental and physical wellness.

2. **What happened**: The facilitator conducting the debrief asks each person to briefly describe what they saw, heard, and experienced during the incident.

3. **What we did well**: The facilitator conducting the debrief will ask each person to briefly describe what the team did well in responding and dealing with the incident.

4. **How we can improve**: The facilitator conducting the debrief will ask each person to briefly describe what they believe the team (we) can improve upon in future incidents. Be positive!

BEHAVIORAL HEALTH
INCIDENT DEBRIEF PROCESS FORM

Conducting an Incident Debrief

- ☑ After a workplace violence incident, it is important that **all personnel involved in the incident meet immediately following the incident to debrief.**
- ☑ The debrief should be **led and documented by the supervisor and/or person in charge on duty** at the time of the incident, in coordination with security personnel.

FOUR PRIMARY STEPS TO CONDUCTING AN INCIDENT DEBRIEF:

1. **Wellness Check:** The facilitator conducting the debrief *asks each person* involved and gets a *verbal acknowledgement* of their **mental** and **physical wellness**.
    - The debrief leader will **assist in determining if anyone requires immediate or follow up medical treatment** as a result of *injury sustained* as a *result of the incident*.
    - If any personnel are identified as *sustaining injury* or *experiencing extensive stress* as a result of the incident, the agency will need to **follow up and provide further support and resources**, in line with the facilities policy & procedures.

2. **What Happened:** The facilitator conducting the debrief *ask each person* to briefly **describe what they saw, heard and experienced** during the incident.
    - It is important to assist in creating an environment within the debrief that allows **ALL individuals involved** to appropriately decompress and gain their composure prior to returning to regular job duties.

3. **What Did We Do Well:** The facilitator conducting the debrief will a*sk each person* to briefly **describe what the team (we) did well** in responding and dealing with the incident?
    - Often, individuals *immediately following an event* will still be experiencing a **high level of adrenaline**. This is especially true for those who may have not experienced a violent event very often.

4. **What Can we Improve Upon:** The facilitator conducting the debrief will ask each person to briefly describe what they believe the team (we) can improve upon in future incidents? Positive!!
    - An individual still experiencing an *adrenaline rush*, may not be aware of their need to decompress or how the incident may have impacted them emotionally and/or mentally. Because of this, as a **TEAM**, ensure that you encourage each other to take a moment and *assess your ability to return to your regular job duties*.

Staff should debrief after every workplace violence incident, *regardless of the severity*. Often times a brief discussion of the events and outcome is enough. Other times, a more intensive debriefing is needed. Debriefs are **always POSITIVE!** After action corrections should be *done at a later date*.

Remember: The goal of debriefing is to **reduce the chances of Post-Traumatic Stress Disorder** (PTSD) and **Post-Traumatic Stress Symptoms**.

A) Wellness Check: _____

B) What Happened: _____

C) What Did We Do Well: _____

D) What Can We Improve Upon: _____

Behavioral Health Crisis & De-Escalation Intervention Training
© Personal Safety Training Inc. | AVADE® Training

Post-Incident Documentation

Who–What–Where–When–Why–How?
The first rule in post-incident documentation is the "who, what, where, when, why, and how" rule of reporting. After writing an incident narrative, double-check to see if you have included the first rule of reporting.

Witnesses: Who was there?
Make sure to include anyone who was a witness to the incident. Staff, visitors, guests, and support services (police, fire, EMS, etc.) can be valuable witnesses should an incident be litigated.

Narrative characteristics
A proper narrative should describe in detail the characteristics of the violent offender/predator.

Before, during, and after
A thorough incident report will describe what happened before, during, and after the incident. Details matter!

First person vs. third person
The account of an incident can be described in the first person or the third person. This can be specific to your agency protocols or the preference of the person documenting the incident.

Post-follow-up (track and trend)
Most agencies use electronic documentation, which allows for easy retrieval, tracking, and trending. Using technology assists agencies in following up and initiating proactive corrections.

Follow standard operating procedures
Whether handwriting incident reports or using electronic documentation and charting, staff should consistently and thoroughly document all incidents relating to violence in the workplace.

Elements of Reporting Self-Defense Force

After any situation involving the defense of yourself or another person, proper documentation and reporting are crucial. The events of the assault or attempted assault should be reported to police/security. Police/security will document the incident and start an investigation. You should also document the account for your personal records. This can protect you in a possible legal situation that could arise out of using force to defend yourself. As you document your account of the incident, make sure to report to police/security any details you missed during your initial report to them.

What type of force/self-defense/technique was used during the incident?
Be specific in your documentation regarding the type of control, defense, and force used during the incident.

How long did the incident and resistance last?
Important to note the length of the resistance, as this is a factor relative to exhaustion and increasing the level of force.

Was any de-escalation used?
Verbal and non-verbal de-escalation techniques should be noted.

Were you in fear of injury (bodily harm) to yourself, others, or the subject?

Fear is a distressing emotion aroused by a perceived threat, impending danger, evil, or pain.

If so, why?

Fear is a basic survival mechanism occurring in response to a specific stimulus, such as pain or the threat of danger.

Explain thoroughly, and make sure to document completely.

The importance of documentation cannot be over-emphasized. Documentation ensures proper training standards are met, policies and procedures are understood, certification standards are met, liability and risk management are mitigated, and departmental and organizational requirements are maintained.

Every person must take into consideration their moral, legal, and ethical beliefs and rights, and understandings when using any type of force to defend themselves or others. Personal Safety Training Inc. makes no legal declaration, representation, or claim as to what force should be used or not used during a self-defense/assault incident or situation. Each individual must take into consideration their ability, agency policies and procedures, and laws in their state and/or country.

IF YOU OR SOMEONE YOU KNOW IS IN CRISIS AND CONSIDERING SELF-HARM OR SUICIDE:

- Call 911 for emergency services.
- Visit the nearest hospital emergency room.
- Call or text 988 to connect with the 988 Suicide and Crisis Lifeline, offering 24-hour, confidential support. *Para ayuda en español, llame al 988.*
- Support is also available via live chat at 988lifeline.org. *AVADE® does not monitor this website for crisis messages, provide medical advice, or make referrals.*

PSTI LEGAL DISCLAIMER

The information in this training book is a supplement, not a substitute, for the expertise of qualified healthcare professionals. The content on AVADE® Behavioral Health, sourced from reliable information, does not constitute medical or professional healthcare advice, diagnosis, or treatment. It is crucial to consult healthcare providers for specific guidelines related to medical or behavioral health conditions. This material does not guarantee that any technique or strategy is safe or effective for any specific needs. Personal Safety Training, Inc., does not dictate policies or procedures for behavioral health violence prevention, self-defense tactics, or any physical interventions. Agencies are responsible for developing their own policies and evaluating the recommendations based on their circumstances.

The author and publisher do not guarantee the completeness or accuracy of the information and assume no risk for its use. Any implied warranty are expressly disavowed.

AVADE® Level II Self-Defense Tactics and Techniques Review

> **SELF-DEFENSE FUNDAMENTALS**

> **DEFENSIVE BLOCKING TECHNIQUES**

> **SELF-DEFENSE TACTICS AND TECHNIQUES**

> **POST-INCIDENT RESPONSE, DEBRIEFING, AND DOCUMENTATION**

Workplace violence is, unfortunately, on the rise. By learning and studying the AVADE® strategies, integrating them, teaching them, and modeling them to your co-workers, you can lessen your chances of being a victim of workplace violence. Integrate the AVADE® safety principles into your workplace/life-place for defusing tense situations. Learn to identify the signs and symptoms of potential violence. Above all, learn to trust your instincts and listen to your intuition.

Remember: your best tools for keeping yourself safe are your own mind and personal safety habits.

AVADE® Behavioral Health
LEVEL III

Defensive Control Tactics and Techniques

Introduction to Defensive Control Tactics and Techniques

The goal of this section is to teach defensive control tactics and techniques. Most incidents can be prevented using your awareness, vigilance, and avoidance. However, there may be times when you need to physically control a subject that is out of control and a risk to themselves or others. **After any control tactics and techniques, always follow post-incident responses and documentation procedures.**

Before conducting any physical training, be sure to cover the following safety rules with your class. Safety is the most important rule in physical training.

In today's society, corporations, healthcare, schools, gaming, law enforcement, security, corrections, the military, and protective services agencies realize that defensive control tactics and techniques are essential for protecting themselves and the public they serve. These agencies also understand that mitigating liability begins with proper training and education in defensive control tactics strategies, and techniques.

The AVADE® training program is designed for agencies and staff to reduce the potential of injury and liability risk when lawfully defending themselves or controlling an aggressive individual. The tactics and techniques in this training curriculum are for incidents where the aggressor is physically combative, resistive, and unarmed.

This training manual provides training and education that is designed to empower individuals and to increase awareness, knowledge, skills, and actions regarding the use of force, control and restraint, self-defense, and defending others with defensive control tactics, strategies, and techniques.

This course stresses the importance of knowing your agency's policies and procedures in regard to using force and defending yourself or another person. The AVADE® training is intended to give the trainee the basic understanding of self-defense, use of force, control and restraint, reasonable force, and basic legal definitions of force. Personal Safety Training Inc. makes no legal declaration, representation, or claim as to what force should be used or not used during self-defense, use of force, or assault incident or situation. Each trainee must take into consideration their ability, agency policies and procedures, and laws in the state and country in which they reside.

Most individuals can learn and develop proficiency in the techniques covered in this training course. The course includes the fundamentals of basic defensive tactics, followed by contact and cover positioning, escort strategies and techniques, control and decentralization, prone and supine restraint, and post-incident response and documentation procedures.

AVADE® Training Safety Rules

1. Safety and waiver agreement
Each individual trained *must* complete the **Student Registration and Recertification Form**. The instructor will advise the student how to fill it out and answer any questions pertaining to it.

2. Weapons-free environment
NO WEAPONS are allowed anywhere in the training area. Instructor will advise participants in proper procedures in securing weapons and ammunition. Follow agency policy and procedures.

3. Remove jewelry, etc.
The following should not be worn during a class which involves hands-on training: all jewelry with sharp edges, pins or raised surfaces, or jewelry that encircles the neck.

4. No horseplay
Any participant who displays a disregard for safety to anyone in class will be asked to leave the class. Please practice only the technique currently being taught. **Do not practice unauthorized techniques.**

5. Pat out rule (used for partner techniques)
Upon hearing/feeling/seeing the "PAT," your partner applying the technique will immediately release the pressure of the technique to reduce discomfort/pain. The technique will be immediately and totally released on instructions from the instructor or when a safety monitor says "RELEASE," "STOP," or words similar to them.

6. Be a good "defender" and good "aggressor"
Essentially this means working together with your partner when practicing the techniques. Without cooperation while practicing self-defense or defensive control tactics techniques, time is wasted and injury potential is increased.

7. Practice techniques slowly at first
Gain balance and correctness slowly before practicing for speed. Proceed at the pace directed by your trainer.

8. Check equipment for added safety
The instructor will check *all* equipment used during the training to ensure proper function, working order and safety.

9. Advise instructor of any pre-existing injuries
Any injury or condition that could be further injured or aggravated should be brought to the immediate attention of your instructor, and your partner, prior to participating in any hands-on training.

10. Advise instructor of any injury during class
Any injury, regardless of what it is, needs to be reported to the primary instructor.

11. Safety is everyone's responsibility!
Safety is everyone's responsibility and everyone is empowered to immediately report or *yell out* any safety violation.

12. Training hazards
Always keep any items or training equipment and batons off the floor/ground and out of the way when not in use.

13. Safety markings
Colored wrist bands or blue tape marking is a visual aid for pre-existing injury. **Use caution.**

14. Leaving training area
If you must leave the training area for any reason, please advise your instructor prior to doing so.

AVADE® Level III Defensive Control Tactics Modules

FUNDAMENTALS OF DEFENSIVE CONTROL

CONTACT AND COVER POSITIONING

ESCORT STRATEGIES AND TECHNIQUES

CONTROL AND DECENTRALIZATION TECHNIQUES

POST-INCIDENT RESPONSE, DEBRIEFING, AND DOCUMENTATION

HEALTHCARE RESTRAINT HOLDS AND APPLICATIONS

Use of Force

> Use of force is a term that describes the right of an individual or authority to settle conflicts or prevent certain actions by applying measures to either:
> - dissuade another party from a particular course of action, OR
> - physically intervene to stop or control them.

Use of Force Awareness

Any use of force must be justified and legally warranted. When any force is used, the staff person must take into consideration their ability, agency policies and procedures, and laws in the state and country in which they reside. Unauthorized or inappropriate use of force may expose the staff person/agency to criminal/civil liability.

Center for Medicaid Services

AVADE® Level III Training aligns with the Center for Medicaid Services (CMS) COP § 482.13(e) (2). Restraint or seclusion may only be used when less restrictive interventions have been determined to be ineffective to protect the patient, a staff member, or others from harm.

Any intervention other than verbal de-escalation should only be used when it "is used for the management of violent or self-destructive behavior that jeopardizes the immediate physical safety of the patient, a staff member, or others," as defined by CMS.

Individuals (staff) *must* have a strong understanding of their agency policies and procedures regarding the use of force and self-defense.

VIOLENT OR SELF-DESTRUCTIVE BEHAVIOR CONTINUUM

This continuum of authority/care for using physical intervention reflects the minimum federal standard for restraint and seclusion as defined by CMS in *42 CFR § 482.13 (e) - Condition of participation: Patient's rights*.

Restraint or seclusion may only be used when less restrictive interventions have been determined to be ineffective in protecting the patient, a staff member, or others from harm.

Any intervention other than verbal de-escalation should only be used when it *"is used for the management of violent or self-destructive behavior that jeopardizes the immediate physical safety of the patient, a staff member, or others,"* as defined by CMS.

An agency's policies and procedures ultimately outline a person's responsibilities during restraint and seclusion interventions. Restraint and seclusion laws in some states may outline more job titles that have the authority to authorize restraint or seclusion for observed violent or self-destructive behavior.

1. PHYSICIAN OR LICENSED PRACTITIONER
A physician or licensed practitioner has the highest authority to order a patient into restraints or seclusion.

2. CHARGE NURSE/NURSE
If a patient provider is not present, the charge nurse or any nurse typically has the next highest authority to order a patient into restraints or seclusion.

3. BEHAVIORAL HEALTH STAFF, AVADE® CERTIFIED STAFF, LEO-SECURITY
When a doctor or nurse is not present, certain staff may intervene to stop violent or self-destructive behavior in an emergent situation.

4. ALL STAFF
All staff must be able to articulate in documentation "violent or self-destructive behavior that jeopardizes the immediate physical safety of the patient, a staff member, or others," as defined by *(CMS) COP §482.13(e)(2)* that leads up to the restraint or seclusion intervention.

Personal Safety Training Inc. makes no legal declaration, representation or claim as to what force should be used or not used during a self-defense, use of force incident, or assault incident or situation. Each trainee must take into consideration their ability, agency policies and procedures and laws in the state and country in which they reside.

MODULE 1

Fundamentals of Defensive Control

The foundation of the AVADE® hands-on tactics and techniques

Module 1: Fundamentals of Defensive Control

Every tactic and technique requires the use of fundamental laws. If you don't understand the fundamental rules of self-defense, your ability to defend yourself is compromised. A basic understanding and use of these laws will give you an advantage in a situation where you might need to use force to defend yourself or another person.

> **Fun·da·men·tal** (from the Latin medieval: *fundāmentālis*: late Middle English)
> —synonyms 1. Indispensable, primary.
> —adjective 1. Serving as, or being an essential part of, a foundation or basis; basic; underlying: *fundamental principles; the fundamental structure.*

Fundamentals of Defensive Control Overview

Stance | Balance | Stability

Defensive Movements

Core Energy Principle

Defensive Verbalization

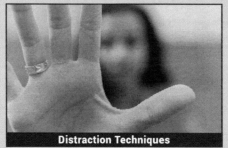
Distraction Techniques

Escape Strategies

Reactionary Gap

Hand Positions

On Target Training

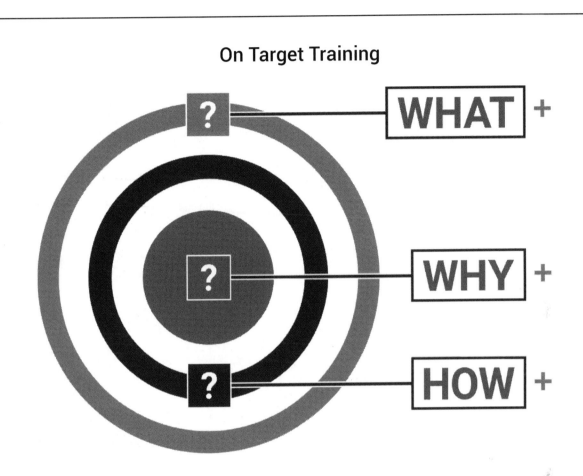

1. WHAT?
The WHAT describes a technique or tactic. The first step in teaching a hands-on technique is to explain what the technique is by the name of it. For example, we will be learning about defensive movement, and the first defensive movement technique is forward shuffle.

2. HOW?
The HOW is the manner or method, the technique or tactic is performed. The second step in teaching a hands-on technique is to explain and demonstrate how to do it. This step should be done a couple of times so that students can see it fully and completely.

3. WHY?
And most importantly is the WHY. It's the purpose, reason, intention, justification, or motive of a technique or tactic. The third step and most important step in teaching hands-on techniques are to explain why the technique is done a certain way and why you should have this technique in your arsenal of defenses. Without this understanding, the student is not bought into believing that the technique is needed or effective.

To really understand a technique or tactic, you must know the WHY (bullseye).

STANCE | BALANCE | STABILITY: BLADED STANCE

THE BLADED (DEFENSIVE) STANCE

All techniques are performed from the bladed stance/position.

Objective: Demonstrate how to correctly position your body to protect your vulnerable line and maintain stance, balance, and stability.

PERFORMANCE: BLADED STANCE

1. Face the clock (diagram on PowerPoint or imagine a clock in front of you) with your feet shoulder-width apart.
2. Step straight back with either left or right foot. Usually, individuals prefer to have their dominant foot to the rear.
3. If you stepped back with your right foot, turn your feet and body to the one o'clock position. If you stepped back with your left foot, turn your feet and body to the eleven o'clock position.
4. Keep your weight equal on both feet, and your knees slightly bent.

Caution: When back foot is behind front foot, you are positioned like being on a skateboard (common mistake - not stable).

PERFORMANCE: STABILITY TEST (BLADED STANCE)

Partner exercise (A and B)

1. Partner A places his/her feet together. Partner B gently pushes Partner A to the front, back, left side, and right side. Reverse roles.
2. Partner A stands with his/her feet shoulder-width apart. Partner B gently pushes partner A to the front, back, left side, and right side. Reverse roles.
3. Partner A now assumes the bladed stance. Partner B gently pushes Partner A to the front, back, left side, and right side. Reverse roles.

> **The Bladed Stance protects your "Vulnerable Line" away from the subject.**

DEFENSIVE MOVEMENTS: FORWARD SHUFFLE

Forward movement is used to engage a subject for control or defense.

FORWARD SHUFFLE

This defensive movement involves being able to move forward while maintaining balance and stability. All defensive tactics techniques are enhanced with defensive movement.

Objective: Demonstrate how to move forward correctly.

PERFORMANCE: FORWARD MOVEMENT

1. Assume the bladed stance.
2. Take a short step forward with your front foot (shuffle).
3. Follow up with a short step forward using your rear foot.
4. Continue forward, using forward shuffling movement.

Caution: If the feet come together, balance and stability are compromised (common mistake).

> The rule of defensive movement is:
> The foot that is closest to the direction you want to go always moves first.

DEFENSIVE MOVEMENTS: REAR SHUFFLE

Rear movement is used to disengage from an aggressor.

REAR SHUFFLE

This defensive movement involves being able to move to the rear (backward) while maintaining balance and stability. All defensive tactics techniques are enhanced with defensive movement.

Objective: Demonstrate how to correctly move to the rear.

PERFORMANCE: REAR MOVEMENT

1. Assume the bladed stance.
2. Take a short step back with the rear foot (shuffle).
3. Follow up with a short step back using your front foot.
4. Continue backward, using the rear shuffling movement.

Caution: If the feet come together, balance and stability are compromised (common mistake).

Caution: Backpedaling is another common mistake.

Caution: Beware of obstacles in your environment.

> The rule of defensive movement is:
> The foot that is closest to the direction you want to go always moves first.

DEFENSIVE MOVEMENTS: SIDE-TO-SIDE SHUFFLE

Side-to-side movement is used to avoid an attack from an aggressor.

SIDE-TO-SIDE SHUFFLE

This defensive movement involves being able to move side to side while maintaining balance and stability. All defensive tactics techniques are enhanced with defensive movement.

Objective: Demonstrate how to correctly move side to side.

PERFORMANCE: SIDE-TO-SIDE MOVEMENT

1. Assume the bladed stance.
2. Take a short step to the right using your right foot.
3. Follow up with a short step to the right using your left foot.
4. Take a short step to the left using your left foot.
5. Follow up with a short step to the left using your right foot.

Caution: If the feet come together, balance and stability are compromised (common mistake).

Caution: Crossing feet up is another common mistake.

Caution: Beware of obstacles in your environment.

> The rule of defensive movement is:
> The foot that is closest to the direction you want to go always moves first.

DEFENSIVE MOVEMENTS: FORWARD AND REAR PIVOTING

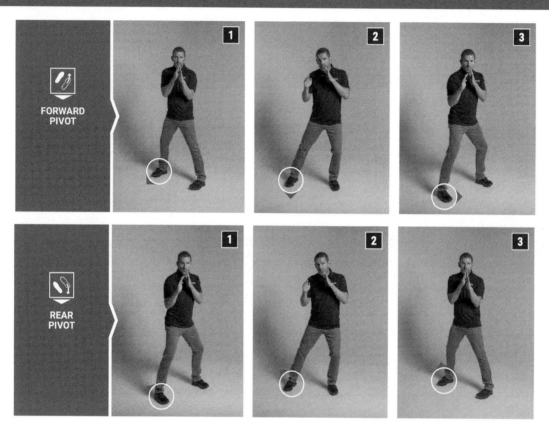

Pivoting is used to reposition or to enhance your energy when using personal defensive techniques or defensive control tactics.

FORWARD AND REAR PIVOTING

This defensive movement involves being able to pivot forward or back while maintaining balance and stability. All defensive tactics techniques are enhanced with defensive movement.

Objective: Demonstrate how to correctly pivot forward and backward.

PERFORMANCE: PIVOTING (FORWARD & BACK)

1. Assume the bladed stance.
2. Take an arcing step forward with your rear foot (forward pivot).
3. Take an arcing step backward with your front foot (rear pivot).
4. When pivoting forward or backward, always remain balanced and stable.
5. Pivots can be small movements or up to a 360-degree pivot.

Caution: If the feet come together, balance and stability are compromised (common mistake).

Caution: Crossing feet up is another common mistake.

Caution: Beware of obstacles in your environment.

ROBOT EXERCISE (THE BEST SELF-DEFENSE TECHNIQUE!)

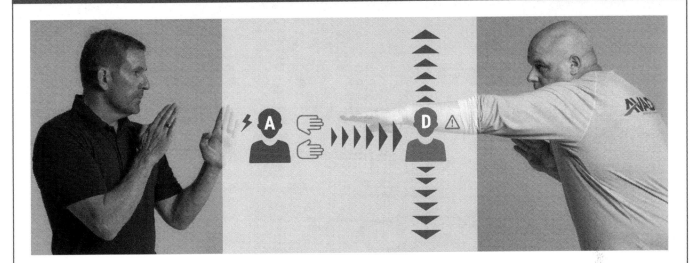

DEFENSIVE MOVEMENT "ROBOT EXERCISE"

The robot exercise involves being able to move in a lateral motion (side to side) to avoid an attack that is coming at you from a distance of 4' away or greater.

Objective: Demonstrate how to correctively avoid a forward attack by moving out of the way.

PERFORMANCE: "ROBOT EXERCISE"

1. The defender assumes a bladed defensive stance.
2. From 4–6' away, the attacker places hands out directly toward the defender.
3. Attacker moves forward toward the defender, attempting to gently touch either shoulder of the defender.
4. The defender waits for the last moment to move to either side, away from the attack.
5. Using sounds and/or movements will assist the defender in distracting the attacker.
6. Once out of the attack zone, defender can proceed to keep moving away from the attacker.

Caution: Do not move too late!

Caution: Do not move too soon, or the attacker will have time to adjust (reaction time) and follow/track you.

Caution: Crossing feet up is another common mistake.

Caution: Beware of obstacles in your environment.

CORE ENERGY PRINCIPLE

Energy and power are generated and developed from the core of the human body, even though a lot of emphasis is placed on the body's extremities.

The Core Energy Principle will:

- give you an advantage over aggressive subjects
- provide you power for counter blocks
- provide you power for defenses
- help you control and decentralize a physically resistive subject

CORE ENERGY

Our central and most essential part of our strength and power is our core energy. Without core energy, we rely on our extremities, which are not as strong as our central core. All defensive tactics techniques utilize this essential principle.

Objective: Demonstrate how to correctly use your core energy.

PERFORMANCE: CORE ENERGY

Partner exercise (A and B)

1. Partner A faces Partner B with his/her elbows away from their core.

2. Partner B moves forward toward Partner A. Partner A pushes Partner B back by pushing at their shoulders. How did it go? Reverse roles.

3. Partner A again faces Partner B with his/her elbows down towards their core. Partner B moves forward toward Partner A. Partner A pushes Partner B back by pushing at their shoulders. How did it go? Reverse roles.

- Provides direction to the aggressor
- Mitigates liability risk for you and the agency

Defensive Verbalization

During all defenses, use loud, repetitive defensive verbalizationsno!

NO!

STOP!

GET BACK!

STOP RESISTING!

BREAK YOUR FALL!

WE'RE GOING TO THE GROUND!

TURN YOUR HEAD

WE'RE GOING TO THE WALL!

Why use defensive verbalization?
- Creates witnesses
- Establishes authority
- Keeps you breathing
- May be used as a distraction
- Alerts others of a confrontation

The Art of Distraction

> The Art of Distraction is a process by which we can buy valuable time to escape, defend, or control.

Distractions affect the senses, which take time for the mind to process the new information. Distractions have been used since ancient times. A valuable advantage!

- **Sounds:** Using a loud scream or yell can cause a momentary delay.
- **Movements:** Using your hands, eyes, and body can distract and cause a momentary delay.
- **Psychological:** Asking a question that is out of the ordinary can cause them a mental delay.
- **Lights:** Flashlights, the sun, emergency lights, etc., can cause a delay.

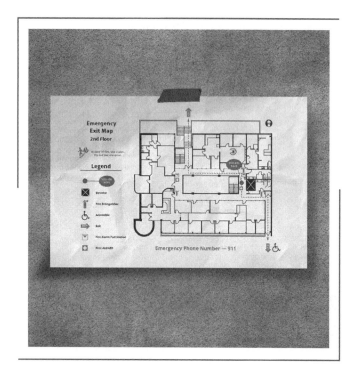

Escape Strategies

Escape is the act or instance of breaking free from danger or threat or from being trapped, restrained, confined, or isolated against your will.

Planning is the cognitive process of thinking about what you will do in the event of something happening.

REACTIONARY GAP EXERCISE

The "Reactionary Gap" is 4–6 feet: The distance between and you and an aggressor in which your ability to react/respond is impaired due to the close proximity of the aggressor.

When we are approaching individuals who are in the Assault Cycle (stressed, intoxicated, angry, escalated), we should approach them at a 45-degree angle versus approaching them head-on. We then proceed with our 5 Habits and maintain the appropriate distance from them.

- Action beats reaction within the Reactionary Gap.
- When we are too close to an individual, it can cause them anxiety and escalate them.
- When we lean in, we appear to be closer than we really are.
- A minimum distance of 4–6 feet is always recommended.
- Avoid using statements that can escalate a person.

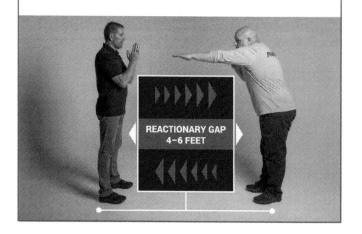

REACTIONARY GAP EXERCISE, PART ONE

"Reactionary Gap" is the distance between and individual and an aggressor in which the ability to react is impaired due to the close proximity of the aggressor.

1. Form two lines with participants facing each other at approximately 10' apart.
2. Have **Line A** approach **Line B** until they are arm's length away from them and able to touch their shoulder.
3. Have both **Line A** and **Line B** place their hands in the prayer position.
4. **Line A** will begin by quickly touching **Line B**'s shoulder with either hand. (Always come back to the prayer position. The touching of the shoulder is simulating an unarmed attack.)
5. **Line B** will try to defend against the shoulder attack by blocking with either hand or moving out of the way.
6. Reverse the roles of attacker and defender.
7. How did it go? Who didn't get hit?

> "Action beats reaction within the Reactionary Gap"

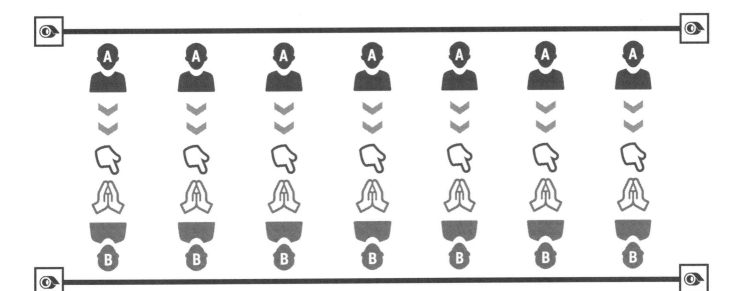

REACTIONARY GAP EXERCISE, PART TWO

"Reactionary Gap" is the distance between and individual and an aggressor in which the ability to react is impaired due to the close proximity of the aggressor.

1. Form two lines with participants facing each other at approximately 10' apart.
2. Now instruct Line B to stop Line A as they approach with 4–6' of distance away from them.
3. Line A will again attack Line B's shoulder from this new distance (4–6'). Notice that Line A must lunge in, in order to reach Line B's shoulder.
4. Line B, again will defend by blocking with either hand or moving out of the way.
5. How did it go, Line B?
6. Reverse the roles of attacker and defender.

> The minimum distance needed in order to react to an unarmed attack is 4–6' away from the attacker.

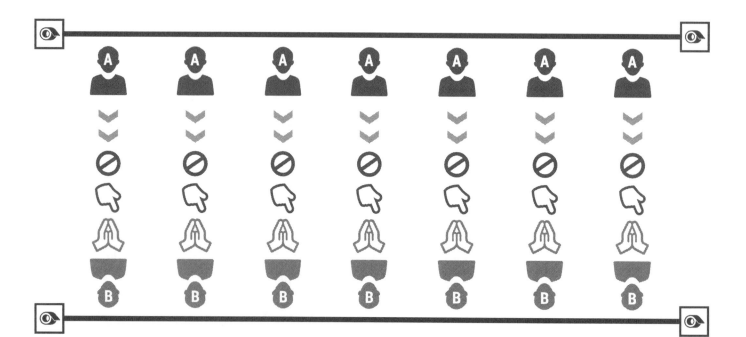

HAND POSITIONS

There are five basic hand positions.

Objective: Demonstrate how to correctly use your hands in the open, authority, stop, caution, and directive positions.

PERFORMANCE: OPEN OR AUTHORITY HAND POSITIONS

1. Assume the bladed stance.
2. Position your arms with your elbows down and your palms facing upward (Open).
3. Position your arms with your elbows down and your palms down (Authority).

PERFORMANCE: STOP OR CAUTION HAND POSITIONS

1. Assume the bladed stance.
2. Position your arms with your elbows down and your palms facing outward (Stop).
3. The non-verbal message says, "Don't come close to me," or a non-threatening message if you are moving forward (Caution).

PERFORMANCE: DIRECTIVE HAND POSITIONS

1. Assume the bladed stance.
2. Position your arms/hands, pointing with your open hand in the direction you want them to go (Directive).

Caution: Do not point when giving directions, as pointing is perceived as a derogatory gesture.
Caution: Closing your hands into a fist position may send a message of aggression.

Contact and Cover Positioning

MODULE 2

The primary strategy of the Defensive Tactics System™

Module 2:
Contact and Cover Positioning

Contact and Cover (Team Positioning) is the main strategy for the AVADE® Level III Defensive Control Tactics System. Contact and Cover techniques are used by individuals during situations where they are dealing with a subject(s). The purpose of the technique is to deter a situation from getting out of control, and to improve the individual's safety by having other individuals in a constant state of preparation to act in the event that the situation gets out of control.

Contact and Cover should be used for all situations involving subjects and witnesses.

Contact (team leader)
The contact individual is the focal point for the subject (the aggressor), as this individual is the primary communicator giving directions to the subject. In many situations, the contact individual(s) will initiate communications.

In the pictures, the contact individual is communicating with the subject, which may act as a distraction, allowing cover individuals (team members) to move in and escort subject or gain physical control if needed/approved. The contact individual should have a prearranged "cue" (verbal or non-verbal) alerting the cover individuals to initiate any engagement.

Cover (team members)
The role of the cover individual(s) is to watch subject(s) for any attempt to flee or assault the contact individual. The cover individual(s) should be ever-vigilant, ready to respond, and ready to alert the contact individual of a suspicious activity or an imminent attempt at assault.

> Special Note: Cover individuals should maintain their distance (stay back) until needed (see top picture on the right). Moving in too soon may cause the subject to feel cornered.

INITIAL CONTACT FRONT: 1-PERSON (PT. 1)

INITIAL CONTACT FRONT (1-PERSON)

This is a technique that teaches individuals how to safely approach a subject and make initial contact.

Objective: Demonstrate how to safely approach a subject while moving forward with defensive movement to make physical contact.

Note: A 2-person Initial Contact is safer as you have controlled both arms of the aggressor.

Note: This technique can be done to the front or behind the subject. It is safer to perform from behind the subject.

PERFORMANCE: INITIAL CONTACT FRONT (1-PERSON)

1. Move forward towards the subject at a 45-degree angle.
2. Use defensive movement and keep your hands in a cautious position.
3. Your body should be bladed away (vulnerable line) from the subject. Left side forward on the left side of the subject, and right side forward on the right side of the subject.
4. Firmly capture the elbow of the subject with both hands (thumbs up).
5. Bring your shoulder slightly forward to further protect your vulnerable line if you are in front of the subject. Avoid this if you are behind the subject.

Caution: Armed individuals should keep their gun side back and away from the subject regardless of their approaching side.

Caution: Approaching a subject to the front is more dangerous for the individual than approaching from behind.

...continued, INITIAL CONTACT FRONT: 1-PERSON (PT. 2)

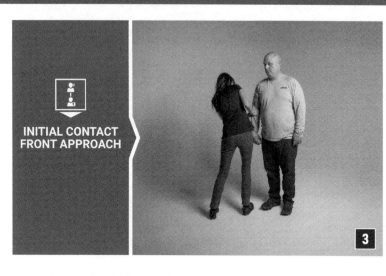

INITIAL CONTACT FRONT (1-PERSON)

This is a technique that teaches individuals how to safely approach a subject and make initial contact.

Objective: Demonstrate how to safely approach a subject while moving forward with defensive movement to make physical contact.

Note: A 2-person Initial Contact is safer as you have controlled both arms of the aggressor.

Note: This technique can be done to the front or behind the subject. It is safer to perform from behind the subject.

PERFORMANCE: INITIAL CONTACT FRONT (1-PERSON)

1. Move forward towards the subject at a 45-degree angle.
2. Use defensive movement and keep your hands in a cautious position.
3. Your body should be bladed away (vulnerable line) from the subject. Left side forward on the left side of the subject, and right side forward on the right side of the subject.
4. Firmly capture the elbow of the subject with both hands (thumbs up).
5. Bring your shoulder slightly forward to further protect your vulnerable line if you are in front of the subject. Avoid this if you are behind the subject.
6. Once initial contact/control is established, pivot behind the subject.

Caution: Armed individuals should keep their gun side back and away from the subject regardless of their approaching side.

Caution: Approaching a subject to the front is more dangerous for the individual than approaching from behind.

INITIAL CONTACT FRONT: 2-PERSON (PT. 1)

INITIAL CONTACT FRONT APPROACH

INITIAL CONTACT FRONT (2-PERSON)

This is a technique that teaches individuals how to safely approach a subject and make initial contact.

Objective: Demonstrate how to safely approach a subject while moving forward with defensive movement to make physical contact.

Note: A 2-person Initial Contact is safer as you have controlled both arms of the aggressor.

Note: This technique can be done to the front or behind the subject. It is safer to perform from behind the subject.

PERFORMANCE: INITIAL CONTACT FRONT (2-PERSON)

1. Move forward towards the subject at a 45-degree angle.
2. Use defensive movement and keep your hands in a cautious position.
3. Your body should be bladed away (vulnerable line) from the subject. Left side forward on the left side of the subject, and right side forward on the right side of the subject.
4. Firmly capture the elbow of the subject with both hands (thumbs up).
5. Bring your shoulder slightly forward to further protect your vulnerable line if you are in front of the subject. Avoid this if you are behind the subject.

Caution: Armed individuals should keep their gun side back and away from the subject regardless of their approaching side.

Caution: Approaching a subject to the front is more dangerous for the individual than approaching from behind.

...continued, INITIAL CONTACT FRONT: 2-PERSON (PT. 2)

INITIAL CONTACT FRONT APPROACH

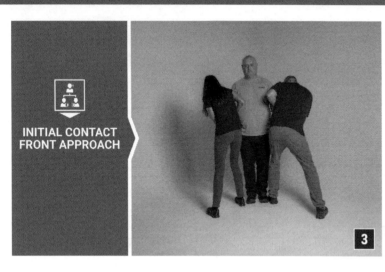

INITIAL CONTACT FRONT (2-PERSON)

This is a technique that teaches individuals how to safely approach a subject and make initial contact.

Objective: Demonstrate how to safely approach a subject while moving forward with defensive movement to make physical contact.

Note: A 2-person Initial Contact is safer as you have controlled both arms of the aggressor.

Note: This technique can be done to the front or behind the subject. It is safer to perform from behind the subject.

PERFORMANCE: INITIAL CONTACT FRONT (2-PERSON)

1. Move forward towards the subject at a 45-degree angle.
2. Use defensive movement and keep your hands in a cautious position.
3. Your body should be bladed away (vulnerable line) from the subject. Left side forward on the left side of the subject, and right side forward on the right side of the subject.
4. Firmly capture the elbow of the subject with both hands (thumbs up).
5. Bring your shoulder slightly forward to further protect your vulnerable line if you are in front of the subject. Avoid this if you are behind the subject.
6. Once initial contact/control is established, pivot behind the subject.

Caution: Armed individuals should keep their gun side back and away from the subject regardless of their approaching side.

Caution: Approaching a subject to the front is more dangerous for the individual than approaching from behind.

INITIAL CONTACT REAR: 1-PERSON

INITIAL CONTACT REAR (1-PERSON)

This is a technique that teaches individuals how to safely approach a subject and make initial contact.

Objective: Demonstrate how to safely approach a subject while moving forward with defensive movement to make physical contact.

Note: A 2-person Initial Contact is safer as you have controlled both arms of the aggressor.

Note: This technique can be done to the front or behind the subject. It is safer to perform from behind the subject.

PERFORMANCE: INITIAL CONTACT REAR (1-PERSON)

1. Move forward towards the subject at a 45-degree angle.
2. Use defensive movement and keep your hands in a cautious position.
3. Your body can be bladed away (to protect your vulnerable line) from the subject, but it is not necessary. Left side forward on left of subject and right side forward on the right side of the subject.
4. Firmly capture the elbow of the subject with both hands (thumbs up).

Caution: Armed individuals should keep their gun side back and away from the subject regardless of their approaching side.

Caution: Approaching a subject to the front is more dangerous for the individual than approaching from behind.

INITIAL CONTACT REAR: 2-PERSON

INITIAL CONTACT REAR (2-PERSON)

This is a technique that teaches individuals how to safely approach a subject and make initial contact.

Objective: Demonstrate how to safely approach a subject while moving forward with defensive movement to make physical contact.

Note: A 2-person Initial Contact is safer as you have controlled both arms of the aggressor.

Note: This technique can be done to the front or behind the subject. It is safer to perform from behind the subject.

PERFORMANCE: INITIAL CONTACT REAR (2-PERSON)

1. Move forward towards the subject at a 45-degree angle.
2. Use defensive movement and keep your hands in a cautious position.
3. Your body can be bladed away (to protect your vulnerable line) from the subject, but it is not necessary. Left side forward on left of subject and right side forward on the right side of the subject.
4. Firmly capture the elbow of the subject with both hands (thumbs up).

Caution: Armed individuals should keep their gun side back and away from the subject regardless of their approaching side.

Caution: Approaching a subject to the front is more dangerous for the individual than approaching from behind.

CONTACT AND COVER: 2-PERSON (PT. 1)

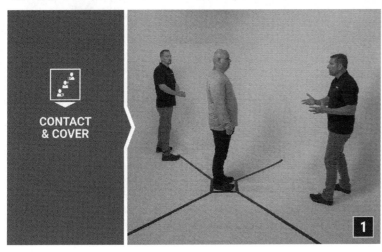 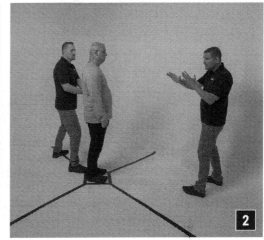

CONTACT AND COVER (2-PERSON)

This is a technique that teaches individuals how to safely approach a subject and make contact using a team approach.

Objective: Demonstrate how to safely approach a subject using contact and cover in a team approach.

PERFORMANCE: CONTACT AND COVER (2-PERSON)

1. The contact staff person is in front of the subject at a 45-degree angle.
2. The cover staff person is behind the subject at a 45-degree angle.
3. The contact staff person will initiate cover to move in and apply the initial contact technique by using verbal and nonverbal cues.
4. The nonverbal cue could be the contact staff person scratching their head.
5. The verbal cue could be the use of the word "green" in the context of a psychological distraction.

Caution: If the cover staff person moves in too soon, it could escalate the situation by not allowing the contact person enough time to attempt to de-escalate the subject.

Caution: Armed individuals should keep their gun side back and away from the subject regardless of their approaching side.

Caution: Approaching a subject to the front is more dangerous for the individual than approaching from behind.

Note: A 3-person Contact and Cover is safer as you have controlled both arms of the subject.

...continued, CONTACT AND COVER: 2-PERSON (PT. 2)

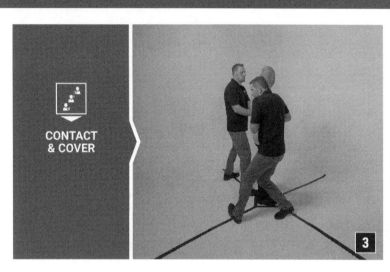
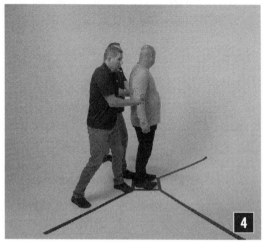

CONTACT AND COVER (2-PERSON)

This is a technique that teaches individuals how to safely approach a subject and make contact using a team approach.

Objective: Demonstrate how to safely approach a subject using contact and cover in a team approach.

PERFORMANCE: CONTACT AND COVER (2-PERSON)

6. Once the cover has made initial contact, the subject will more than likely turn towards the cover staff person.
7. Immediately, the contact staff person will move into initial contact from the front to gain control and then pivot behind the subject.
8. From here, both the contact and cover staff are behind the subject at a 45-degree angle using the initial contact technique.
9. Once this control is established, the staff can transition into a hands-on escort.

Caution: If the cover staff person moves in too soon, it could escalate the situation by not allowing the contact person enough time to attempt to de-escalate the subject.

Caution: Armed individuals should keep their gun side back and away from the subject regardless of their approaching side.

Caution: Approaching a subject to the front is more dangerous for the individual than approaching from behind.

Note: A 3-person Contact and Cover is safer as you have controlled both arms of the subject.

CONTACT AND COVER: 3-PERSON

CONTACT AND COVER: 3-PERSON

This is a technique that teaches individuals how to safely approach a subject and make contact using a team approach.

Objective: Demonstrate how to safely approach a subject using contact and cover in a team approach.

PERFORMANCE: CONTACT AND COVER: 3-PERSON

1. The contact staff person is in front of the subject at a 45-degree angle.
2. The cover staff are behind the subject at 45-degree angles.
3. The contact staff person will initiate the cover staff to move in and apply the initial contact technique by using verbal and nonverbal cues.
4. The nonverbal cue could be the contact staff person scratching their head.
5. The verbal cue could be the use of the word "green" in the context of a psychological distraction.
6. Once this control is established, the cover staff can transition into a hands-on escort while the contact staff person clears a path for them to follow.

Caution: If the cover staff persons move in too soon, it could escalate the situation by not allowing the contact person enough time to attempt to de-escalate the subject.

Caution: Armed individuals should keep their gun side back and away from the subject regardless of their approaching side.

Caution: Approaching a subject to the front is more dangerous for the individual than approaching from behind.

MODULE 3

Escort Strategies and Techniques

Techniques for safely moving cooperative and uncooperative subjects.

Module 3:
Escort Strategies and Techniques

Escort techniques are often used to safely move a person from one location to another. These techniques are commonly employed in various contexts, including security, law enforcement, healthcare, and protective services. The goal is to ensure the safety and well-being of the person being escorted while minimizing potential risks or threats during the transportation process.

Escort (es-kawrt)
Noun
1. A group of persons, or a single person, accompanying another or others for protection, guidance, or courtesy.
2. An armed guard, as a body of soldiers or ships.
3. Protection, safeguard, or guidance on a journey.

Verb (used with object)
1. To attend or accompany as an escort.

Strategy (strat-i-jee)
Noun
1. Also strategics. the science or art of combining and employing the means of war in planning and directing large military movements and operations.
2. The use or an instance of using this science or art.
3. A plan, method, or series of maneuvers or stratagems for obtaining a specific goal or result.

Technique (tek-neek)
Noun
1. The manner and ability with which an artist, writer, dancer, athlete, or the like employs the technical skills of a particular art or field of endeavor.

ESCORT STRATEGIES AND TECHNIQUES: 1-PERSON

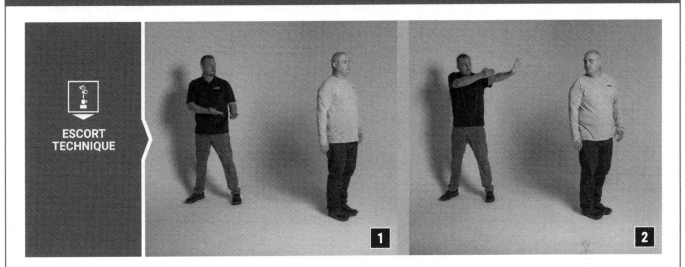

ESCORT TECHNIQUE (1-PERSON)

This is a technique that teaches individuals how to safely escort a cooperative subject.

Objective: Demonstrate how to safely escort a cooperative subject using proper distancing, verbal communication, and non-verbal communication.

PERFORMANCE: ESCORT TECHNIQUE (1-PERSON)

1. Maintain a 45-degree angle and distance of 4-6 feet behind the individual.
2. Direct the subject where you want them to go.
3. Use proper verbal and non-verbal skills.
4. Do not point; use open hand gestures.
5. Maintain awareness.

Caution: If the subject stops and moves towards you, use verbal and non-verbal communication, and defensive movements.

ESCORT STRATEGIES AND TECHNIQUES: 2-PERSON

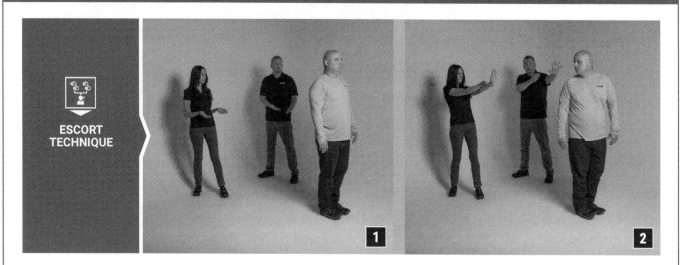

ESCORT TECHNIQUE (2-PERSON)

This is a technique that teaches individuals how to safely escort a cooperative subject.

Objective: Demonstrate how to safely escort a cooperative subject using proper distancing, verbal communication, and non-verbal communication.

PERFORMANCE: ESCORT TECHNIQUE (2-PERSON)

1. Maintain a 45-degree angle and distance of 4-6 feet behind the individual.
2. Direct the subject where you want them to go.
3. Use proper verbal and non-verbal skills.
4. Do not point; use open hand gestures.
5. Maintain awareness.

Caution: If the subject stops and moves towards you, use verbal and non-verbal communication, and defensive movements.

HANDS-ON ESCORT TECHNIQUE: 1-PERSON

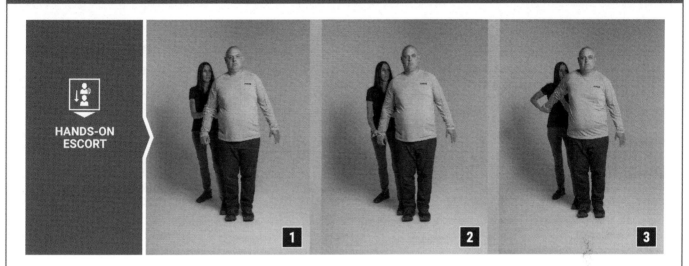

HANDS-ON ESCORT TECHNIQUE (1-PERSON)

This is a technique that teaches an individual how to escort a subject using light subject control.

Objective: Demonstrate how to safely escort a passive-resistive subject using light subject control with proper hand and body positioning.

PERFORMANCE: HANDS-ON ESCORT TECHNIQUE (1-PERSON)

1. Begin in the initial contact position.
2. If you are on the right side of the subject, your right-hand slides down and grips the wrist. Same for the left side.
3. Bring the subject's gripped wrist to the side of your body (holstered position).
4. The subject's palm should be facing upward, and above any defensive tools you may be carrying.
5. Maintain a 45-degree angle behind the subject and escort them to the desired location.

Caution: When gripping the appropriate wrist, the web of your hand should be on the ulna side of the subject's wrist. This ensures that their core strength is eliminated due to proper positioning.

Caution: When initiating the hands-on escort and when moving the subject, remember to stay at a 45-degree angle behind the subject.

HANDS-ON ESCORT TECHNIQUE: 2-PERSON

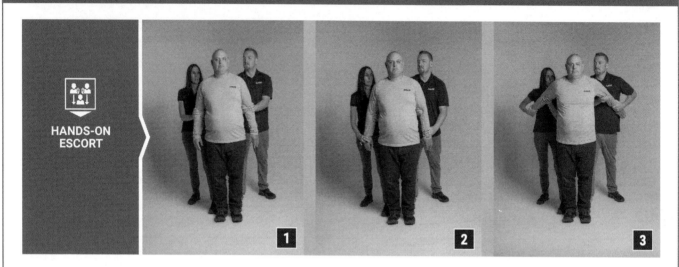

HANDS-ON ESCORT TECHNIQUE (2-PERSON)

This is a technique that that teaches an individual how to escort a subject using light subject control.

Objective: Demonstrate how to safely escort a passive-resistive subject using light subject control with proper hand and body positioning.

PERFORMANCE: HANDS-ON ESCORT TECHNIQUE (2-PERSON)

1. Begin in the initial contact position.
2. If you are on the right side of the subject, your right-hand slides down and grips the wrist. Same for the left side.
3. Bring the subject's gripped wrist to the side of your body (holstered position).
4. The subject's palm should be facing upward, and above any defensive tools you may be carrying.
5. Maintain a 45-degree angle behind the subject and escort them to the desired location.

Caution: When gripping the appropriate wrist, the web of your hand should be on the ulna side of the subject's wrist. This ensures that their core strength is eliminated due to proper positioning.

Caution: When initiating the hands-on escort and when moving the subject, remember to stay at a 45-degree angle behind the subject.

Caution: Both individuals acting with the same timing and control can reduce the possibility of escalation.

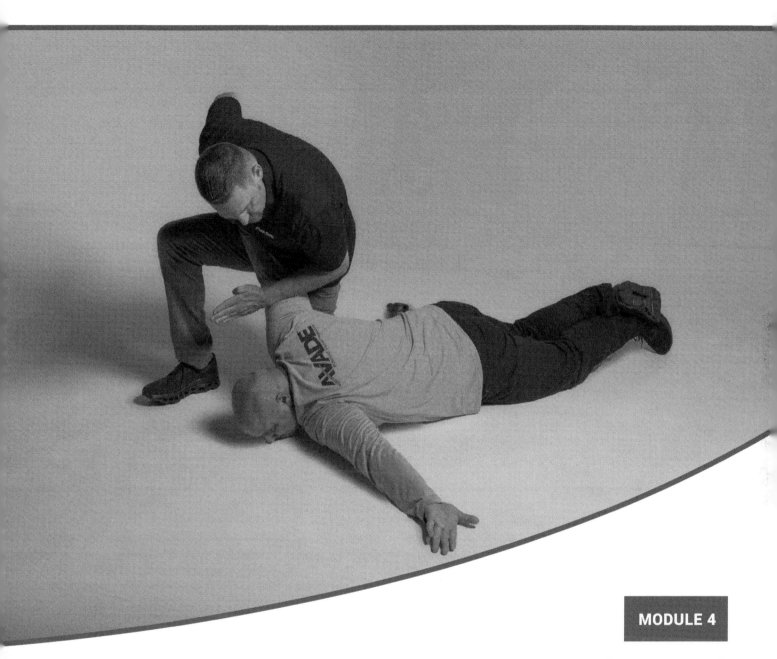

MODULE 4

Control and Decentralization

Techniques for dealing with violent and aggressive behavior

Module 4:
Control and Decentralization

Controlling and decentralizing a combative individual helps ensure the safety of themselves and others. It prevents the escalation of conflicts that may lead to physical harm or damage.

Control (kuhn-trohl)
Noun

1. The act or power of controlling; regulation; domination or command.
2. The situation of being under the regulation, domination, or command of another. Verb (used with object)
3. To exercise restraint or direction over; dominate: command.
4. To hold in check; curb.

Decentralize (dee-sen-truh-lahyz)
Verb

1. To distribute the administrative powers or functions of (a central authority) over a less concentrated area.
2. To disperse (something) from an area of concentration.
3. To undergo decentralization.

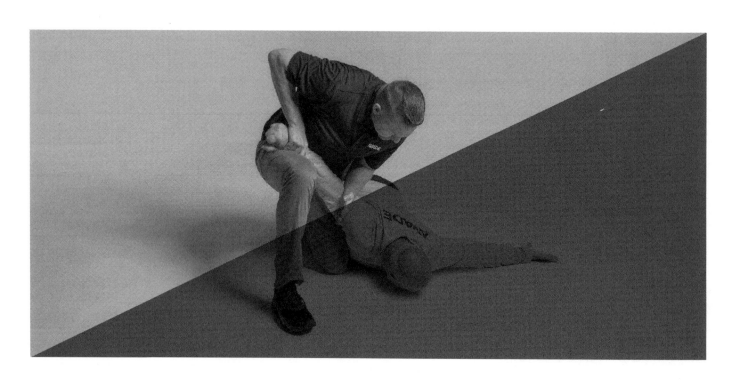

ONE-ARM TAKEDOWN (PT. 1)

ONE-ARM TAKEDOWN

This is a technique that teaches an individual how to decentralize a resistive subject using a takedown control technique. This technique is for a subject who is displaying violent or self-destructive behavior towards themselves or others.

Objective: Demonstrate how to control a subject using a one-arm takedown for a subject who is actively resisting.

PERFORMANCE: ONE-ARM TAKEDOWN

1. Begin in the hands-on escort position.
2. The individual will place their wrist onto the tricep of the subject (2–3 inches above the elbow).
3. The individual will then apply pressure to the tricep while moving forward or pivoting to the rear.

Caution: Be aware of your environment and what direction you are moving the resistive subject towards.

CONTINUALLY MONITOR THE SUBJECT AND SEEK MEDICAL ATTENTION IF NEEDED.

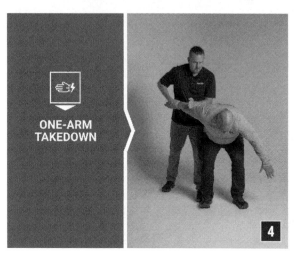

ONE-ARM TAKEDOWN

This is a technique that teaches an individual how to decentralize a resistive subject using a takedown control technique. This technique is for a subject who is displaying violent or self-destructive behavior towards themselves or others.

Objective: Demonstrate how to control a subject using a one-arm takedown for a subject who is actively resisting.

PERFORMANCE: ONE-ARM TAKEDOWN

4. Use loud, defensive verbalizations (e.g., NO, STOP, STOP RESISTING, WE'RE GOING DOWN, BREAK YOUR FALL) to direct the aggressor to stop resisting you and to direct them down.
5. Continue to use movement and pressure on the tricep to direct the aggressor to the ground.

Caution: Be aware of your environment and what direction you are moving the resistive subject towards.

Caution: The prone position is a temporary position that may predispose the subject to breathing difficulties.

PRONE CONTROL IS A TEMPORARY POSITION!

CONTINUALLY MONITOR THE SUBJECT AND SEEK MEDICAL ATTENTION IF NEEDED.

PRONE CONTROL POSITION

PRONE CONTROL POSITIONS

PRONE POSITION CAUTION

- Individuals in a prone position may have difficulty breathing.
- Monitor individuals and place them on their side, seated position, or get them up as soon as possible.

POSITIONAL ASPHYXIA

Positional asphyxia is a form of asphyxia that occurs when someone's position prevents them from breathing adequately. A small but significant number of people die suddenly and without apparent reason during restraint by police, prison (corrections) officers, and healthcare staff. Positional asphyxia may be a factor in some of these deaths. Research has suggested that restraining a person in a face-down position is likely to cause greater restriction of breathing than restraining a person face up.

Many law enforcement and health personnel are now taught to avoid restraining people face down or to do so only for a very short period of time.

PRONE CONTROL IS A TEMPORARY POSITION!

CONTINUALLY MONITOR THE SUBJECT AND SEEK MEDICAL ATTENTION IF NEEDED.

STANDING THE PRONE SUBJECT (PT. 1)

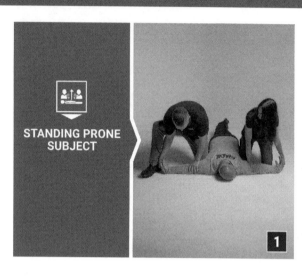

STANDING PRONE SUBJECT

STANDING THE PRONE SUBJECT

This is a technique that teaches an individual(s) how to stand a prone controlled subject.

Objective: Demonstrate how to stand a subject who has been placed in a prone controlled position (one or two individuals are needed).

PERFORMANCE: STANDING THE PRONE SUBJECT

1. Once control is established, verbalize to the subject to place their hands in the pushup position.
2. Direct them to push their knees up under them to prepare to stand.
3. Maintain contact with the subject's arms and wrists.

Caution: Verbalization and constant control is the key to standing a prone controlled subject. Maintain your balance and be prepared to escape if needed.

PRONE CONTROL IS A TEMPORARY POSITION!

...continued, STANDING THE PRONE SUBJECT (PT. 2)

STANDING PRONE SUBJECT

STANDING THE PRONE SUBJECT

This is a technique that teaches an individual(s) how to stand a prone controlled subject.

Objective: Demonstrate how to stand a subject who has been placed in a prone controlled position (one or two individuals are needed).

PERFORMANCE: STANDING THE PRONE SUBJECT

4. Once subject is on their hands and knees, step back 45 degrees behind them as you holster their hands to your sides.
5. Direct subject to place one knee up in front of them. Allow them to bring their chest up, so that this is possible.
6. Direct subject to now bring their other foot forward so that they can be escorted.

Caution: Verbalization and constant control is the key to standing a prone controlled subject. Maintain your balance and be prepared to escape if needed.

PRONE CONTROL IS A TEMPORARY POSITION!

ESCORTING THE COMBATIVE SUBJECT

ESCORTING THE COMBATIVE SUBJECT

This is a technique that teaches an individual(s) how to escort a combative/violent subject.

Objective: Demonstrate how to escort a combative/violent subject using the combative subject escort technique (one or two individuals are needed).

PERFORMANCE: ESCORTING THE COMBATIVE SUBJECT

1. From the kneeling position, have the subject raise one knee.
2. You will need to have the subject raise their torso in order to get them to place one knee in front of them.
3. Ask the subject to then bring their other knee up and stand into a bent over position.
4. From this position (combative escort), you can direct subject to another location for a wall control technique, or to a bed for a supine restraint.
5. Use loud, repetitive, defensive verbalizations (e.g., NO, STOP, STOP RESISTING) to direct the aggressor to stop resisting you.

Caution: Verbalization and constant control is the key to standing a prone controlled subject. Maintain your balance and be prepared to escape if needed.

REAR ARM CONTROL TECHNIQUE: 1-PERSON

 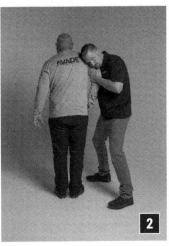 

REAR ARM CONTROL TECHNIQUE (1-PERSON)

This is a technique that teaches an individual how to control a resistive subject from the escort technique. This technique is for a subject who is displaying violent or self-destructive behavior towards themselves or others.

Objective: Demonstrate how to control a resistive subject using the rear arm control technique from the hands-on escort position (one or two individuals are needed).

PERFORMANCE: REAR ARM CONTROL TECHNIQUE (1-PERSON)

1. Begin in the hands-on escort position.
2. The subject becomes resistive by pushing their arm backward.
3. The individual moves with the resistance and repositions him/herself turning 90 degrees towards the aggressor.
4. The individual pulls the resistive subject's arm into his/her core.
5. Use loud, repetitive, defensive verbalizations (e.g., NO, STOP, STOP RESISTING) to direct the aggressor to stop resisting you.

Caution: Tuck your head into the shoulder of the aggressor. This will prevent the aggressor from striking you with a rear headbutt.

REAR ARM CONTROL TECHNIQUE: 2-PERSON

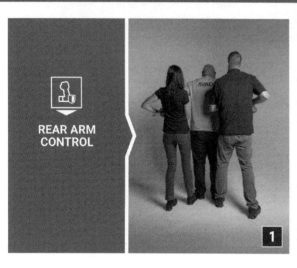

REAR ARM CONTROL TECHNIQUE (2-PERSON)

This is a technique that teaches an individual how to control a resistive subject from the escort technique. This technique is for a subject who is displaying violent or self-destructive behavior towards themselves or others.

Objective: Demonstrate how to control a resistive subject using the rear arm control technique from the hands-on escort position (one or two individuals are needed).

PERFORMANCE: REAR ARM CONTROL TECHNIQUE (2-PERSON)

1. Continue to control the arm in your core by pulling it into you.
2. Reposition your hand on the wrist; bring your fingertips onto the resistive subject's knuckles.
3. Gently bring the subject's arm upward into their lower back as you bring the subject's fingertips towards you.
4. Use loud, repetitive, defensive verbalizations (e.g., NO, STOP, STOP RESISTING) to direct the aggressor to stop resisting you.

From the rear arm control, you can escort the subject and/or handcuff the subject.

Caution: Tuck your head into the shoulder of the aggressor. This will prevent the aggressor from striking you with a rear headbutt.

WALL CONTROL TECHNIQUE

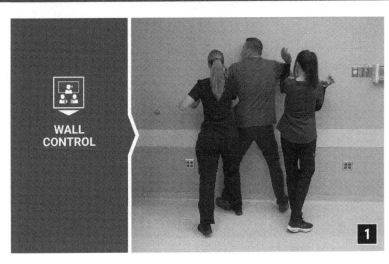

WALL CONTROL TECHNIQUE

This is a technique that teaches an individual how to decentralize and control a resistive subject and place them against a wall. This technique is for a subject who is displaying violent or self-destructive behavior towards themselves or others.

Objective: Demonstrate how to control a resistive subject using the wall control technique from the hands-on escort position (two individuals are needed).

PERFORMANCE: WALL CONTROL TECHNIQUE

1. Begin in the hands-on escort position.
2. The individuals will place their wrist onto the tricep of the subject (2-3 inches above the elbow) while walking the subject towards a wall.
3. Continue to place the individual on the wall (have subject turn their head to the side) and position your feet closest to the subject on the inside of their feet.
4. Bring the subject's arms out to the side and continue to use your wrist or hands on the subject's triceps.
5. Use loud, repetitive, defensive verbalizations (e.g., NO, STOP, STOP RESISTING) to direct the aggressor to stop resisting you.

Caution: Be aware of your environment and what direction you are moving the resistive subject towards.

Caution: The wall control position is a temporary position that may predispose the subject to breathing difficulties.

CONTINUALLY MONITOR THE SUBJECT AND SEEK MEDICAL ATTENTION IF NEEDED.

RESTRAINT CHAIR HOLDS AND APPLICATION (PT. 1)

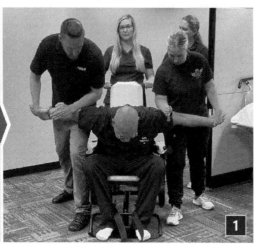
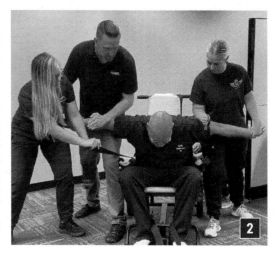

RESTRAINT CHAIR HOLDS AND APPLICATION

This is a technique that teaches individuals how to safely place a patient in the restraint chair and apply restraint chair restraints.

Objective: Demonstrate how to safely place the combative patient into the restraint chair and restrain them with proper hand and body positioning.

PERFORMANCE: RESTRAINT CHAIR HOLDS AND APPLICATION

1. Using the combative escort technique or the wall control technique, two staff members will walk the patient backward and direct them into the restraint chair.
2. Once in the chair, two staff members will maintain control of the patient, who will be bent forward at the waist.
3. A third staff member will hold the restraint chair securely and/or lock its wheels.
4. Waist/lap restraint will be applied while staff members remain in control of the patient who is still bent forward.
5. One or two staff members will then apply the ankle restraints while the patient is still bent forward and controlled by the initial two staff members.

Caution: Do not secure the waist/lap restraint snugly until all restraints have been applied.

Caution: When applying ankle restraints, ensure you position yourself carefully to avoid being kicked or kneed by the patient. Proper positioning is crucial.

Always:

- Follow agency policies and procedures in regard to restraint and seclusion.
- Report and document immediately.
- **Continually monitor the subject and seek medical attention if needed.**

...continued, RESTRAINT CHAIR HOLDS AND APPLICATION (PT. 2)

RESTRAINT CHAIR HOLDS AND APPLICATION

This is a technique that teaches individuals how to safely place a patient in the restraint chair and apply restraint chair restraints.

Objective: Demonstrate how to safely place the combative patient into the restraint chair and restrain them with proper hand and body positioning.

PERFORMANCE: RESTRAINT CHAIR HOLDS AND APPLICATION

6. Once ankle restraints have been applied, the two initial staff members will allow the patient to sit back and place the patient's forearms onto the armrest of the restraint chair.

7. One or two additional staff members will then apply the wrist restraints while the initial two staff members secure the patient's arm with the initial contact hand position technique.

8. Once wrist restraints have been applied a staff member will move to the back of the restraint chair for shoulder restraint application. The two initial staff members will remain in position to steady the patient for the shoulder restraint application.

9. Once the shoulder restraint has been applied and checked for proper fit, the waist/lap restraint will also be secured and checked for proper fit.

10. Staff will ensure that all restraints are properly fitted: waist/lap, ankles, wrists, and shoulder restraints.

Caution: Follow the manufacturer's guidelines when using the Restraint Chair.[1]

Always:

- Follow agency policies and procedures in regard to restraint and seclusion.
- Report and document immediately.
- **Continually monitor the subject and seek medical attention if needed.**

1 https://restraintchair.com/

Restraint Chair Holds and Application Studies

McLean Hospital Study[1]

A team of nurses from McLean Hospital published a study on the safety and effectiveness of restraint chairs.

- **Study purpose:** To examine the safety and efficacy of restraint chairs compared to traditional four-point restraints in psychiatric settings.

- **Research team:** McLean nurses and leaders including Nicole Visaggio, Kristen Kichefski, Jeanne McElhinney, Thomaskutty B. Idiculla, Luciana R.A. Pennant, and Scott C. Young.

- **Publication:** April 2018 edition of the Archives of Psychiatric Nursing

- **Hypothesis:** Restraint chairs would lead to shorter restraint episodes, increased oral medication intake, and fewer injuries.

- **Methodology:** Data collected over one year (May 1, 2014, to May 1, 2015) from three large psychiatric hospitals in the northeastern U.S.

- **Findings:**
  - **Medication intake:** Patients in restraint chairs more likely to take medication orally.
  - **Injuries:** Fewer staff injuries with restraint chairs compared to four-point restraints.
  - **Patient positioning:** Upright positioning in the chair aids communication and de-escalation, making patients feel less vulnerable.

- **Anecdotal evidence:** Nurses observed benefits for both patients and staff, including reduced time in restraints and increased willingness to take medication orally.

- **Future research:** Phase two to investigate nursing staff perceptions of the restraint chair versus four-point restraints, hypothesizing the chair is more dignified, humane, and clinically safer.

- **Recommendation:** Encouragement for other psychiatric institutions to consider adopting restraint chairs as a safer alternative.

Fairfield University Study[2]

The Marion Peckham Egan School of Nursing and Health Studies at Fairfield University produced a "qualitative study of nurses' experience with the restraint chair versus four-point restraint."

- **Authors:** Nicole Visaggio, Kathryn Phillips, Sharon Milne, Jeanne McElhinney, Scott C. Young

- **Study purpose:** To explore psychiatric nurses' experiences with the restraint chair compared to traditional four-point restraints.

- **Method:** Three focus groups conducted with psychiatric registered nurses at a large psychiatric hospital in the northeastern United States.

---

1 https://www.mcleanhospital.org/news/mclean-nurses-publish-study-safety-and-effectiveness-restraint-chairs

2 https://digitalcommons.fairfield.edu/cgi/viewcontent.cgi?article=1240&context=nursing-facultypubs

- **Findings:**
  - **Decision to restrain**
    - Safety: Primary reason for using restraints.
    - Last resort: Used only after other interventions fail.
    - Tough decision: Ethical and psychological challenges in deciding to restrain.
  - **Comparison: Chair vs. Four-Point Restraints**
    - Easier to use: Less physical force required.
    - Enhances therapeutic relationship: Better communication and eye-level interaction.
    - More humane: Seen as more respectful and dignified.
    - Less traumatic: Reduces risk of re-traumatizing patients.
    - Comforting: Some patients find the chair comforting.
    - Four points for supine: Preferred if the patient is already lying down.
  - **Patient Experience**
    - Fear and anger: Common emotions during restraint.
    - Thankful and remorseful: Express gratitude and remorse post-restraint.
- **Conclusion:** The restraint chair is a safe and effective alternative to traditional four-point restraints, improving patient dignity and therapeutic relationships. Further research is recommended to validate these findings across different settings and explore patient perspectives.

CHILD CONTROL TECHNIQUE: STANDING (OPTIONAL)

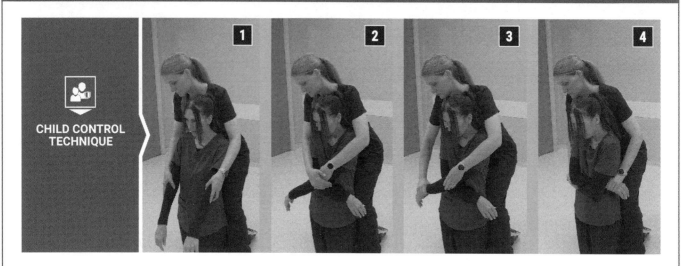

CHILD CONTROL TECHNIQUE: STANDING (OPTIONAL)

This is a technique that teaches staff how to temporarily control a child who is displaying violent or self-destructive behavior towards themselves or others.

Objective: Demonstrate how to approach, position, and safely control a child in this temporary position until they can regain control.

PERFORMANCE: CHILD CONTROL TECHNIQUE—STANDING (OPTIONAL)

1. Safely approach the child from behind and make initial contact on the child's elbows with your thumbs in an upward position.
2. Once initial contact is established, bring the child's elbows in front of their body.
3. Safely release your inner hand and place it on top of your outer hand, controlling both elbows.
4. Your outer hand will slide down to the child's wrist while your inner hand holds both elbows.
5. Your inner hand will now slide down to the remaining wrist of the child.
6. Bring the child's outer elbow under their inner elbow.
7. Maintain position, stay aware, and prepare to have the child go to a seated position if needed.

Caution: Keep your head back and away from the child's head as they may toss their head around and be able to head butt you.

Caution: Do not bend the child forward as this may make it difficult for the child to breathe.

Note: Continue to verbalize to the child while directing them to stop resisting/hurting themselves.

CHILD CONTROL TECHNIQUE: SEATED (OPTIONAL)

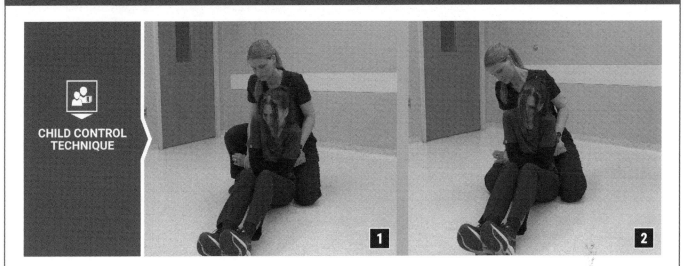

CHILD CONTROL TECHNIQUE: SEATED (OPTIONAL)

This is attechnique that teaches staff how to temporarily control a child who is displaying violent or self-destructive behavior towards themselves or others.

Objective: Demonstrate how to approach, position, and safely control a child in this temporary position until they can regain control.

PERFORMANCE: CHILD CONTROL TECHNIQUE—SEATED (OPTIONAL)

1. To place the child in a seated position, you will need to drop down to one knee.
2. You will then bring your other knee down.
3. To further secure the child, you may need to bring your knees together to hold the child.
4. Maintain position, stay aware, and prepare to disengage once the child has gained control.

Caution: Keep your head back and away from the child's head as they may toss their head around and be able to head butt you.

Caution: Do not bend the child forward as this may make it difficult for the child to breathe.

Caution: Child control techniques are temporary! Disengage immediately once the child regains control.

Note: Continue to verbalize to the child while directing them to stop resisting/hurting themselves.

MODULE 5

Post-Incident Response, Debriefing, and Documentation

Guidelines to follow after encountering a crisis incident

Module 5:
Post-Incident Response, Debriefing, and Documentation

Post-Incident Response

Post-incident response, debriefing, and documentation are essential steps in managing workplace violence incidents. The post-incident response involves immediate actions to ensure safety, provide medical and psychological support, and communicate with staff. Debriefing allows affected employees to discuss the incident, gather information, identify gaps in procedures, and develop improvement strategies. Comprehensive documentation is crucial for legal compliance, providing evidence for investigations, aiding learning and improvement, and maintaining accountability. These processes help organizations manage the aftermath of incidents, support employees, and enhance future prevention and response strategies.

Post-incident responses include:

Triage (medical/hazmat)
Triage is the process of determining the priority of patients' or victims' treatments based on the severity of their condition. Initial first-aid treatment and protocols for hazardous materials and clean-up should be handled immediately.

Report the incident
Report the incident to police, security, risk management, human resources, etc. Follow standard operating procedures in reporting incidents.

Consider all involved
Staff, guests, visitors, patients, or anyone who was witness to the incident should be treated accordingly for medical and stress debriefing.

Provide for incident debriefing
Debriefing allows those involved with the incident to process the event and reflect on its impact. Depending on the situation, a thorough debriefing may need to take place. Even those not specifically involved in an incident may suffer emotional and psychological trauma.

Critical Incident Stress Debriefing (CISD)
CISD is a specific technique designed to assist others in dealing with physical or psychological symptoms that are generally associated with critical incident trauma exposure.

Research on the effectiveness of critical incident debriefing techniques has demonstrated that individuals who are provided critical stress debriefing within a 24- to 72-hour window after experiencing the critical incident have lower levels of short- and long-term crisis reactions and psychological trauma.

Employee Assistance Programs (EAP)

EAPs are intended to help employees deal with work or personal problems that might adversely impact their work performance, health, and well-being. EAPs generally include assessment, short-term counseling, and referral services for employees and their household members. Employee benefit programs offered by many employers, typically in conjunction with health insurance plans, provide for payment for EAPs.

Document incident to include any follow-up investigations

Post-incident documentation is absolutely critical for reducing liability risk, preventing recurrences, and assisting in follow-up investigations.

Initiate corrective actions to prevent recurrences

Preventing similar future incidents involves taking proactive corrective actions. Agency management, supervision, security, risk management, employee safety committees, the environment of care committee, etc., should initiate, track, and follow up on corrective actions.

Post-Incident Debriefing

Post-incident stress debriefing involves methods designed to help manage stress after a traumatic event. These techniques focus on providing emotional support, promoting mental well-being, and fostering a sense of safety and stability among affected individuals. Debriefing sessions typically include discussing the incident, expressing feelings, and receiving professional guidance to process the experience. These methods aim to alleviate stress, prevent long-term psychological effects, and support the overall recovery process.

> **The goal of debriefing is to reduce the chance of Post-Traumatic Stress symptoms and Post-Traumatic Stress Disorder (PTSD).**

Post-incident debriefing includes:

- **Always debrief.** Staff should debrief after every workplace violence incident, regardless of the severity. Oftentimes a brief discussion of the events and outcome is enough. Other times, a more intensive debriefing is needed.

- **Talk to co-workers.** Almost all workers have experienced or witnessed some type of workplace violence incident. Your co-workers can be a great resource to vent your concerns about your feelings after an incident.

- **Acknowledge humanness.** As humans, we are susceptible to the frailties of human nature. This acknowledgement creates an awareness that it is okay to seek and ask for help.

- **Be aware of post-event feelings.** Having the knowledge and awareness that you may experience strong feelings from an event can give you the confidence to seek help and discuss feelings with others.

- **Take advantage of your Employee Assistance Program (EAP).** Agencies realize that feelings may persist for longer than you might expect after an incident. Employee Assistance Programs can benefit employees and help them deal with post-incident stress or other work/personal problems. EAPs are intended to help employees deal with problems or issues that might adversely affect their work performance, health, and well-being. EAPs generally include assessment, short-term counseling, and referral services for employees and their household members.

- **Know the signs and symptoms of Post-Traumatic Stress Disorder (PTSD).** PTSD is a psychological reaction occurring after experiencing a highly stressful event (such as wartime combat, physical violence, or a natural disaster). It's usually characterized by depression, anxiety, flashbacks, recurrent nightmares, and avoidance of reminders of the event.

- **Take the time to follow up with other staff.** As human beings, we often focus on the needs of others and not ourselves. Take the time to discuss workplace incidents, your feelings about the incidents, and how incidents in the workplace could improve.

- **Critical Incident Stress Debriefing (CISD).** Individuals who are exposed to an assault situation (as a witness or a victim) should consider some level of critical incident debriefing or counseling. The final extent of any traumatic situation may never be known or realistically estimated in terms of trauma, loss, and grief. In the aftermath of any critical incident, psychological reactions are quite common and are fairly predictable. CISD can be a valuable tool following a traumatic event.

Conducting an Incident Debrief

Staff should debrief after every workplace violence incident, regardless of the severity. Oftentimes a brief discussion of the events and outcome is enough. Other times, a more intensive debriefing is needed. **Debriefs are always positive!** After action, corrections should be done at a later date.

There are four primary steps for conducting an Incident Debrief:

1. **Wellness check:** The facilitator conducting the debrief asks each person involved and gets a verbal acknowledgement of their mental and physical wellness.

2. **What happened:** The facilitator conducting the debrief asks each person to briefly describe what they saw, heard, and experienced during the incident.

3. **What we did well:** The facilitator conducting the debrief will ask each person to briefly describe what the team did well in responding and dealing with the incident.

4. **How we can improve:** The facilitator conducting the debrief will ask each person to briefly describe what they believe the team (we) can improve upon in future incidents. Be positive!

BEHAVIORAL HEALTH
INCIDENT DEBRIEF PROCESS FORM

▸ Conducting an Incident Debrief

- ☑ After a workplace violence incident, it is important that **all personnel involved in the incident meet immediately following the incident to debrief**.
- ☑ The debrief should be **led and documented by the supervisor and/or person in charge on duty** at the time of the incident, in coordination with security personnel.

FOUR PRIMARY STEPS TO CONDUCTING AN INCIDENT DEBRIEF:

1. **Wellness Check:** The facilitator conducting the debrief *asks each person* involved and gets a *verbal acknowledgement* of their **mental** and **physical wellness**.
   - The debrief leader will **assist in determining if anyone requires immediate or follow up medical treatment** as a result of *injury sustained* as a *result of the incident.*
   - If any personnel are identified as *sustaining injury* or *experiencing extensive stress* as a result of the incident, the agency will need to **follow up and provide further support and resources**, in line with the facilities policy & procedures.

2. **What Happened:** The facilitator conducting the debrief *ask each person* to briefly **describe what they saw, heard and experienced** during the incident.
   - It is important to assist in creating an environment within the debrief that allows **ALL individuals involved** to appropriately decompress and gain their composure prior to returning to regular job duties.

3. **What Did We Do Well:** The facilitator conducting the debrief will *ask each person* to briefly **describe what the team (we) did well** in responding and dealing with the incident?
   - Often, individuals *immediately following an event* will still be experiencing a **high level of adrenaline**. This is especially true for those who may have not experienced a violent event very often.

4. **What Can we Improve Upon:** The facilitator conducting the debrief will ask each person to briefly describe what they believe the team (we) can improve upon in future incidents? Positive!!
   - An individual still experiencing an *adrenaline rush*, may not be aware of their need to decompress or how the incident may have impacted them emotionally and/or mentally. Because of this, as a **TEAM**, ensure that you encourage each other to take a moment and *assess your ability to return to your regular job duties.*

Staff should debrief after every workplace violence incident, *regardless of the severity.* Often times a brief discussion of the events and outcome is enough. Other times, a more intensive debriefing is needed. Debriefs are **always POSITIVE!** After action corrections should be *done at a later date.*

Remember: The goal of debriefing is to **reduce the chances of Post-Traumatic Stress Disorder** (PTSD) and **Post-Traumatic Stress Symptoms**.

A) **Wellness Check:** _____

B) **What Happened:** _____

C) **What Did We Do Well:** _____

D) **What Can We Improve Upon:** _____

Behavioral Health Crisis & De-Escalation Intervention Training
© Personal Safety Training Inc. | AVADE® Training

Post-Incident Documentation

Who–What–Where–When–Why–How?
The first rule in post-incident documentation is the "who, what, where, when, why, and how" rule of reporting. After writing an incident narrative, double-check to see if you have included the first rule of reporting.

Witnesses: Who was there?
Make sure to include anyone who was a witness to the incident. Staff, visitors, guests, and support services (police, fire, EMS, etc.) can be valuable witnesses should an incident be litigated.

Narrative characteristics
A proper narrative should describe in detail the characteristics of the violent offender/predator.

Before, during, and after
A thorough incident report will describe what happened before, during, and after the incident. Details matter!

First person vs. third person
The account of an incident can be described in the first person or the third person. This can be specific to your agency protocols or the preference of the person documenting the incident.

Post-follow-up (track and trend)
Most agencies use electronic documentation, which allows for easy retrieval, tracking, and trending. Using technology assists agencies in following up and initiating proactive corrections.

Follow standard operating procedures
Whether handwriting incident reports or using electronic documentation and charting, staff should consistently and thoroughly document all incidents relating to violence in the workplace.

Elements of Reporting Self-Defense Force

After any situation involving the defense of yourself or another person, proper documentation and reporting are crucial. The events of the assault or attempted assault should be reported to police/security. Police/security will document the incident and start an investigation. You should also document the account for your personal records. This can protect you in a possible legal situation that could arise out of using force to defend yourself. As you document your account of the incident, make sure to report to police/security any details you missed during your initial report to them.

What type of force/self-defense/technique was used during the incident?
Be specific in your documentation regarding the type of control, defense, and force used during the incident.

How long did the incident and resistance last?
Important to note the length of the resistance, as this is a factor relative to exhaustion and increasing the level of force.

Was any de-escalation used?
Verbal and non-verbal de-escalation techniques should be noted.

Were you in fear of injury (bodily harm) to yourself, others, or the subject?

Fear is a distressing emotion aroused by a perceived threat, impending danger, evil, or pain.

If so, why?

Fear is a basic survival mechanism occurring in response to a specific stimulus, such as pain or the threat of danger.

Explain thoroughly, and make sure to document completely.

The importance of documentation cannot be over-emphasized. Documentation ensures proper training standards are met, policies and procedures are understood, certification standards are met, liability and risk management are mitigated, and departmental and organizational requirements are maintained.

Every person must take into consideration their moral, legal, and ethical beliefs and rights, and understandings when using any type of force to defend themselves or others. Personal Safety Training Inc. makes no legal declaration, representation, or claim as to what force should be used or not used during a self-defense/assault incident or situation. Each individual must take into consideration their ability, agency policies and procedures, and laws in their state and/or country.

IF YOU OR SOMEONE YOU KNOW IS IN CRISIS AND CONSIDERING SELF-HARM OR SUICIDE:

- Call 911 for emergency services.
- Visit the nearest hospital emergency room.
- Call or text 988 to connect with the 988 Suicide and Crisis Lifeline, offering 24-hour, confidential support. *Para ayuda en español, llame al 988.*
- Support is also available via live chat at 988lifeline.org. AVADE® does not monitor this website for crisis messages, provide medical advice, or make referrals.

PSTI LEGAL DISCLAIMER

The information in this training book is a supplement, not a substitute, for the expertise of qualified healthcare professionals. The content on AVADE® Behavioral Health, sourced from reliable information, does not constitute medical or professional healthcare advice, diagnosis, or treatment. It is crucial to consult healthcare providers for specific guidelines related to medical or behavioral health conditions. This material does not guarantee that any technique or strategy is safe or effective for any specific needs. Personal Safety Training, Inc., does not dictate policies or procedures for behavioral health violence prevention, self-defense tactics, or any physical interventions. Agencies are responsible for developing their own policies and evaluating the recommendations based on their circumstances.

The author and publisher do not guarantee the completeness or accuracy of the information and assume no risk for its use. Any implied warranty are expressly disavowed.

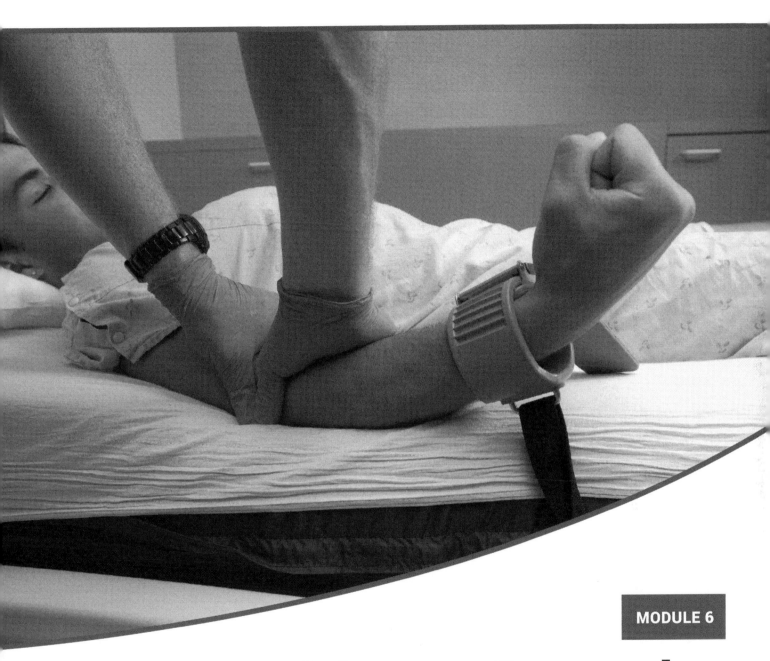

MODULE 6

Healthcare Restraint Holds/Applications

Best practices and procedures for restraining a violent patient

Module 6:
Healthcare Restraint Holds and Applications

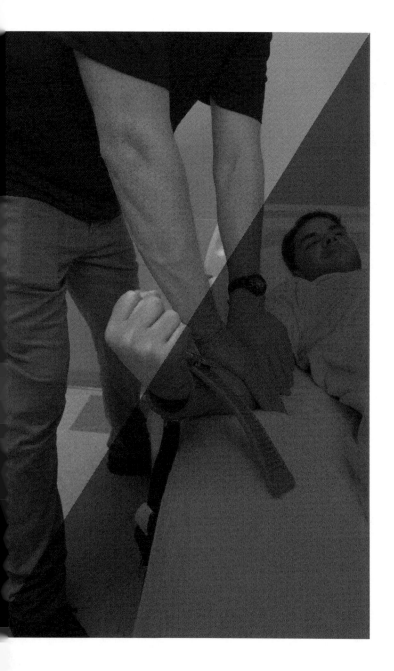

Use of Restraints

- Using restraints to control violence is acceptable in certain cases, but clinical policy and procedures must be rigidly adhered to.

- Restraint use is a very controversial subject and not always understood by staff. Acceptability of restraint use should be carefully identified and approved by medical staff.

- Agencies should seek to reduce the use of physical restraints and therapeutic holds through risk assessment and early intervention with less restrictive measures.

- AVADE® Level III Training aligns with the Center for Medicaid Services (CMS) COP 482.13(e)(2). Restraint or seclusion may only be used when less restrictive interventions have been determined to be ineffective to protect the patient, a staff member, or others from harm.

- Any intervention other than verbal de-escalation should only be used when it "is used for the management of violent or self-destructive behavior that jeoparadizes the immediate physical safety of the patient, a staff member, or others," as defined by CMS.

SUPINE HOLDING POSITION

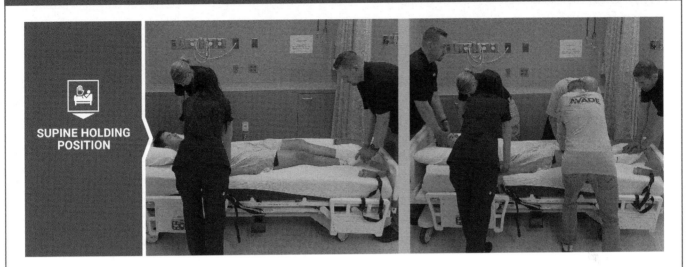

SUPINE HOLDING POSITION

SUPINE HOLDING POSITION

The above pictures depict a four-point healthcare holding position for a behavioral/violent person restraint application. This technique is for a subject who is displaying violent or self-destructive behavior towards themselves or others.

Objective: Demonstrate how to hold and apply healthcare restraints to a combative/violent individual.

PERFORMANCE: SUPINE HOLDING POSITION

1. Once staff (two persons) have placed an individual on the bed, they (plus other staff) will hold patient down on either side of the elbow and knee. Not on joint!
2. A staff person can then apply restraints to the ankles and wrists.
3. Keeping one-arm raised above the head reduces the individual's ability to use their core strength and resist.
4. A staff person may be needed to control the individual's head (do not turn their head).
5. A staff person may be needed to control the individual's feet until restraints can be applied (pigeon toe position).

Note: Restraints can be removed one at a time in a process called "contracting with the patient." Follow your SOPs.

Always follow agency policies and procedures in regard to restraint and seclusion.

Always report and document immediately.

SUPINE RESTRAINT POSITION

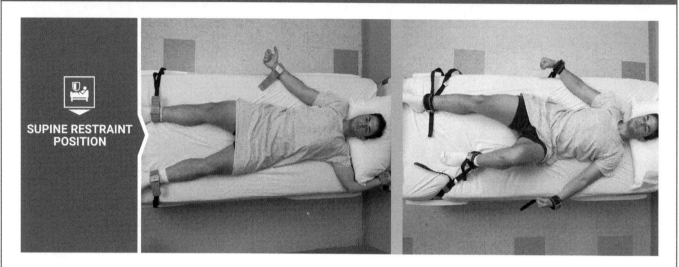

SUPINE RESTRAINT POSITION

The above pictures depict a four-point healthcare restraint for a behavioral/violent person restraint application. This technique is for a subject who is displaying violent or self-destructive behavior towards themselves or others.

Objective: Demonstrate how to hold and apply healthcare restraints to a combative/violent individual.

PERFORMANCE: SUPINE RESTRAINT POSITION

1. Once staff (two persons) have placed an individual on the bed, they (plus other staff) will hold patient down on either side of the elbow and knee. Not on joint!
2. A staff person can then apply restraints to the ankles and wrists.
3. Keeping one-arm raised above the head reduces the individual's ability to use their core strength and resist.
4. A staff person may be needed to control the individual's head (do not turn their head).
5. A staff person may be needed to control the individual's feet until restraints can be applied (pigeon toe position).

Note: Restraints can be removed one at a time in a process called "contracting with the patient." Follow your SOPs.

Always follow agency policies and procedures in regard to restraint and seclusion.

Always report and document immediately.

LEVEL III · MODULE 6

AVADE Behavioral Health Advanced Student Guide | Healthcare Restraint Holds/Applications Page | 335

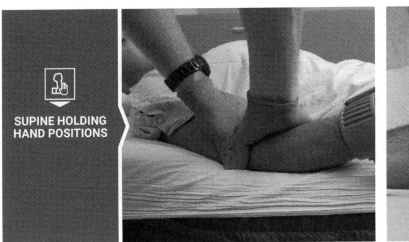
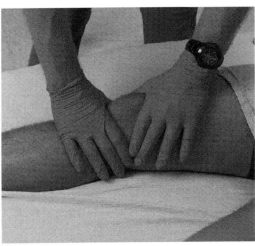

SUPINE HOLDING HAND POSITIONS: Holding the limbs for the application of restraints is achieved by grasping either side of the knee and either side of the elbow **with both hands**. Ensure no pressure is exerted on the joints. For better leverage, lock your arms and position your shoulders directly over your hands.

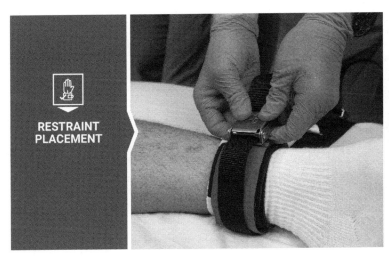
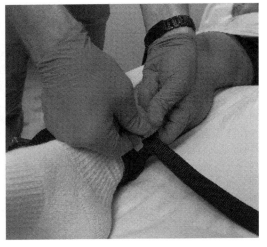

RESTRAINT PLACEMENT: The placement of restraints involves initially attaching them to the bed. It's crucial to note that beds may vary, so securing restraints should be preplanned before any incident. Once attached to the bed, the restraints are then applied to the patient's wrists and ankles.

Note: Whenever restraining a patient, ensure thorough checks for the proper placement, correct fit, secure locking of restraints, and comprehensive documentation.

Always follow agency policies and procedures in regard to restraint and seclusion.

Always report and document immediately.

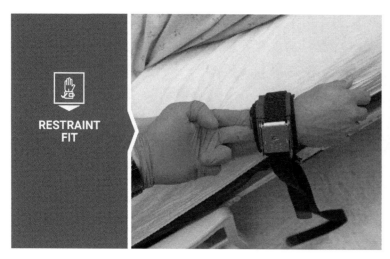
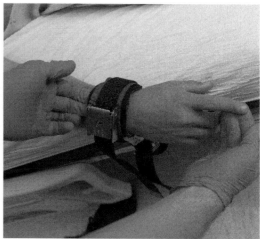

RESTRAINT FIT: When checking for proper restraint fit, insert your index and middle fingers into the restraint (refer to the picture above). There should be ample room to do so comfortably. Restraints must be appropriately fitted to ensure proper blood circulation. Capillary refill, which ensures circulation to the fingertips, is assessed by pressing the patient's nailbed or fingertip. Regardless of pigmentation, the nailbed or fingertip color should change, and normal color should return once pressure is released.

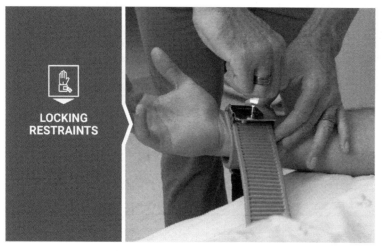
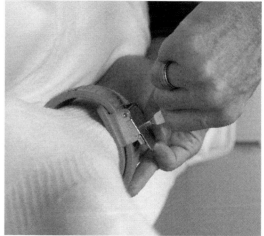

LOCKING RESTRAINTS: Not all restraints are equipped with locking mechanisms. If using restraints with locks, it is crucial to understand how these mechanisms work and to ensure you have the appropriate key for unlocking them.

Note: Whenever restraining a patient, ensure thorough checks for the proper placement, correct fit, secure locking of restraints, and comprehensive documentation.

Always follow agency policies and procedures in regard to restraint and seclusion.

Always report and document immediately.

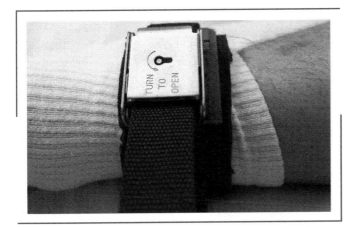

Six Core Strategies© for Reducing Seclusion and Restraint Use Alignment

The Six Core Strategies© are evidence-informed methods proven to be effective in minimizing instances of seclusion and restraint. This comprehensive approach was initially formulated in the United States by the Medical Directors Council of the National Association of State Mental Health Program Directors (NASMHPD).

Strategy 1 | Leadership Toward Organizational Change

The primary approach to reduce instances of seclusion and restraint (S/R), known as "Leadership toward Organizational Change," involves the active participation of senior facility leadership, including the CEO, CNO, and COO. This strategy entails defining a vision for S/R reduction, implementing a targeted performance improvement plan, and ensuring continuous oversight through a public health prevention approach and a multi-disciplinary performance improvement team.

To support this strategy, evidence-based tools include the Six Core Strategies© checklist for leadership and the Reflective Guide for Senior Leaders. These tools offer a structured framework for leaders to follow and assess their progress in implementing the strategy.

Evidence-based tools to support Strategy 1:

- Six Core Strategies© Checklist for Leadership
- Reflective Guide for Senior Leaders

Strategy 2 | Use of Data to Inform Practice

To achieve a successful reduction in seclusion and restraint (S/R), it is essential to gather data at the individual unit level. This approach includes the following steps: establishing baseline data, consistently monitoring facility usage, tracking demographics, involuntary medication use, and injuries associated with S/R events. Moreover, it involves setting improvement goals for comparative monitoring over time. This strategy aims to comprehensively assess and address factors contributing to S/R instances.

Evidence-based tools to support Strategy 2:

- AVADE® 4-Step Debriefing Tool
- Six Core Strategies for Reducing Seclusion and Restraint Use© Planning Tool

Strategy 3 | Workforce Development

The strategy revolves around establishing a treatment environment founded on recovery principles and trauma-informed care to proactively prevent coercion and conflicts. Implementation entails thorough staff training, education, and human resource development. This includes incorporating training on the application of seclusion and restraint (S/R), choice-oriented treatment activities, and individualized person-centered treatment planning. To ensure effectiveness, there is a focus on maintaining consistent communication and supervision. This approach aims to equip staff with the necessary knowledge and skills for the reduction of S/R incidents.

Evidence-based tools to support Strategy 3:

- Staff and Patient Development Support Plan

Strategy 4 | Use of S/R Prevention Tools

The strategy encompasses the integration of tools and assessments into facility policies and individual consumer recovery plans, with a focus on promoting individualized treatment to reduce instances of seclusion and restraint (S/R). Implementation involves the utilization of assessment tools, universal trauma assessments, de-escalation surveys, person-first language, environmental changes, and sensory modulation interventions. These measures aim to teach emotional self-management skills and create a personalized approach to treatment.

Evidence-based tools to support Strategy 4:

- Six Core Strategies for Reducing Seclusion and Restraint Use© Planning Tool

Strategy 5 | Consumer Roles in Inpatient Settings

The strategy actively engages consumers, children, families, and external advocates at all organizational levels to minimize instances of seclusion and restraint. Implementation encompasses their participation in event oversight, monitoring, debriefing interviews, peer support services, and significant roles in key facility committees. Additionally, there is elevated supervision by executive staff, with a focus on addressing ADA (Americans with Disabilities Act) issues in job descriptions, expectations, work hours, and communication. This approach aims to include diverse perspectives and ensure a collaborative effort in reducing seclusion and restraint.

Evidence-based tools to support Strategy 5:

- Staff and Patient Development Support Plan

Strategy 6 | Debriefing Techniques

The strategy places a strong emphasis on conducting a comprehensive analysis of each seclusion and restraint (S/R) event to shape policies and proactively prevent future occurrences. It recommends debriefing activities, including immediate post-event analysis and formal problem analysis using root cause analysis (RCA) steps. The approach acknowledges the need for flexibility in facilities treating children and frequently using holds. This analytical process aims to provide valuable insights that inform policies and contribute to a continuous improvement approach in minimizing S/R incidents.

Evidence-based tools to support Strategy 6:

- Six Core Strategies© Checklist for Leadership
- AVADE® 4-Step Debriefing Tool
- Psychological First Aid, John Hopkins Method (recommended by SAMHSA)

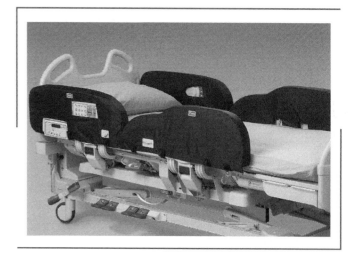

Risk Factors for Restraints

- Patients who smoke
- Positional asphyxiation
- Patients with deformities
- Lack of continuous monitoring
- Improper restraining techniques
- Incomplete medical assessment
- Improper restraints, room, and beds
- Insufficient staff orientation and training

- Supine position may predispose them to aspiration
- Prone position may predispose them to suffocation

Strategies for Reducing Risk

- Reduce the use of physical restraints and holds through risk assessments and early interventions.
- Clarify restraint use in clinical protocols.
- See alternatives to restraint use (de-escalation techniques).
- Enhance staff orientation/education regarding alternatives and proper application.
- Develop structured procedures and competencies for consistent application of restraints.
- Develop safety guidelines and continuous observation of those restrained.
- Apply the "one-hour" rule.
- Utilize patient quiet rooms/seclusion rooms.
- Revise the staffing model.
- Increase awareness of medical/surgical versus behavioral restraints.
- Comply with the Joint Commission on Accreditation of Healthcare Organizations (JCAHO) and state/federal standards.
- If the patient is restrained in the supine position, ensure that the patient's head is free to rotate and, when possible, that the head of the bed is elevated to minimize the risk of aspiration.
- If the patient must be controlled in the prone position, ensure that the airway is unobstructed at all times (do not cover or bury the patient's face). Ensure that the patient can expand their lungs to properly breathe (do not put any pressure on their back). *Special caution is required for children, elderly patients, and very obese patients.*

- Never place a towel, bag, or other cover over a patient's face.
- Do not restrain a patient in a bed with unprotected split side rails.
- Do not use certain types of restraints, such as high vests and waist restraints.
- Ensure the patient is properly searched and free of weapons and smoking materials.
- Limit access from friends and family.
- Policies and procedures should be adhered to for all healthcare restraint applications/holds.

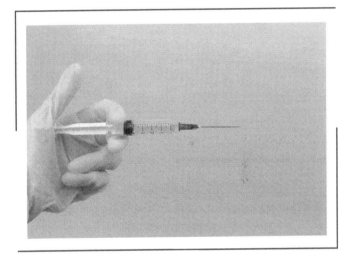

Chemical Restraints (Emergency Medications)

A chemical restraint is a form of medical restraint in which a drug is used to restrict the freedom of movement of a patient, or in some cases, to sedate a patient. These are used in emergency, acute, and psychiatric settings to control aggressive patients who are interfering with their care or who are otherwise harmful to themselves or others.

Drugs that are often used as chemical restraints include benzodiazepines (such as Lorazepam/Ativan), Midazolam (Versed), or Diazepam (Valium). Haloperidol (Haldol) is a drug chemically unrelated to benzodiazepines and is also popular for chemical restraint, without the potentially dangerous side effects of benzodiazepine drugs.

Any use of chemical restraints must be authorized and administered by a licensed clinician or doctor.

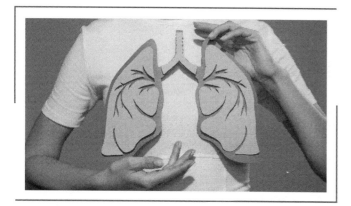

Positional Asphyxia

> **Positional asphyxia is a form of asphyxia that occurs when someone's position prevents them from breathing adequately.**

A small but significant number of people die suddenly and without apparent reason during restraint by police, prison (corrections) officers, and healthcare staff. Positional asphyxia may be a factor in some of these deaths.

- Positional asphyxia is a potential danger of some physical restraint techniques.
- People may die from positional asphyxia by simply getting themselves into a breathing-restricted position they cannot get out of, either through carelessness or as a consequence of another accident.

Research has suggested that restraining a person in a face-down position is likely to cause greater restriction of breathing than restraining a person face up. Many law enforcement and health personnel are now taught to avoid restraining people face down or to do so only for a very short period of time.

Risk factors that may increase the chance of death include obesity, prior cardiac or respiratory problems, alcohol intoxication, illicit drugs use (such as cocaine), excited delirium (see below) or bizarre/frenzied behavior.

Excited Delirium

> **Excited delirium is a controversial term used to explain the deaths of individuals in police custody, in which the person being arrested or restrained shows some combination of agitation, violent or bizarre behavior, insensitivity to pain, elevated body temperature, or increased strength. It has been listed as a cause of death by some medical examiners.**

The term has no formal medical recognition and is not recognized in the Diagnostic and Statistical Manual of Mental Disorders. There may also be a controversial link between "excited delirium" deaths and the use of tasers to subdue agitated people.

Almost all subjects who have died during restraint have engaged in extreme levels of physical resistance against the restraint for a prolonged period of time.

Other issues in the way the subject is restrained can also increase the risk of death; for example, kneeling or otherwise placing weight on the subject and particularly any type of restraint hold around the subject's neck.

AVADE® Level III Defensive Control Tactics and Techniques Review

FUNDAMENTALS OF DEFENSIVE CONTROL

CONTACT AND COVER POSITIONING

ESCORT STRATEGIES AND TECHNIQUES

CONTROL AND DECENTRALIZATION TECHNIQUES

POST-INCIDENT RESPONSE, DEBRIEFING, AND DOCUMENTATION

HEALTHCARE RESTRAINT HOLDS AND APPLICATIONS

Workplace violence is, unfortunately, on the rise. By learning and studying the AVADE® strategies, integrating them, teaching them, and modeling them to your co-workers, you can lessen your chances of being a victim of workplace violence. Integrate the AVADE® safety principles into your workplace/life-place for defusing tense situations. Learn to identify the signs and symptoms of potential violence. Above all, learn to trust your instincts and listen to your intuition. Remember: your best tools for keeping yourself safe are your own mind and personal safety habits.

About the Author

David Fowler is the founder and president of (PSTI) Personal Safety Training Incorporated and AVADE® Training, located in Coeur d' Alene, ID. He is responsible for the overall management and operations of PSTI and AVADE®, which offers seminars, training, consulting, and protective details. Since 1990, David has been involved in security operations, training, and protective details.

He is the author of the SOCS® (Safety Oriented Customer Service) program and training manual, as well as the AVADE® Personal Safety Training and Workplace Violence Prevention programs and training manuals. He is also the author of the book *Be Safe Not Sorry: The art and science of keeping you and your family safe from crime and violence*. David has worked with thousands of individuals and hundreds of agencies and corporations throughout the United States and Canada. His presentations have included international, national, and local seminars. David's thorough understanding of safety and security and martial science adds an exciting and interesting approach to his style of presentation.

David is a certified master instructor in several nationally recognized training programs such as Workplace Violence Prevention (AVADE®), Pepper Spray Defense™, Handcuffing Tactics™, Security Oriented Customer Service (SOCS®), Defensive Tactics System™ (DTS™), Defense Baton™, Security Incident Reporting System™ (SIRS™) and AVADE® Personal Safety Training. David has certified and trained thousands of individuals in these programs and others throughout the United States and abroad.

He is a graduate of (ESI) Executive Security International's Advanced Executive Protection Program and the Protective Intelligence and Investigations program. He is also a member of ASIS (American Society for Industrial Security), The International Law Enforcement Educators and Trainers Association (ILEETA), and the International Association of Healthcare Safety and Security (IAHSS).

David brings insight, experience, and a passion for empowering people and organizations utilizing the training programs and protective services that he offers here in the United States and in other countries. He is considered by many to be the most dynamic and motivational speaker and trainer in the security and personal safety industry.

David is happily married to the love of his life, Genelle Fowler. They live in Coeur d' Alene, ID, and have five children and three grandchildren. David and Genelle have committed their lives to serve others through the mission of safety. Both David and Genelle travel extensively, providing training and consulting to corporations throughout North America.

Bibliography, Reference Guide, and Recommended Reading

AVADE Training.
   https://personalsafetytraining.com/

Personal Safety Training.
   https://personalsafetytraining.com/

AVADE Learning.
   https://avadeelearning.com

AVADE Instructor.
   https://www.avadeinstructor.com

AVADE Student Guides.
   https://www.avade-studentguides.com/

"Active Shooter Incidents in the United States in 2014 and 2015." (FBI, 2016), https://www.fbi.gov/file-repository/activeshooterincidentsus_2014-2015.pdf.

Adams, Terry, and Rob, Adams. *Seminar Production Business: Your Step by Step Guide to Success.* Canada: Entrepreneur Press, 2003.

Albrecht, Steve. *Surviving Street Patrol: The Officer's Guide to Safe and Effective Policing.* Boulder, CO: Paladin Press, 2001.

Amdur, Ellis. *Dueling with O-sensei: Grappling with the Myth of the Warrior Sage.* Seattle, WA: Edgework, 2000.

Andersen, Peter A. *The Complete Idiot's Guide to Body Language.* Indianapolis, IN: Alpha Books, 2004.

Andrews, Andy. *The Travelers Gift: Seven Decisions that Determine Personal Success.* Nashville, TN: Nelsen Books, 2002.

Arapakis, Maria. *Soft Power: How to Speak Up, Set Limits, and Say No Without Losing Your Lover, Your Job, or Your Friends.* New York, NY: Warner Books, Inc. 1990.

Artwhohl, Alexis and Loren Christensen. *Deadly Force Encounters: What Cops Need to Know to Mentally and Physically Prepare for and Survive a Gunfight.* Boulder, CO: Paladin Press, 1997.

Ayoob, Massad. "10 Cases Where An Armed Citizen Took Down An Active Shooter." *Athlon Outdoors.* 2015. http://www.personaldefenseworld.com/2015/03/10-cases-where-an-armed-citizen-took-down-an-active-shooter/#10-cases-where-an-armed-citizen-took-down-an-active-shooter-2.

Berkowitz, Bonnie and Chris Alcantara. "The Terrible Numbers that Grow with Each Mass Shooting." *The Washington Post.* 2021. https://www.washingtonpost.com/graphics/2018/national/mass-shootings-in-america/?noredirect=on&utm_term=.35ae4b2837e4.

Blair, J. Pete and Katherine W. Schweit, "A Study of Active Shooter Incidents in the United States Between 2000 and 2013." *FBI.* 2014. https://www.fbi.gov/file-repository/active-shooter-study-2000-2013-1.pdf/view.

Bottom Line Publications, Editors. *The World's Greatest Treasury of Health Secrets.* Stamford, CT: Bottom Line Publications, 2006.

Branca, Andrew. *The Law of Self-Defense: The Indispensable Guide for the Armed Citizen*. Maynard, MA, 2016.

Brown, Tom. *Survival Guides: Americas Bestselling Wilderness Series*. New York, NY: Berkley Books, 1984.

Byrnes, John D. *Before Conflict: Preventing Aggressive Behavior*. Lanham, Maryland: Scarecrow Press, 2002.

Canfield, Jack, and Janet Switzer. *The Success Principles: How to Get from Where You Are to Where You Want to Be*. New York, NY: Harper Collins Publishers, 2005.

Carnegie, Dale. *Golden Book*. https://www.dalecarnegie.com/en/resources/dale-carnegies-secrets-of-success.

Carnegie, Dale. *How to Win Friends and Influence People*. New York, NY: Pocket Books, 1936.

Casteel, Carri and Corinne Peek-Asa. "Effectiveness of Crime Prevention Through Environmental Design (CPTED) in Reducing Robberies." *PubMed, National Library of Medicine*. Accessed December 27, 2023. www.pubmed.ncbi.nlm.nih.gov/10793286/.

Centers for Disease Control and Prevention (CDC). "Fast Facts: Preventing Intimate Partner Violence." Accessed December 27, 2023. https://www.cdc.gov/violenceprevention/intimatepartnerviolence/fastfact.html.

Centers for Disease Control and Prevention (CDC). "Violence in the Workplace." Current Intelligence Bulletin #57. 1996. http://www.cdc.gov/niosh/docs/96-100/.

Changingminds.org. "Eyes Body Language." Accessed December 27, 2023. www.changingminds.org/techniques/body/parts_body_language/eyes_body_language.htm.

Chicago Police Training Bulletin. "Positional Asphyxia." Volume XXXVI, Number 2, 1995. www.aele.org/law/2008ALL12/chicago.pdf.

Chodron, Thubten. *Working With Anger*. Ithaca, NY: Snow Lion Publication, 2001.

Christenson, Loren. *Defensive Tactics: Modern Arrest and Control Techniques for Today's Police Warrior*. Washington, DC: Turtle Press, 2008

Christenson, Loren. *Fighting in the Clinch: Vicious Strikes, Street Wrestling, and Gouges for Real Fights*. Boulder, CO: Paladin Press, 2009

Christensen, Loren. *The Way Alone: Your Path to Excellence in the Martial Arts*. Boulder, CO: Paladin Press, 1987.

Christensen, Loren. *Warriors: On Living with Courage, Discipline, and Honor*. Boulder, CO: Paladin Press, 2004.

Comfort, Ray. *The Evidence Bible, NKJV*. Alachua, FL: Bridge-Logos Publishers, 2011.

Counter Assault. http://counterassault.com/

Covey, Stephen R. *The 7 Habits of Highly Effective People: Powerful Lessons in Personal Change*. NY, NY: Fireside, 1989.

Covey, Stephen R. *The 8th Habit: From Effectiveness to Greatness*. Washington D.C.: Free Press, 2004.

Cybersecurity and Infrastructure Security Agency. "De-escalation Series." 2021. https://www.cisa.gov/resources-tools/resources/de-escalation-series.

Davis, Joseph A., Ph.D., LL.D.(hon), B.C.E.T.S., F.A.A.E.T.S. "Providing Critical Incident Stress Debriefing (CISD) to Individuals and Communities in Situational Crisis." *American Academy of Experts in Traumatic Stress*. Accessed December 27, 2023. https://www.aaets.org/traumatic-stress-library/providing-critical-incident-stress-debriefing-cisd-to-individuals-and-communities-in-situational-crisis.

DeBecker, Gavin. *Fear Less: Real Truth about Risk, Safety, and Security in a Time of Terrorism*. Boston, New York, London: Little Brown and Company, 2002.

DeBecker, Gavin. *Protecting the Gift: Keeping Children and Teenagers Safe (and Parents Sane)*. New York, NY: A Dell Trade Paperback, 1999.

DeBecker, Gavin. *The Gift of Fear*. New York, NY: Dell Publishing, 1997.

DeBecker, Gavin; Tom Taylor; and Jeff Marquart. *Just 2 Seconds: Using Time and Space To Defeat Assassins*. Studio City, CA: Gavin de Becker Center for the Study and Reduction of Violence; First Edition (2008).

DeMasco, Steve. T*he Shaolin Way: 10 Modern Secrets of Survival from a Shaolin Kung Fu Grandmaster*. New York, NY: Harper, 2006.

Department of Homeland Security. "Active Shooter: How to Respond." Accessed December 27, 2023. https://www.dhs.gov/xlibrary/assets/active_shooter_booklet.pdf.

Deshimaru, Taisen. *The Zen Way to the Martial Arts: A Japanese Master Reveals the Secrets of the Samurai*. New York, NY: Penguin Compass, 1982.

Dimitrius, Jo-Ellan, Ph.D., and Mark Mazzarella. *Reading People: How to Understand People and Predict Their Behavior—Anytime, Anyplace*. New York, NY: Ballantine Books, 1999.

Divine, Mark. *The Way of the SEAL: Think Like an Elite Warrior to Lead and Succeed*. White Plains, NY: Readers Digest, 2016.

Don't Name Them. http://www.dontnamethem.org/.

Drudi, Dino and Mark Zak. "Work-related multiple-fatality incidents." *U.S. Bureau of Labor Statistics*, accessed December 27, 2023. www.bls.gov/mlr/2004/10/art2full.pdf.

Duwe, Grant. "A Circle of Distortion: The Social Construction of Mass Murder in the United States." *Western Criminology Review* 6 (1), 59-78 (2005). https://www.westerncriminology.org/documents/WCR/v06n1/article_pdfs/duwe.pdf.

Dyer, Wayne. *The Power of Intention; Learning to Co-Create Your World Your Way*. Carlsbad, CA: Hay House, 2004.

Eckman, Paul. *Emotions Revealed: Recognizing Faces and Feelings to Improve Communication and Emotional Life*. New York, NY: Henry Holt and Company, 2007.

Eckman, Paul. *Telling Lies*. New York and London: WW. Norton Company, 1991.

Eggerichs, Emerson. *Love and Respect: The Love She Most Desires and the Respect He Desperately Needs*. Thomas Nelson; 1st edition, 2004.

Fedeal Bureau of Investigation. "Active Shooter Incidents in the United States in 2014 and 2015." Accessed December 27, 2023. https://www.fbi.gov/file-repository/activeshooterincidentsus_2014-2015.pdf/view.

Federal Bureau of Investigations. "Active Shooter Incidents in the United States in 2016 and 2017." 2018. https://www.fbi.gov/file-repository/active-shooter-incidents-us-2016-2017.pdf/view.

Federal Bureau of Investigation. "Active Shooter Incidents in the United States in 2019." Accessed December 27, 2023. https://www.fbi.gov/file-repository/active-shooter-incidents-in-the-us-2019-042820.pdf/view.

Federal Bureau of Investigation. "Active Shooter Safety Resources." Accessed December 27, 2023. https://www.fbi.gov/how-we-can-help-you/active-shooter-safety-resources.

Federal Bureau of Investigation. "Making Prevention a Reality: Identifying, Assessing, and Managing the Threat of Targeted Attacks." Accessed December 27,

2023. https://www.fbi.gov/file-repository/making-prevention-a-reality.pdf/view.

Federal Emergency Management Agency (FEMA). "Fire/Emergency Medical Services Department Operational Considerations and Guide for Active Shooter and Mass Casualty Incidents." Accessed December 27, 2023. https://www.usfa.fema.gov/downloads/pdf/publications/active_shooter_guide.pdf.

FEMA Emergency Management Institute. "IS-907: Active Shooter: What You Can Do." Accessed December 27, 2023. http://training.fema.gov/EMIWeb/IS/is907.asp.

Follman, Mark; Gavin Aronsen; and Deanna Pan. "US Mass Shootings, 1982–2023: Data From Mother Jones' Investigation." Mother Jones, 2023. www.motherjones.com/politics/2012/12/mass-shootings-mother-jones-full-data.

Fowler, David. Be Safe Not Sorry: The Art and Science of Keeping You and Your Family Safe from Crime and Violence. Coeur d Alene, ID: Personal Safety Training, Inc., 2011.

Fowler, David. Survive an Active Shooter: Awareness, Preparedness, and Response for Extreme Violence. Coeur d Alene, ID: Personal Safety Training, Inc., 2019.

Fowler, David. To Serve and Protect: Providing Service While Maintaining Safety in the Workplace. Coeur d Alene, ID: Personal Safety Training, Inc., 2015.

Fowler, David. Violence In The Workplace: Education, Prevention, and Mitigation. Coeur d Alene, ID: Personal Safety Training, Inc., 2012.

Fox Labs. https://foxlabs.com/search?q=pepper+spray&options%5Bprefix%5D=last

Funakoshi, Gichin. Karate-Do My Way of Life. Tokyo, New York, London: Kodansha International, 1975.

Funakoshi, Gichin. The Twenty Guiding Principles of Karate. Tokyo, New York, London: Kodansha International, 2012.

Gallups, Carl. Be Thou Prepared: Equipping the Church for Persecution and Times of Trouble. WND Books, 2015.

Gardner, Daniel. The Science of Fear: How the Culture of Fear Manipulates Your Brain. London: Penguin Books Ltd, 2009.

Garner, Bryan. Black's Law Dictionary: Seventh Edition. St. Paul, MN: West Group, 1999.

Gilligan, James. Violence: Reflections on a National Epidemic. New York, NY: Vintage Books, 1996

Gladwell, Malcolm. Blink. New York, NY: Little, Brown and Company, 2005.

Glennon, Jim. Arresting Communication: Essential Interaction Skills for Law Enforcement. Elmhurst, IL: LifeLine Training and Caliber Press, 2010.

Goleman, Daniel. Emotional Intelligence. New York, NY: Bantam Books, 2005.

Gray, John. Beyond Mars and Venus. Better Life Media, DVD and CD, 2004.

Gregory, Hamilton. Public Speaking for College and Career: Fifth Edition. Boston, MA: McGraw-Hill, 1999.

Gross, Linden. Surviving A Stalker: Everything You Need to Know to Keep Yourself Safe. New York, NY: Marlowe and Company, 2000.

Grossman, Dave and Loren Christensen. On Combat: The Psychology of Deadly Conflict in War and Peace. Warrior Science Publications, 2008.

Grossman, Dave and Gloria DeGaetano. Stop Teaching Our Kids to Kill: A Call to Action Against TV, Movie, and Video Game Violence. New York, NY: Crown Publishers, 1999.

Occupational Safety and Health Administration (OSHA). "Guidelines for Preventing Workplace Violence for Health Care and Social Service Workers." Accessed December 27, 2023. www.osha.gov/Publications/osha3148.pdf.

Gun Violence Archive. https://www.gunviolencearchive.org/.

Halek, G. "Here Are 5 Times Concealed Carriers Have Stopped Mass Shootings." Concealednation.org, 2015. http://concealednation.org/2015/10/here-are-5-times-concealed-carriers-have-stopped-mass-shootings/.

Harrell, Erika, Ph.D. "Workplace Violence, 1993-2009 National Crime Victimization Survey, and the Census of Fatal Occupational Injuries." Bureau of Justice Statistics, 2011. www.bjs.ojp.gov/content/pub/pdf/wv09.pdf.

Harrell, Keith. Attitude is Everything: 10 Life-Changing Steps to Turning Attitude Into Action. New York, NY: Harper Collins Publishing, 1999.

Harvard Business School Press. The Results Driven Manager: Dealing with Difficult People. Boston, MA: Harvard Business School Press, 2005.

Hawaii Workplace Violence Working Group Committee. "Workplace Violence: Prevention, Intervention, and Recovery." 2001. https://ag.hawaii.gov/cpja/files/2013/01/WVfull.pdf.

Hawkins, David R, MD. Power vs. Force: The Hidden Determinants of Human Behavior. Sedona, AZ: Veritas, 2004.

Houzz.com. "What Is Capsaicin? What Are Scoville Heat Units?" Accessed December 27, 2023. http://faq.gardenweb.com/faq/lists/pepper/2002075348029538.html.

Hyams, Joe. Zen in the Martial Arts. Toronto, New York, London, Sydney, Auckland: Bantam Books, 1982.

Jeltsen, Melissa. "We're Missing the Big Picture on Mass Shootings." Huffington Post, 2015. www.huffingtonpost.com/entry/massshootings-domestic-violence-women_us_55d3806ce4b07addcb44542a.

Kanarak, Mike Lee; John Pelligrini; Jim Wagner; Richard Ryan; Michael Janich; and Kelly McCann. The Ultimate Guide to Reality-Based Self-Defense. South Korea: Black Belt Books, 2010.

Kane, Lawrence A. Surviving Armed Assaults. Boston, MA: YMAA Publication Center, 2006.

Kinnaird, Brian. Use of Force: Expert Guidance for Decisive Force Response. Flushing, NY: Looseleaf Law Publications, 2003.

Klofas, John "Summary of Research on Mass Murder." Rochester Institute of Technology, 2009. www.rit.edu/liberalarts/sites/rit.edu.liberalarts/files/documents/our-work/2009-11.pdf.

Krebs, Dennis; KC Henry; and MB Gabriele. When Violence Erupts: A Survival Guide for Emergency Responders. St. Louis, Baltimore, Philadelphia, Toronto: The C.V. Mosby Company, 1990.

Lanier, Sandra. Workplace Violence: Before, During, and After. Alexandria, VA: ASIS International, 2003.

Larkin, Tim, and Chris Ranck-Buhr. How to Survive The Most Critical 5 Seconds of Your Life. Sequim, WA: The TFT Group, 2008.

Larkin, Tim. When Violence is the Answer: Learning How to Do What It Takes When your Life Is at Stake. New York: NY: Little, Brown and Company, 2017.

Lawler, Jennifer. Dojo Wisdom: 100 Simple Ways to Become a Stronger, Calmer, More Courageous Person. New York, NY: Penguin Compass, 2003.

Leaf, Caroline. Switch on Your Brain: The Key to Peak Happiness, Thinking, and Health. Grand Rapids, MI: Baker Books, 2013.

Lee, Bruce. *Tao of Jeet Kune Do*. Santa Clarita, CA: Ohara Publications, 1975.

Lee, Johnny. *Addressing Domestic Violence in the Workplace*. Amherst, MA: HRD Press, Inc., 2005.

Lee, Linda. *The Bruce Lee Story*. Santa Clarita, CA: Ohara Publications, 1989.

Lion, John, MD. *Evaluation and Management of the Violent Patient: Guidelines in the Hospital and Institution*. Springfield, IL: Charles C. Thomas Publisher, 1972.

Little, John. *The Warrior Within: The Philosophies of Bruce Lee to Better Understand the World Around You and Achieve a Rewarding Life*. Chicago, IL Contemporary Books, 1996.

Loehr, James, and Jeffrey Migdwo. *Breathe In Breathe Out: Inhale Energy and Exhale Stress By Guiding and Controlling Your Breathing*. Alexandria, VA: Time-Life Books, 1986.

Loomis, Dana, Ph.D.; Stephen W. Marshall, Ph.D.; Susanne H. Wolf, RN, MPH; Carol W. Runyan, Ph.D.; John D. Butts, M.D. "Effectiveness of Safety Measures Recommended for Prevention of Workplace Homicide." *The Journal of the American Medical Association*, 2002. http://jama.jamanetwork.com/article.aspx?articleid=194680.

Lorenz, Konrad. *On Aggression*. New York, NY: MJF Book, 1963.

Lynch, Kellie, Ph.D. and TK Logan, Ph.D. "Assessing Challenges, Needs, and Innovations of Gender-Based Violence Services During the Covid-19 Pandemic." *The Trace*, accessed December 27, 2023. https://www.documentcloud.org/documents/20498812-covid-gender-based-violence-final-report.

MACE. http://www.mace.com/.

Machowicz, Richard J. *Unleash The Warrior Within: Develop the Focus, Discipline, Confidence, and Courage You Need to Achieve Unlimited Goals*. New York, NY: Marlowe and Company, 2002.

Mackay, Harvey. "Harvey Mackay's Column This Week." Weekly e-mail publication. www.harveymackay.com.

MacYoung, Marc "Animal." *A Professional's Guide to Ending Violence Quickly: How Bouncers, Bodyguards, and Other Security Professionals Handle Ugly Situations*. Boulder, CO: Paladin Press, 1996.

Maggio, Rosalie. *How to Say It: Choice Words, Phrases, Sentences, and Paragraphs for Every Situation*. New York, NY: Prentice-Hall Press, 2001.

Maltz, Maxwell, MD. *Psycho-Cybernetics: A New Way to Get More Living Out Of Life*. New York, NY: Essandress, 1960.

Marcinko, Richard. *The Rogue Warriors Strategy For Success*. New York, NY: Pocket Books, 1997.

Mason, Tom and Mark Chandley. *Managing Violence and Aggression: A Manual for Nurses and Health Care Workers*. Edinburgh: Churchill Livingstone, 1999.

McGrew, James. *Think Safe: Practical Measures to Increase Security at Home, at Work, and Throughout Life*. Hilton Head Island, SC: Cameo Publications, 2004.

McTaggart, Lynne. *The Intention Experiment: Using Your Thoughts to Change Your Life and the World*. New York, NY: Free Press, 2007.

Medina, John. *Brain Rules: 12 Principles for Surviving and Thriving at Work, Home, and School*. Seattle, WA: Pear Press, 2008.

Meserve, Evelyn F., Editor. *Basic Training Manual and Study Guide for Healthcare Security Officers, 5th edition*. Lombard, IL: International Association for Healthcare Security and Safety, 2010.

Miller, Rory. *Facing Violence: Preparing for the Unexpected-Ethically, Emotionally, Physically, Without Going to Prison*. Wolfeboro, NH: YMAA Publication Center, 2011.

Miller, Rory. *Training For Sudden Violence: 72 Practical Drills*. Wolfeboro, NH YMAA Publication Center, 2016.

MOAB Training International, Inc. "MOAB® Instructor Manual." 2009.

Monadnock Police Training Council. "MDTS Instructor Manual." 2003.

Monadnock Police Training Council. "MEB Instructor Manual." 2003.

Monadnock Police Training Council. "PR-24® Instructor Manual." 2003.

Murphy, Joseph, Ph.D., D.D. *The Power of Your Subconscious Mind*. New York, Toronto, London, Sidney, Auckland: Bantam Books, 2000.

Musashi, Miyamoto. Translated by Thomas Cleary. *The Book of Five Rings*. Boston, London: Shambhala, 2003.

Nater, Felix P. "Ten Tips to Mitigate Workplace Violence and Threats." *Security Magazine*, accessed December 27, 2023. www.securitymagazine.com/articles/83329-10-tips-to-mitigate-workplace-violence-and-threats.

National Institute of Justice. "Oleoresin Capsicum: Pepper Spray as a Force Alternative." 1994. https://www.ncjrs.gov/pdffiles1/nij/grants/181655.pdf.

NISVS. "National Data on Intimate Partner Violence, Sexual Violence, and Stalking." Accessed December 27, 2023. https://www.cdc.gov/violenceprevention/pdf/nisvs-fact-sheet-2014.pdf.

Norris, Chuck. *The Secret Power Within: Zen Solutions to Real Problems*. New York, NY: Broadway Books, 1996.

Norris, Chuck. *Winning Tournament Karate*. Burbank, CA: Ohara Publications, 1975.

Nowicki, Ed. *Total Survival*. Powers Lake, MI: Performance Dimensions, 1993.

Occupational Safety and Health Administration (OSHA). "Recommendations for Workplace Violence Prevention Programs in Late-Night Retail Establishments." 2009. https://www.osha.gov/sites/default/files/publications/osha3153.pdf.

Occupational Safety and Health Administration (OSHA). "Workplace Violence." Accessed December 27, 2023. http://www.osha.gov/SLTC/workplaceviolence/.

Omartian, Stormie. *Prayer Warrior: The Power of Praying Your Way to Victory*. Eugene, OR: Harvest House Publishers, 2013

Ouellette, Roland W. *Management of Aggressive Behavior*. Powers Lake, WI: Performance Dimensions, 1993.

Palumbo, Dennis. *The Secrets of Hakkoryu Jujutsu: Shodan Tactics*. Boulder, CO: Paladin Press, 1987.

Parker, S.L. *212, the Extra Degree*. Youngsville, LA: Walk the Talk Company, 2005.

Patire, Tom. *Tom Patire's Personal Protection Handbook*. New York, NY: Three Rivers Press, 2003.

Peale, Norman Vincent. *Six Attitudes for Winners*. Wheaton, IL: Tyndale House Publishers, Inc., 1989.

Peale, Norman Vincent. *The Power of Positive Thinking*. New York, NY: Ballantine Books, 1956.

Pease, Allan, and Barbara. *The Definitive Book of Body Language*. New York, NY: Bantam Dell, 2004.

Perkins, John; Al Ridenhour; and Matt Kovsky. *Attack Proof: The Ultimate Guide to Personal Protection*. Champaign, IL: Human Kinetics, 2000.

Personal Protection Consultants, Inc. "OCAT® Instructor Manual." 2009.

Personal Protection Consultants, Inc. "PATH® Instructor Manual." 2009.

Personal Safety Training, Inc. "AVADE® Active Shooter Instructor Manual." Current version.

Personal Safety Training, Inc. "AVADE® De-Escalation Instructor Manual." Current version.

Personal Safety Training, Inc. "AVADE® Defense Baton™ Instructor Manual." Current version.

Personal Safety Training, Inc. "AVADE® Defensive Tactics System™ Instructor Manual." Current version.

Personal Safety Training, Inc. "AVADE® Handcuffing Tactics™ Instructor Manual." Current version.

Personal Safety Training, Inc. "AVADE® Healthcare Defensive Tactics System™ Instructor Manual." Current version.

Personal Safety Training, Inc. "AVADE® Home Healthcare Instructor Manual." Current version.

Personal Safety Training, Inc. "AVADE® Pepper Spray Defense™ Instructor Manual." Current version.

Personal Safety Training, Inc. "AVADE® SIRS™ Safety Incident Reporting System Instructor Manual." Current version.

Personal Safety Training, Inc. "AVADE® Street Smarts™ Instructor Manual." Current version.

Personal Safety Training, Inc. "AVADE® Workplace Violence Prevention Instructor Manual." Current version.

Personal Safety Training, Inc. "SOCS® Instructor Manual." Current version.

Pietsch, William. *Human Be-ing: How to Have a Creative Relationship Instead of a Power Struggle*. New York, NY: Lawrence Hill and Company Publishers Inc, 1974

Police Magazine. "Video: Kansas Active Shooter Kills 3, Wounds 14, Before Being Stopped by Single 'Heroic' Officer." 2016. http://www.policemag.com/channel/patrol/news/2016/02/26/video-kansas-active-shooter-kills-3-wounds-14-before-being-stopped-by-single-heroic-officer.aspx.

PPCT Management Systems, Inc. "Defensive Tactics Instructor Manual." 2005.

Purpura, Philip. *The Security Handbook: Second Edition*. Boston, MA: Butterworth Heinemann, 2003.

Rail, Robert R. *The Unspoken Dialogue: Understanding Body Language and Controlling Interviews and Negotiations*. Kansas City, KS: Varro Press, 2001.

Ralston, Peter. *Cheng Hsin: The Principles of Effortless Power*. Berkeley, CA: North Atlantic Books, 1989.

Ratey, John J. *Spark: The Revolutionary New Science of Exercise and the Brain*. New York, NY: Little, Brown and Co., 2008.

Rawls, Neal. *Be Alert, Be Aware, Have a Plan: The Complete Guide to Protecting Yourself, Your Home, Your Family*. Guilford, CT: Globe Pequot Press, 2002.

Romano, Stephen; Micòl E. Levi-Minzi; Eugene A. Rugala; and Vincent B. Van Hasselt. "Workplace Violence Prevention: Readiness and Response." *FBI Law Enforcement Bulletin*, 2011. https://leb.fbi.gov/articles/featured-articles/workplace-violence-prevention-readiness-and-response.

Rugala, Eugene A. and Arnold R. Isaacs, editors. "Workplace Violence: Issues in Response." *FBI Law Enforcement Bulletin*, accessed December 27, 2023. http://www.fbi.gov/stats-services/publications/workplace-violence.

SABRE. http://www.sabrered.com/.

SAMHSA's National Center for Trauma-Informed Care. https://www.traumainformedcare.chcs.org/.

Sandford, John, and Paula. *The Transformation of the Inner Man*. S. Plainfield, NJ: Bridge Publishing, Inc. 1982.

Schneier, Bruce. "The Psychology of Security (Part 1)." *Scheiner*, 2008. http://www.schneier.com/essay-155.html.

Schweit, Katherine W., J.D. "Addressing the Problem of the Active Shooter." *FBI Law Enforcement Bulletin*, 2013. https://leb.fbi.gov/articles/featured-articles/addressing-the-problem-of-the-active-shooter.

Security Magazine. "FBI: 4 Percent of Active Shooters Since 2002 Were Female." Accessed December 27, 2023. http://www.securitymagazine.com/articles/83930-fbi-4-percent-of-active-shooters-since-2002-were-female.

Sjodin, Terri. *New Sales Speak: The 9 Biggest Sales Presentation Mistakes and How to Avoid Them*. Better Life Media. DVD and CD 2004.

Soo, Chee, *The Chinese Art of T'ai Chi Ch'uan: The Taoist Way to Mental and Physical Health*. Wellingborough, Northamptonshire: The Aquarian Press, 1984.

Staley, Charles. *The Science of Martial Arts Training*. Burbank, CA: Multi-Media Books, 1999.

Strong, Sanford. *Strong on Defense: Survival Rules to Protect You and Your Family from Crime*. New York, NY: Pocket Books, 1996.

Sygnatur, Eric and Toscano, Guy. "Work-related Homicides: The Facts." *U.S. Bureau of Labor Statistics*, 2000. www.bls.gov/opub/mlr/cwc/work-related-homicides-the-facts.pdf.

Tarani, Steve. *PreFense: The 90% Advantage—Preventing Bad Things from Happening to Good People*. Tarani Press, 2014.

The Free Dictionary. "Capsicum." Accessed December 27, 2023. http://www.thefreedictionary.com/capsicum.

The Joint Commission. "Sentinel Event." Accessed December 27, 2023. www.jointcommission.org/SentinelEvents/SentinelEventAlert/sea_40.htm.

Theriault, Jean Yves. *Full Contact Karate*. Chicago, IL: Contemporary Books, Inc., 1983.

Thompson, George. *Verbal Judo (Updated Edition)*. New York, NY: William Morrow Paperbacks, 2013.

Tsunetomo, Yamamoto. *Hagakure: The Book of the Samurai*. Tokyo, New York, London: Kodansha International, 1979.

Turner, James T. *Violence in the Medical Care Setting*. Rockville, MD: Aspen Systems Corporation, 1984.

Tzu, Sun. *The Art of War (Samuel B. Griffith's Interpretation)*. Oxford University Press, 1993.

U.S. Department of Justice. "Active Shooter: Recommendations and Analysis for Risk Mitigation." 2012. https://www.ojp.gov/ncjrs/virtual-library/abstracts/active-shooter-recommendations-and-analysis-risk-mitigation

U.S. Bureau of Labor Statistics. "Injuries, Illnesses, and Fatalities." Accessed December 27, 2023. https://www.bls.gov/iif/home.htm.

U.S. Department of Homeland Security. "Active Shooter: How to Respond." 2008. https://www.dhs.gov/xlibrary/assets/active_shooter_booklet.pdf.

U.S. Department of Homeland Security. "If You See Something, Say Something." Accessed December 27, 2023. https://www.dhs.gov/see-something-say-something.

U.S. Department of Homeland Security. "Recent Active Shooter Incidents Highlight Need for Continued Vigilance." 2012. https://info.publicintelligence.net/DHS-FBI-ActiveShooters.pdf.

U.S. Department of Homeland Security. "Stop the Bleed." Accessed December 27, 2023. https://www.dhs.gov/stopthebleed.

U.S. Secret Service. "National Threat Assessment Center." Accessed December 27, 2023. https://www.secretservice.gov/protection/ntac/.

Ueshiba, Kisshomaru. *The Spirit of Aikido*. Tokyo, New York, London: Kodansha International, 1987.

Van Horne, Patrick, and Jason Riley. *Left of Bang: How the Marine Corps' Combat Hunter Program Can Save Your Life*. New York and Los Angeles: Black Irish Entertainment LLC, 2014.

Volokh, Eugene. "Do civilians with guns every stop mass shootings?" *The Washington Post*, 2015. https://www.washingtonpost.com/news/volokh-conspiracy/wp/2015/10/03/do-civilians-with-guns-ever-stop-mass-shootings/?utm_term=.8373a89601ea.

Wallace, Bill. *The Ultimate Kick: The Wallace Method to Winning Karate*. Burbank, CA, Unique Publications, 1987.

Wassell, James T. "Workplace violence intervention effectiveness: A systematic literature review." *Safety Science*, Volume 47, Issue 8, October 2009. www.sciencedirect.com/science/article/pii/S092575350800218X.

Webster, Noah. *Webster's Dictionary*. New York, NY: Modern Promotions/Publishers, 1984.

Wikipedia. "2011 Seal Beach shooting." Last modified 2023. https://en.wikipedia.org/wiki/2011_Seal_Beach_shooting.

Wikipedia. "2011 Tucson shooting." Last modified 2023. https://en.wikipedia.org/wiki/2011_Tucson_shooting.

Wikipedia. "2012 Aurora, Colorado shooting." Last modified 2023. https://en.wikipedia.org/wiki/2012_Aurora_shooting.

Wikipedia. "Active shooter." Last modified 2023. https://en.wikipedia.org/wiki/Active_shooter.

Wikipedia. "Chemical restraint." Last modified 2023. http://en.wikipedia.org/wiki/Chemical_restraint.

Wikipedia. "Colorado Springs Planned Parenthood shooting." Last modified 2023. https://en.wikipedia.org/wiki/Colorado_Springs_Planned_Parenthood_shooting.

Wikipedia. "Excited delirium." Last modified 2023. http://en.wikipedia.org/wiki/Excited_delirium.

Wikipedia. "Pepper spray." Last modified 2023. http://en.wikipedia.org/wiki/Pepper_spray.

Wikipedia. "Positional asphyxia." Last modified 2023. http://en.wikipedia.org/wiki/Positional_asphyxia.

Wikipedia. "Sandy Hook Elementary School shooting." Last modified 2023. https://en.wikipedia.org/wiki/Sandy_Hook_Elementary_School_shooting.

Wikipedia. "Virginia Tech shooting." Last modified 2023. https://en.wikipedia.org/wiki/Virginia_Tech_shooting.

Willis, Brian. *W.I.N. 2: Insights Into Training and Leading Warriors*. Calgary, Alberta, Canada: Warrior Spirit Books, 2009.

Workplace Violence 911. "The Workplace Violence Prevention eReport." Accessed December 27, 2023. http://www.workplaceviolence911.com/preventionreport.

ZARC International. http://www.zarc.com/.

AVADE® Training Programs

The only way to deal with conflict and avoid violence of any type is through awareness, vigilance, avoidance, defensive training, and escape planning (AVADE).

David Fowler, President of Personal Safety Training Inc. (PSTI), specializes in nationally recognized training programs that empower individuals, increase confidence, and promote pro-active preventative solutions.

OSHA, Labor and Industries, Joint Commission, State WPV Laws, and the Department of Health all recognize that programs like PSTI's are excellent preventive measures to reduce crime, violence, and aggression in the workplace.

Personal Safety Training Inc. is committed to providing the finest level of training and service to you and your employees. Whether you are an individual or represent an agency, we have the Basic and Instructor Course Certifications that you need.

CONTACT US TODAY!

Personal Safety Training Inc. | AVADE® Training
P.O. Box 2957 Coeur d'Alene, ID 83816 | Phone: 208-664-5551 | Fax: 208-664-5556 | Email: info@personalsafetytraining.com
personalsafetytraining.com | avadetraining.com

PSTI | AVADE® Offers Multiple Training Options for Your Organization

On-Site Training
We will come to you! No need to send staff away for training. PSTI will come to your place of business and train your staff.

Train-the-Trainer (Instructor Seminars)
The most cost-effective way to implement PSTI Training courses for your organization. We can come to you for instructor courses or you can send staff to one of our upcoming seminars.

Combo Classes
Combination classes are where Basic Training and Instructor Training are combined during on-site training. It is a great way to introduce PSTI Training with our initial instruction and then continue on with your own instructors.

E-Learning
Are you looking for a training solution to integrate a Workplace Violence Prevention Program in order to meet compliance standards for both State and Federal guidelines? The AVADE® E-Learning programs offer a great solution to give your staff an introductory yet comprehensive training program that can be completed as needed.

Course Duration Options
PSTI offers multiple options and course durations from introductory to advanced training. Course lengths range from: 2-hr. Introductory Courses, 1/2 Day Training Sessions, 1-Day Classes, 2-Day Classes, and Train-the-Trainer (Instructor Classes).

AVADE® Training Programs Serve Multiple Industries

HEALTHCARE

CORPORATE

SECURITY

GAMING

CHURCHES

CONTACT US TODAY!
Personal Safety Training Inc. | AVADE® Training
P.O. Box 2957 Coeur d'Alene, ID 83816 | Phone: 208-664-5551 | Fax: 208-664-5556 | Email: info@personalsafetytraining.com
personalsafetytraining.com | avadetraining.com

AVADE® Training Courses for You and Your Agency

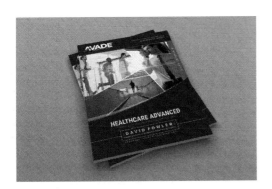

AVADE® Workplace Violence Prevention

avadetraining.com

The AVADE® WPV Training is offered as a Basic and Instructor level course for private corporations, healthcare, security, and agencies wanting to educate, prevent, and mitigate the risk of violence to their employees.

AVADE® De-Escalation

avadedeescalation.com

When individuals are in crisis, you are either escalating or de-escalating them. The AVADE® De-Escalation Training is designed to educate, prevent, and mitigate the risk of escalation, aggression, and violence in the workplace.

AVADE® Active Shooter

avadeactiveshooter.com

The AVADE® Active Shooter Training is designed to increase awareness, preparedness, and response to extreme violence. The philosophy of education, prevention, and mitigation is the cornerstone of this training program.

CONTACT US TODAY!

Personal Safety Training Inc. | AVADE® Training

P.O. Box 2957 Coeur d'Alene, ID 83816 | Phone: 208-664-5551 | Fax: 208-664-5556 | Email: info@personalsafetytraining.com

personalsafetytraining.com | avadetraining.com

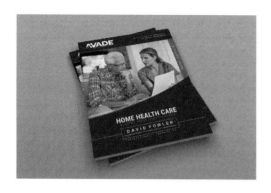

AVADE® Home Healthcare

avadehomehealthcare.com

The AVADE® Home Healthcare Training program is designed to educate, prevent, and mitigate aggression and violence for workers in the Home Healthcare and Hospice industry.

AVADE® DTS™ (Defensive Tactics System)

dts-training.com

The AVADE® DTS™ Training program covers basic defensive tactics, control techniques, and defensive interventions. This course includes stance, movement, escort techniques, takedowns, defensive blocking, active defense skills, weapon retention, handcuffing, post-incident response and documentation, and more.

AVADE® HDTS™ (Healthcare Defensive Tactics System)

hdts-training.com

The AVADE® HDTS™ Training program for healthcare covers basic defensive tactics, control techniques, and defensive interventions. This course includes all of the DTS techniques/modules listed above and a special healthcare module for patient restraint techniques.

AVADE® Handcuffing Tactics™

handcuffingtactics.com

Training in the use of plastic, chain, or hinged handcuffs. Standing, kneeling, and prone handcuffing techniques are covered. In this training course you will also learn defensive tactics fundamentals, proper positioning, nomenclature, risk factors, and post-incident response and documentation.

CONTACT US TODAY!

Personal Safety Training Inc. | AVADE® Training

P.O. Box 2957 Coeur d'Alene, ID 83816 | Phone: 208-664-5551 | Fax: 208-664-5556 | Email: info@personalsafetytraining.com

personalsafetytraining.com | avadetraining.com

AVADE® Defense Baton™

defensebaton.com

Training in the use of an expandable bat, straight stick, or riot control baton. Techniques and topics in this training include: vulnerable areas of the body, stance, movement, blocks, control holds, counter techniques, draws, and retention techniques.

AVADE® Pepper Spray Defense™

pepperspraydefense-training.com

Tactical and practical concepts of when and how to use pepper spray in a variety of environmental situations. Aerosol pepper is a great less-than-lethal control and defense option for agencies that encounter violence and aggression.

AVADE® SIRS™ (Safety Incident Reporting System)

sirs-training.com

The AVADE® SIRS™ Training program teaches staff how to effectively and intelligenty write safety incident reports. Documentation of safety incidents is absolutely critical to your agency's ability to track and trend, reduce liability, and share vital information.

SOCS® (Safety Oriented Customer Service)

socstraining.com

SOCS® Training teaches staff how to identify and provide great customer service while maintaining safety in the workplace. The core concept of the training is to be able to provide excellent service without having to think about it. Creating habits, skills and taking action, for exceptional customer service is the goal of the SOCS® Training program.

CONTACT US TODAY!

Personal Safety Training Inc. | AVADE® Training

P.O. Box 2957 Coeur d'Alene, ID 83816 | Phone: 208-664-5551 | Fax: 208-664-5556 | Email: info@personalsafetytraining.com

personalsafetytraining.com | avadetraining.com